HUMAN RIGHTS, DIGNITY AND AUTONOMY IN HEALTH CARE AND SOCIAL SERVICES: NORDIC PERSPECTIVES

HUMAN RIGHTS, DIGNITY AND AUTONOMY IN HEALTH CARE AND SOCIAL SERVICES: NORDIC PERSPECTIVES

Henriette Sinding Aasen
Rune Halvorsen
António Barbosa da Silva
(eds.)

EAP

Distribution for Germany:
BWV Berliner Wissenschafts-Verlag
Axel-Springer-Straße 54 b
D-10117 Berlin
Tel.: +49 30 84 17 70-0
Fax: +49 30 84 17 70-21

Distribution for Austria:
Neuer Wissenschaftlicher Verlag
Argentinierstraße 42/6
A-1040 Wien
Tel.: +43 1 535 61 03-24
Fax: +43 1 535 61 03-25

Distribution for other countries:
Intersentia Publishers
Groenstraat 31
BE-2640 Mortsel
Belgium
Tel.: +32 3 680 15 50
Fax: +32 3 658 71 21

Human Rights, Dignity and Autonomy in Health Care and Social Services: Nordic Perspectives
Henriette Sinding Aasen, Rune Halvorsen and António Barbosa da Silva (eds.)

ISBN Intersentia 978-90-5095-877-6
ISBN Berliner Wissenschafts-Verlag 978-3-8305-1650-7
ISBN Neuer Wissenschaftlicher Verlag 978-3-7083-0612-4
D/2009/7849/32
NUR 828

PREFACE

THE WELFARE STATE AND PROTECTION OF INDIVIDUAL AUTONOMY

The protection of the autonomy of the individual is a cornerstone of modern thinking on human rights, with roots back to the Age of Enlightenment and the ethical philosophies of humanism, affirming the dignity and worth of all human beings. Today the 1950 European Convention on Human Rights and Fundamental Freedoms (Article 5) and the 1966 UN Covenant on Civil and Political Rights (Article 9) state as an overreaching principle that everyone has the right to liberty and personal security.

In liberal political theory human rights are seen not merely as moral principles in legal clothing but also as instruments for creating and maintaining a democratic society and social stability. Enlightened political discourse and the invisible hand of market economy both presuppose individual freedom and personal security. Thus for a rational organization of society, protecting the rights of citizens *collectively* through a democratic government cannot suffice. Even when based on a popular mandate, '[p]ower tends to corrupt, and absolute power corrupts absolutely'.[1] Thus establishing and securing certain inalienable individual rights, based upon the principle of equal protection of autonomy and freedom for all members of society, also becomes necessary.

The human rights set forth in eighteenth and early nineteenth century political theory and constitutions sprung out of dismal experiences with absolute monarchy. This background is reflected in the liberal constitutions of the period, when a main objective was to protect the citizen against abuse of power by the government. Human rights are generally defined as negative rights – *freedom from* various kinds of government interference – with the main positive right being the right to equal protection under the law.

---

1 British historian John Emerich Edward Dalberg Acton in a letter to Bishop Mandell Creighton in 1887.

Through the nineteenth and the first part of the twentieth century it became evident that mere negative rights and the formal requirement of equal protection of liberal constitutions did not suffice for creating a just society with substantive – not merely formal – autonomy for all citizens. A famous summation of the moral criticism of classical liberalism lies in Anatole France's ironic comment: 'The law, in its majestic equality, forbids the rich as well as the poor to sleep under bridges, to beg in the streets, and to steal bread'.[2]

But the strongest driving force behind the emergence and development of the welfare state in its early stages was political concern for social stability and the need to stem revolutionary movements. Thus we find the roots of modern welfare state social security systems in Otto von Bismarck's late nineteenth century conservative Germany.[3]

From these two roots – a radical moral criticism as voiced by Anatole France and a conservative political strategy as implemented by Otto von Bismarck – a modern welfare state founded on a multiplicity of rationales has developed. While social justice is the most visible rationale, and most often cited, economic and political theory and concerns are equally important. To create and maintain an efficient, functioning democracy, one needs to have mechanisms for keeping the bulk of the population within the social fabric of society. People who are marginalized because of poverty, poor health or lack of education cannot be a useful part of the workforce of the country; they cannot be expected to be loyal to the ruler's system of government, and they may constitute a disruptive or even revolutionary force, threatening law and order. The state must have a programme for *autonomy repair*, where those individuals falling through the ordinary social network are caught by a state safety net that takes care of them and, if possible, re-establishes them as self-supporting and independent citizens.

These challenges have also become an *international* concern. The development of a world-wide market economy presupposes certain minimum standards for work and living conditions for the labour force in the competing countries. Substandard work and living conditions in one country will adversely affect others competing in the same market either through loss of profit or through a Gresham's law effect, forcing states with higher standards of welfare out of the international market.[4]

---

2 A. France, *The Red Lily*, 1894.

3 See e.g. S. B. Fay, 'Bismarck's Welfare State', *Current History*, Vol. XVIII, January 1950.

4 Sir Thomas Gresham, 1519–1579, to whom is wrongly attributed the observation that 'bad money drives out the good'.

This concern is one important factor behind the development of the welfare state as a global model, as reflected in the 1966 UN Covenant on Economic, Social and Cultural Rights, Articles 11 and 12, which recognizes an adequate standard of living and the highest attainable standard of physical and mental health as the equal and inalienable rights of all members of the human family.

Taken literally, the Covenant is more ambitious than realistic, as also reflected in the absence of any potent remedies against states that do not fulfil their obligations. Nevertheless, the Covenant is an important instrument of international law through the strong ideological message it conveys, because it establishes the basic principles of the welfare state as a social contract between the individual state and its citizens.

Whilst this departure from a traditional liberalistic political philosophy, based upon a notion of a negative concept of freedom (i.e. absence of government intervention) is a necessary shift, it is not without certain serious dangers. When social inclusion and care for the unfortunate become major concerns for the government, the dangers of paternalism and forced uniformity arise.

The welfare state itself, however, did not create these dangers. Paupers, the sick, the unemployed, vagabonds, criminals and people with mental impairment have always been considered a threat to a well-organized society. Whilst the welfare state's treatment of these groups is by no means harsher or less humane than that of previous periods, the nets catching and protecting members of these groups tend to gradually grow finer. Our tolerance for eccentricity and deviation has decreased. At the same time the ambitions and the self-assurance of the professionals entrusted the task of implementing the ideals of the welfare state have been growing to a point where they sometimes pose a serious threat to the autonomy and integrity of the individual: 'the doctor knows best'.

But perhaps the greatest threat to the autonomy of the individual springs from a disparity between the expressed ambitions of welfare state governments and their ability or willingness to allocate sufficient economic resources to social and health services. This disparity commonly leads not only to substandard treatment or services but also to the use of various forms of coercion in situations where adequate health care and social rehabilitation could have been given and received voluntarily had the necessary resources been available. For some of the most vulnerable recipients of welfare state services, proper health care and social rehabilitation based upon consent and cooperation are replaced with forced care and treatment, and rigorous social control, sometimes completely obliterating the autonomy of the individual. The use of force and other types of coercion in treatment and care becomes a vehicle for achieving budgetary balance within the sector or the institution, thereby making it possible for politicians to underfund welfare services.

In such a situation an overriding concern for lawmakers, civil servants within the sector, and scholars of social and health law must be to protect and develop the rights and the autonomy of citizens in the face of the combined forces of professional paternalism and administrative budget control. Our major challenge is to see to it that the protection of autonomy and dignity is not merely a privilege for healthy and well-adjusted citizens but also a right for those who depend on help from the government for coping with health or social problems.

This task is two-fold. We must contribute to developing and bringing the right to health and social security, as set forth in the UN Covenant on Economic, Social and Cultural Rights, into general recognition as a binding obligation for national governments. At the same time we must work to strengthen the protection of the integrity and autonomy of the individual against the development of a paternalistic social and health bureaucracy. The best of intentions may lead to disastrous results in a welfare state that does not realize the seriousness of these challenges. To maintain the legitimacy of the modern welfare state as a political programme, the governments must recognize the seriousness of these challenges and the need to allocate adequate professional and economic resources to face them. The welfare state needs our constant critical attention if we are to prevent it from becoming a paternalistic caricature of the humanitarian and political ideals upon which it is meant to be based.

Jan Fridthjof Bernt

ABOUT THE EDITORS AND CONTRIBUTORS

António Barbosa da Silva (Dr.) is professor of mental health and systematic theology at Ansgar Theological Seminary, Kristiansand, Norway. His research interests comprises the fields of philosophy of religion, inter-religious dialogue, Jewish-Christian relation, cultural confrontation, Christian ethics, healthcare ethics, the philosophy of healthcare sciences, the theoretical foundations of qualitative methods and approaches.

Jan Fridthjof Bernt (Dr.) is professor of public law at The Faculty of Law, University of Bergen, Norway. His main research interests are administrative law, local government law, social- and health law and legal theory. Bernt has been the head of several government law commissions, e.g. The Commission on New Legislation on Involuntary Psychiatric Care and The Commission on Coordination of Primary Social Care and Health Care.

Rune Halvorsen (Dr.) is senior researcher at NOVA Norwegian Social Research, Oslo, Norway. His main research interests are international and comparative welfare policy, European social regulation policy, and driving forces in European social policy development.

Mette Hartlev (PhD and LL.D) is professor in health Law at the University of Copenhagen, Denmark. Her main research interests are health law, biolaw and bioethics, law, science and technology studies, and patient rights in international law.

Bjørn Hvinden (Dr.) is professor and head of research at NOVA Norwegian Social Research, Oslo, Norway. He is currently leader of a Nordic Centre of Excellence in Welfare Research (www.reassess.no). His main research interests are comparative welfare policy, Europeanisation, globalisation and social exclusion.

Salla Lötjönen (Dr.) is senior adviser at the Ministry of Justice, Helsinki, Finland. She is also Adjunct Professor (Docent) in Medical- and Bio Law at the University of Helsinki, Finland. Her main research interests include regulation of research on human beings, children's rights and rights of adults with impaired legal capacity.

Marit Skivenes (Dr.) is senior researcher at HEMIL-Centre, University of Bergen, Norway. Her research interests are international child welfare policies, decision-making processes, children's participation, communication and welfare politics.

Henriette Sinding Aasen (Dr.) is professor of public law, University of Bergen, Norway. She is currently the coordinator of the University of Bergen research program on Rule of law and Democracy. Her research interests are human rights, health- and social law and patient rights, focusing on universality of human rights, rights of women and children, patient autonomy, regulation of medical research, dignity in medical treatment, and health as a human right.

ACKNOWLEDGEMENTS

The idea for this volume was born on 10–11 May 2007, when the Faculty of Law, University of Bergen, hosted the seminar *Human rights, dignity and autonomy in health care and social services: Nordic perspectives.* Its primary focus was the concept of human dignity and its relation to individual autonomy in health care and social services. Whilst most of the chapters derive from presentations given at the seminar, the authors have since further developed those contributions for this volume. We thank everyone who has contributed, especially those who have taken the time to produce the texts that make up this book. We also thank those who contributed to the seminar but whose work is not represented here (Georg Høyer, Elisabeth Rynning, Brynhildur Flovenz, Inger Hilde Nordhus and Kirsten Ketscher): this book has greatly benefited from their important knowledge and valuable perspectives. Language editor Natalie Reid has provided invaluable advice in editing this volume. Responsibility for any shortcomings and errors remain with the editors and the authors.

We also wish to thank the two institutions that have provided us with the necessary funds for hosting the seminar and producing this volume: the Faculty of Law, University of Bergen, for financial support of the seminar, and both the Faculty of Law and NOVA Norwegian Social Research for financial support of this publication.

Henriette Sinding Aasen
Rune Halvorsen
António Barbosa da Silva

TABLE OF CONTENTS

CHAPTER 6
COERCIVE TREATMENT AND HUMAN DIGNITY

CHAPTER 7
HUMAN DIGNITY, THE VALUE OF KNOWLEDGE, AND THE LIMITS OF SCIENTIFIC FREEDOM

CHAPTER 8
AUTONOMY AND DIGNITY IN CLINICAL MEDICAL RESEARCH ON ADULTS WITH COGNITIVE IMPAIRMENT

LIST OF ABBREVIATIONS

ALMM	Active Labour Market Measures
CEDAW	Convention on the Elimination of All Forms of Discrimination against Women
CoE	Council of Europe
CRC	Convention on the Rights of the Child
DOP	Disabled People's Organizations
EC	European Commission
ECtHR	European Court of Human Rights
ECHR	European Convention on Human Rights and Fundamental Freedoms
EU	European Union
EU25	The Member States of the European Union from 2004 (Austria, Belgium, Cyprus, Czech Republic, Denmark, Estonia, Finland, France, Germany, Greece, Hungary, Ireland, Italy, Latvia, Lithuania, Luxembourg, Malta, Netherlands, Poland, Portugal, Slovakia, Slovenia, Spain, Sweden, United Kingdom
EU-SILC	European Union Statistics on Income and Living Conditions
GDP	Gross Domestic Product
ICCPR	International Covenant on Civil and Political Rights
ICESCR	International Covenant on Economic, Social and Cultural Rights
NEM	Norwegian National Committee on Medical Research Ethics
NLWO	The Norwegian Labour and Welfare Organization
OECD	Organisation for Economic Co-operation and Development
UDHR	Universal Declaration of Human Rights
UK	United Kingdom
UN	United Nations
US	United States of America
WHO	World Health Organization

INTRODUCTION

Henriette Sinding Aasen, Rune Halvorsen
and António Barbosa da Silva

This volume examines important human rights questions of high relevance for modern welfare states. The overall theme of the volume is the understanding of human dignity, autonomy and human rights in health care and social services in modern welfare states, especially in the Nordic countries. The focus is on vulnerable groups such as children, individuals with cognitive impairment or mental illness, and persons with physical disabilities. Experts in law, philosophy and sociology identify legal, ethical and sociological dilemmas and conflicts in modern welfare services and describe how basic values and rights either are or may come in conflict in concrete situations.

Of particular interest is how the human rights perspective challenges the policies and regulations of modern welfare states while providing the overall normative direction for how to solve ethical, legal and social conflicts or shortcomings. Although the human rights perspective is the dominant one, insights from philosophy and the social sciences provide both a necessary and a fruitful supplement to the legal approach. The volume presents analyses and findings from studies of how human rights are balanced and expressed in the regulation of Nordic welfare services in the twenty-first century, especially for individuals considered in need of help and assistance from others, e.g. children, patients with cognitive impairment and persons with disabilities.

The Nordic welfare states are built on democratic, humanistic ideals and a policy of social justice. All are characterized by their protection of fundamental human rights, both the classic 'negative' civil rights (freedom from unjustified state interventions) and modern 'positive' welfare rights (social rights, entitlements). However, an important aspect of the welfare state has been the risk of paternalism inherent in social policies. The state often confers help and assistance on condition that the individual relinquish personal freedom or autonomy. This situation arises because the state conceives of the lives and habits of the individuals in need as requiring intervention; they are in need of help and thus objects of scrutiny.

Research has demonstrated that Nordic welfare states are characterized by a more active state involvement in citizen well-being than most European countries. The state's involvement has been strong in all social policy areas, with public authorities as the main providers of services.[1] At the same time a high premium has been set on participation in the labour market and social equality.[2] Such normative ideals have created incentives for implementing an active and even interventionist approach to individuals whom public authorities consider in need of support.[3] In the Nordic tradition of active state interventions for achieving ambitious goals of social equality, generous welfare services, and the highest possible employment rate in the working age population, the legal standing of the citizen has received less focus from or control by courts, and legal tribunals have played a minor role.[4] For a long time, social policies have put greater emphasis on meeting collective needs and guaranteeing citizens certain standards of material and physical well-being than on extending individual autonomy and participation. The securing of material rights and entitlements for the population as a whole has received more priority than the protection of individual autonomy.

When it comes to the health care sector, patients with serious mental illness have been the main targets for public interventionism. The use of coercive measures, although limited to patients with serious mental illness under strict conditions, has a long tradition in psychiatric health care. The principle of informed consent is dominant in the field of somatic health care, with exceptions generally accepted only in emergency situations. However, when it comes to children and individuals with cognitive impairment, the picture is more blurred. The Nordic states are still defining a proper balance between the principles of protectionism (public intervention) and individual autonomy.

We therefore believe that the Nordic welfare states represent a particularly interesting case for identifying dilemmas and unsolved issues in the application of a human rights perspective within modern welfare services. Whether individual autonomy and dignity are sufficiently protected in the Nordic welfare system is an ongoing discussion and an open question. Given the risks of paternalism inherent in modern welfare policies, we see a clear need to analyze and discuss the

1 M. Kautto et al. (eds.), *Nordic Welfare States in the European Context* (Routledge, 2001), p. 13.

2 H. M. Hernes, 'Scandinavian Citizenship', 31 *Acta Sociologica*, 3 (1988), 199–215; M. Gullestad, *The Art of Social Relations: Essays on Culture, Social Action and Everyday Life in Modern Norway* (Scandinavian University Press, 1992).

3 G. Broberg and N. Roll-Hansen (eds.) Eugenics and the Welfare State. Sterilization policy in Denmark, Sweden, Norway and Finland (Michigan State University Press, 1997); B. Hvinden (ed.), *Romanifolket og det norske samfunn. Følgene av hundre års politikk for en nasjonal minoritet* [The Roma people and Norwegian society. Consequences of a century's policy towards a national minority] (Fagbokforlaget, 2000).

4 K. Ketscher 2008, *Socialret* [Social law] (Thomson, 2008).

normative basis for modern welfare services, especially in the light of international human rights instruments. The notion of human rights implies that everyone has the right to be treated with respect and dignity, and that individual self-determination or autonomy must be respected as far as possible.

However, in many instances the right to self-determination cannot be respected without a serious risk of violating other rights, such as the right to health. The main theme in this book is the relationship and tension between modern welfare rights and the traditional civil rights protecting individual autonomy. In particular, the book focuses on the legal protection of human dignity and autonomy with regard to vulnerable groups, such as children and persons with disabilities, including individuals with cognitive impairment or mental illness. Many individuals in obvious need of medical treatment and care are not able to give valid informed consent to proposed interventions, thus giving rise to a constant tension between different human rights. The book argues that balancing conflicting human rights calls for invoking human dignity, as human dignity is the core value to be protected through human rights. Thus one of the basic questions is how to protect the human dignity of a person when individual autonomy cannot be (fully) respected, for example with regard to coercive or non-consensual medical treatment of children and individuals with cognitive impairment or mental illness.

The concept of human dignity is also explored in relation to medical research on human subjects not able to give valid consent and in relation to individuals with non-cognitive impairments. For the latter, the problem is not a question of legal capacity for giving valid consent to interventions but rather one of social policy for ensuring non-discrimination and respect for human dignity. The book provides case studies of different situations in which the right to self-determination or individual autonomy is at stake and in which the concept of human dignity is invoked as a way of protecting and balancing conflicting principles, values and rights.

Human rights, dignity and autonomy in health care and social services: Nordic perspectives consists of three main parts. Part I, comprising two chapters, offers a theoretical overview and analysis of basic concepts and the human rights framework, as well as a brief description of some of the tensions between different human rights in modern welfare states. Part II comprises seven chapters offering more details and examples of the concrete tensions in particular areas in which human dignity and autonomy are at stake, such as decision-making involving children in health care and social services, treatment of or care for individuals with mental illness or cognitive impairment, medical research on human subjects, and general protection of the rights of persons with disabilities.

In particular the chapters discuss important provisions in the European Convention on Human Rights and Fundamental Freedoms (ECHR), the Convention for the Protection of Human Rights and Dignity of the Human Being with regard to the Application of Biology and Medicine. Convention on Human Rights and Biomedicine (Biomedicine Convention) and the UN Convention on the Rights of Persons with Disabilities.[5] In addition, the chapters present Nordic domestic legislation as examples of how the provisions in human rights instruments are implemented and how human rights instruments may guide future amendments in national law. Some of the chapters have a general Nordic and comparative perspective, while others focus mainly on law and practice in one of the Nordic countries (primarily Norway). Part III concludes the volume and points to both current and future challenges in the field.

Description of the chapters

Chapter 1 (Barbosa da Silva) analyzes the concepts of autonomy, human dignity and integrity, and their interrelationship with regard to health care ethics, law and basic human rights. This analysis is rooted in Kantian humanism, non-Kantian humanism and a non-humanistic concept of the human being. The chapter argues that Western European health care ethics is dominated by two central normative concepts: *dignity* and *autonomy*. The author argues that human dignity is still used in the Kantian sense, meaning that the intrinsic worth of human life is equal for all human beings. Autonomy, on the other hand, is also used in an empirical and non-Kantian humanistic sense. When the two conflict in health care contexts, the protection of human dignity receives priority. The analysis emphasizes that the Kantian concept of dignity is not only inalienable and equal for all humans but also the normative foundation of the contemporary human rights doctrine.

The chapter discusses five different but logically possible relations between law and morality in the light of two mutually exclusive interpretative traditions: the *natural law* tradition and the *legal positivist* tradition. Each of these traditions presupposes different views of the human being, society and their interrelationship. These views, which can be either humanistic or non-humanistic, constitute the basis for different conceptions of human dignity, which is the ultimate normative foundation of health care and human rights and law. The author maintains that the position of natural law, combined with the Kantian humanistic concept of human dignity, provides the most plausible interpretations of law and morality and their interrelationship.

5 Council of Europe 1950 and 1997, UN 2006.

Chapter 2 (Aasen) analyzes the role of human dignity and human rights in the modern welfare state. Together with Chapter 1, this chapter provides a theoretical overview and a conceptual framework for the rest of the book. It also briefly describes some of the conflicts or tensions between different human rights in modern welfare states, which are beneficent states based not only on 'negative' freedoms and civil rights but also on 'positive' social entitlement rights. Although the principle of self-determination is fundamental, the welfare state is to some extent paternalistic, as it does not leave individuals to their own destiny but takes responsibility for their survival and well-being. This paternalistic aspect of the welfare state is a problem mainly in the case of coercive or non-voluntary interventions in the private sphere of individuals. The human rights framework, protecting both civil and social rights, and with human dignity as its core value, is the overarching normative guideline for the implementation of social policies in modern welfare states. However, the inherent tensions between various human rights need thorough and constant analysis, both separately and in relation to other rights. The balancing of human rights is an ongoing normative process that will continue, along with social, scientific and normative developments, at both national and international levels.

Chapter 3 (Sandberg) examines a child's right to participation in health decisions concerning himself or herself according to the UN Convention on the Rights of Children (CRC) and under Norwegian law. The author argues that Article 12 of the CRC is of particular importance for regulating the right to participation, and that using Article 12 as a moral compass for amending the existing Norwegian law is possible. The author identifies a tension between the autonomy of the child and the protection of the child and its health. In cases of conflicting views between the child and the parents, or between the child and the health personnel, the distinction between regarding the child as an acting subject and regarding him or her as an object to be protected becomes highly visible. Although how to balance the right to participation and the right to health is not self-evident, Sandberg argues that Norwegian law has a scope for strengthening the participatory rights of the individual child.

Chapter 4 (Skivenes) explores children as participants and service users in child welfare cases. The author identifies six reasons for involving children in decision-making processes and four institutional and five individual obstacles that hinder the successful fulfilment of children's right to participation. The chapter studies how experienced Norwegian child welfare workers actually understand and handle children's participation in decision-making processes. The findings show that although children's participation is primarily justified by a need for information, about half the interviewees report that respect for the child's integrity and decisions about the life of the child are important grounds for recognizing the child's right to participate. This finding indicates that children have a relatively prominent role in child welfare work, despite room for improvement. However, when the author asked these welfare workers how they give a child's view due weight in accordance with the age and maturity of the child, the welfare workers displayed uneasiness and a lack of concrete procedures for handling the issue. The few welfare workers who had a clear opinion about how they could give a child's view due weight focused on whether the child had substantial reasons for his or her views and whether the child was consistent in maintaining them.

Chapter 5 (Aasen) discusses the role of informed consent in relation to treatment of individuals with cognitive impairment. The right of giving informed consent to treatment is an important patient right, derived from the general principle of individual autonomy. However, when the person concerned lacks decisional capacity to give valid consent and is in obvious need of health care, the principle of autonomy does not give sufficient protection and is also challenged by the principle of beneficence. The chapter presents the various rights at stake: health, private life, self-determination and liberty, and the right to life and to freedom from torture, inhuman or degrading treatment. It also explores the international and national legal protection of persons with cognitive impairment, including the requirement of qualifying reasons for depriving individuals of their right to give consent to treatment, proper procedures, proportionality, proxy consent and patient participation. Special attention goes to the new Norwegian regulation of coercive measures towards various groups of adults not able to give valid consent, especially elderly individuals with dementia, in the interests of ensuring proper treatment and care. The author emphasizes that the notion of human dignity is essential for reaching a justified understanding of, and balance between, the rights at stake.

Chapter 6 (Hartlev) explores the relationship between various conceptions of human dignity and the use of coercion in psychiatric care. Respect for personal liberty is one of the most widely acknowledged human rights. Curtailment of personal liberty is normally only justifiable in extraordinary situations in which substantial interests of other persons or of society speak in favour of such actions. However, psychiatric care has a long tradition of deprivation of liberty and the use of coercion, a tradition leading to reflections on respect for human dignity. Although the concept of dignity plays an important role both within moral philosophy and in law, the concept is somehow nebulous and in need of clarification. The chapter provides an analysis of human dignity as it is used in human rights law and discusses how various conceptions of it relate to the use of coercion in psychiatric care. The concept of human dignity employed in human rights law appears multifaceted: sometimes human dignity is related to respect for autonomy, sometimes it is related to respect for the intrinsic worth of all human beings, and sometimes it is also related to the obligation for providing dignified conditions of detainment.

The chapter concludes that whether coercion is either in conflict with or supportive of the right to respect for human dignity depends on one's point of departure. Most importantly, the legal concept of dignity requires the regarding of all human beings as individuals with intrinsic worth, thereby providing a reference point for making the difficult decision between respecting a person's autonomous or non-autonomous wishes and offering sufficient psychiatric care for persons who are weak and vulnerable.

Chapter 7 (Barbosa da Silva) discusses the ethical limits of scientific freedom. The author argues that scientific freedom is based on and justified by the value attributed to knowledge. The author also asserts that scientific freedom can be limited by a number of factors such as the responsibility of the researcher, the value of knowledge, the concept of human dignity, and the needs of society and humanity. Human dignity is considered the ultimate justification for the limitation of scientific freedom. The chapter stresses that the need for putting limits on scientific freedom becomes pertinent when vulnerable groups are used as research participants. The chapter clarifies both the meaning of and the ethical justification for scientific freedom. The author emphasizes that the limitation of scientific freedom is ethically justifiable only if human beings are attributed greater value than that attributed to knowledge. The chapter presents and explains twelve logically possible relations between the values attributed to human beings and to knowledge, showing that the universality of the equal value of all human beings is based on the view of the human being as unique, with a special moral status. Finally the author points out that, given human uniqueness and dignity, producers and consumers of scientific knowledge, including researchers and state authorities, are ethically and legally responsible for respecting, defending and promoting limits on scientific freedom.

Chapter 8 (Lötjönen) examines how the concepts of autonomy and dignity have been taken into account in clinical medical research on adults with cognitive impairment, with a special focus on persons with dementia. The author has chosen three central requirements in medical research regulation for closer analysis: primacy of the human being, balance of risks and benefits, and respect for the wishes of a person with cognitive impairment and whose legal capacity for decision-making in matters about his or her own health has therefore been limited. In each area the chapter examines the relevance of autonomy and dignity with respect to Nordic and European regulation. In the regulation of medical research, the concept of human dignity appears mostly in protective provisions, whereas autonomy is regarded mainly as a means of empowerment.

However, the balance between protection and empowerment is not black and white. Research strategies giving a research subject a chance to participate by informing him or her about the project in which he or she is involved, paying attention to the previous wishes of the particular participant, and respecting the signs of objection suggest that different combinations of protection and empowerment of the research subjects will occur. While the Nordic countries are generally the same when it comes to regulating medical research on adults who have been legally incapacitated, some interesting anomalies appear.

Chapter 9 (Halvorsen and Hvinden) argues that the Nordic welfare states have thus far been more successful in providing social security benefits, health care and social services than in obligating employers to be responsible for providing work for persons with disabilities. Neither have the Nordic welfare states been very advanced when it comes to legal obligations for businesses to provide accessibility to goods and services for users or consumers with disabilities. The authors argue that the weaknesses in the system have been generated by limitations in the Nordic cooperative welfare state model as it was constructed after World War II. As the Nordic governments have been reluctant to confront business and employers too strongly, regulatory measures (including legislation) for advancing real opportunities for persons with disabilities to participate in mainstream society have been underdeveloped.

A movement in the direction of more binding legal regulations within Nordic disability protection is likely to be stimulated by the evolving supranational equal treatment policy as it has materialized in the United Nations, the Council of Europe and the European Union. However, the evolving human rights approach to disability in supranational disability law and policy is challenging some of the underlying assumptions of the Nordic welfare state model. Yet the authors argue that the Nordic countries ought to have good opportunities for finding ways of socializing the costs associated with new regulations for advancing employment and accessibility for persons with disabilities, and for avoiding disproportionate burdens on business and employers.

Conclusions

Although *Human rights, dignity and autonomy in health care and social services* focuses on Nordic perspectives and experiences, the chapters identify moral, legal, and policy issues and dilemmas that are relevant for other countries and policy contexts. The Nordic responses to human rights concerns in health care and social services will not necessarily be directly transferable to other institutional contexts, legal traditions and policy cultures, since states have different conditions for providing health care and social services. Nevertheless, as other countries are likely to face similar dilemmas and questions, experiences from the Nordic legal and social context might be useful in their endeavours to apply and implement human rights instruments in health care and social services.

The ideas and arguments that the different chapters present are all based on the ethical philosophies of humanism, affirming the dignity and worth of all human beings. Although as a system of philosophy humanism is a broad category with different schools of thought, they all focus on the universal qualities of human beings when determining what is right and wrong and emphasize personal autonomy and independence. Contemporary humanism has ideological roots dating back to Ancient Greek and Renaissance humanism, whilst the modern human rights doctrine is also based on the eighteenth century idea of 'natural rights'[6], born out of the philosophical humanism centred on human needs and interests.

Philosopher Immanuel Kant (1724–1804), one of the most influential thinkers of modern Europe, developed a form of humanism whose bearing on the human self and its capacity for reasoning is central for our current understanding of human dignity and human rights. Indeed, Kantian humanism is essential for the understanding of modern health care ethics, law and human rights. Human rights, both civil and social, have become an international ethical and legal standard for treating humans with dignity. However, this standard must be constantly applied and implemented in new situations and social settings, with a special focus on protecting vulnerable groups and individuals from violations of their dignity and basic rights, including in health care and social services.

6 Thomas Paine, *Rights of Man*, 1791.

PART I
BASIC CONCEPTS, THEORY AND NORMATIVE FRAMEWORK

CHAPTER 1
AUTONOMY, DIGNITY AND INTEGRITY IN HEALTH CARE ETHICS – A MORAL PHILOSOPHICAL PERSPECTIVE

António Barbosa da Silva

1. INTRODUCTION

This chapter examines the relationship between the concepts of autonomy, dignity and integrity, and their implications for health care and law. These three closely related concepts are central to health care ethics, the normative ethics for all health professionals. These ethics express the moral obligation of all health professionals to save life, prevent sickness, alleviate suffering, promote health, and comfort the patient or client.[1] This goal implies care and respect for the dignity, autonomy and vulnerability of the human being. Health care ethics is conceived here as an umbrella term for medical ethics, nursing ethics, social ethics (e.g. ethics for social workers), etc.

The purpose of this chapter is threefold. First, it will clarify the different meanings of 'autonomy', 'dignity' and 'integrity' to point out which of these are most relevant to health care ethics, law and human rights. The right to health care today is a human right that is both ethical and, within this context, legal. The chapter, providing both a classical humanistic and a non-humanistic view of these three concepts, will indicate not only the differences between them but also their respective consequences for health care ethics. The classical humanistic perspective here means a view of all human beings as equal in dignity, with shared basic rights. By contrast, non-humanistic perspectives deny what humanistic perspectives affirm, especially the universality of human autonomy, dignity and basic human rights.

---

1 J.M. Mann, *Medicine and Public Health, Ethics and Human Rights* (Hastings Center Report, 1997) 6–13.

Second, the chapter will discuss the interrelationship between the three concepts within the humanistic and non-humanistic traditions, as both are relevant to health care ethics, law and human rights. The humanistic viewpoint dominates health care ethics today through its concept of dignity, whereas the non-humanistic viewpoint dominates health care ethics through its concept of autonomy.

Third, in the light of these analyses, the chapter discusses the logical connection between law and ethics – the legally right and the ethically right – to see which of them should have priority when they conflict in health care and law. In addition, I shall argue that, regardless of the relationship between the two, both legal norms and ethical norms presuppose a given concept of the human being and society, in turn implying certain concepts of reality. All of these concepts are relevant to health care ethics, law, human rights and their interrelationship.

2. THE AMBIGUITY OF THE TERMS 'AUTONOMY', 'DIGNITY' AND 'INTEGRITY'

Law philosopher Gerald Dworkin points out at least fourteen meanings of the word 'autonomy':

> ... '[A]utonomy' ... is used sometimes as an equivalent to liberty ..., sometimes as equivalent to self-rule or sovereignty, sometimes as identical with freedom of the will. It is equated with dignity, integrity, individuality, independence, responsibility, and self-knowledge. It is identified with qualities of self-assertion, with critical reflections, with freedom from obligation, with absence of external causation, with knowledge of one's own interests ... It is related to actions, to beliefs, to reasons for acting, to rules, to the will of other persons, to thoughts, and to principles. About the only features held constant from one author to another are that autonomy is a feature of persons and that it is a desirable quality to have.[2]

Dworkin holds that defining the concept of autonomy is not possible, and that autonomy functions as three different ideals: moral, political and social.[3] This chapter deals with autonomy primarily as a moral ideal. As Dworkin points out, 'autonomy' is sometimes used as a synonym for 'dignity' or 'integrity'. Therefore, to show their relevance to health care ethics, law and human rights, I shall begin by specifying some important meanings of these three words and their interrelationship.

---

2 G. Dworkin, *The Theory and Practice of Autonomy. Cambridge Studies in Philosophy* (Cambridge University Press, 1988) p. 6.

3 Ibid., p. 10.

3. AUTONOMY IN KANT'S, POST-KANTIAN, AND NON-HUMANISTIC PHILOSOPHY

3.1. CONCEPTUAL CLARIFICATION

The word 'autonomy' is a combination of two Greek words: *autos* (oneself) and *nomos* (law). The term 'autonomy' is used with different meanings in different academic contexts such as moral philosophy, criminal law, theology and political science. Autonomy is used in ethics to express the idea that a human being possesses the moral law within him- or herself so that he or she needs no outside laws or norms to guide his or her actions.[4] Consequently, a human being is an autonomous, sovereign or self-governing, and responsible agent. Autonomy thus means that the human being is completely different from all other known beings in the universe, in the sense that the human is not totally controlled by the laws of nature. I shall first analyze the eighteenth century philosopher Immanuel Kant's concept of autonomy, then the concept of autonomy in the non-humanistic philosophy. The reason for focusing on Kant is that Kant's understanding of dignity is still used for justifying human equality and basic rights, and it can be used for ultimately justifying distributive social justice as based on the equality of all human beings. The Kantian understanding of dignity is also assumed in the UN Universal Declaration of Human Rights (Articles 1 and 23).

3.1.1. Autonomy as an inherent human property according to Kant

In the European humanistic tradition, autonomy has always been considered a specific moral value belonging to the human being. For Kant autonomy is a unique human feature that distinguishes the human being from all other beings in the world. The ultimate basis for autonomy is another inherent human property that Kant calls reason. Therefore, the concept of autonomy is grounded in the human ability to reason.

3.1.2. Autonomy, human reason and their interrelationship according to Kant

Understanding Kant's view of autonomy and reason calls for understanding his dualistic view of the human being, which we can summarize as follows: the human being is a rational being and a moral agent, belonging to the 'super-sensible' or 'intelligible' world. Thus the human being is independent of the laws of nature, with absolute self-determination or autonomy. The human being is also

4 The term autonomy 'was first applied to the Greek city state. A city had *autonomia* when its citizens made their own laws, opposed to being under the control of some conquering power' (Dworkin, *The Theory and Practice of Autonomy*, p. 108).

an empirical being with desires, inclinations and vulnerability. As an empirical being, the human is subject to the laws of nature (e.g. physical, biological, psychological) and belongs to the empirical, sensible world. Kant explains the human being's relationship to these two different worlds as follows:

> The rational being counts himself [sic.], qua intelligence, as belonging to the intelligible world ... But on the other side, he is conscious of himself as being also a part of the world of sense, where his actions are found as mere appearances of that causality ... these actions as belonging to the world of sense must be viewed as determined by other appearances, namely, desires and inclinations. Therefore, if I were solely a member of the intelligible world, then all my actions would perfectly conform to the principle of the autonomy of a pure will; if I were solely a part of the world of sense, my actions would have to be taken as in complete conformity with the natural law of desires and inclinations, i.e. with the heteronomy of nature.[5]

As this statement shows, a split exists between the intelligible (non-empirical) dimension and the empirical dimension of the human being. Philosopher Poul Lübcke holds that, according to Kant, the split is reconciled as follows: the human being has an inherent feeling of respect (reverence or awe) for moral law, which is spontaneously given by reason.[6] Because of this inherent feeling – which belongs to the human being's intelligible dimension (reason) – the human being can act as a free agent in the empirical world. Furthermore, Kant's solution for the incompatibility between natural necessity (expressed in the laws of nature) and human freedom (independence from these laws), is the following: 'we because of our awareness of belonging to the kingdom of ends and the idea of God, who guarantees that reason functions in the seemingly reasonless nature, can live as if there were a harmony between freedom and nature'.[7] Thus reason is presupposed in both worlds so that autonomy can function. In Kant's view, 'autonomy is a property of the will of moral agents that allows them to act on principles and not be determined by empirical causes'.[8] This 'property of the will' can be defined as the power of the will for self-determination and 'spontaneous causation' of moral actions, in contrast to the natural causation of the laws of nature, e.g. gravity.[9]

Thus Kant's concepts of autonomy, rationality and pure will are primarily metaphysical, not empirical. Kant grounds autonomy in rationality as a non-empirical concept. It is on this concept of autonomy that he bases his concept of

---

5 I. Kant, *Groundwork for the metaphysics of moral*, 2nd Ed., (Hackett Publishing Company, 1981) p. 54.

6 P. Lübcke (ed.) *Filosofilexikonet* [Dictionary of Philosophy] (Forum, 1988) p. 286.

7 Ibid.

8 Dworkin, *The Theory and Practice of Autonomy*, p. 57.

9 Ibid., p. 14f. For 'spontaneous causality', see also W. T. Jones, *A History of Western Philosophy* (Harcourt, Brace and World, 1952) p. 862.

human dignity, as we shall see in Section 4. In Kant's ethics the basic concepts are human rationality, autonomy, will and dignity, all non-empirical concepts.[10]

3.2. AUTONOMY IN POST-KANTIAN HUMANISM

Post-Kantian humanism refers to humanists who lived after Kant and who like him hold that the human being is unique with respect to reason, autonomy and dignity. Nevertheless, in contrast to Kant, they justify human uniqueness by appealing not to metaphysics but to what they regard as essential and unique to the human species. Thus, from a post-Kantian humanist viewpoint, an individual's autonomy is neither a super-sensible property of the human being in the Kantian sense nor a property based on an individual human being's acquired characteristic.[11] It is, however, one of the properties that distinguish the human being from all other beings. Post-Kantian humanists talk about autonomy as freedom conceived in a threefold sense: The individual's freedom of the will (the freedom of indeterminacy), the individual's freedom of choice (the freedom of alternative choice), and the individual's freedom of action (the freedom of self-determination).[12]

An individual's freedom of will means his or her potential or actual ability to think up alternative courses of actions or to understand the differences between alternative actions that other individuals may think up. Freedom of will is also the individual's capacity for reflecting upon his or her desires and choices and preferences so that he or she can voluntarily change them.[13]

An individual's freedom of choice means his or her actual ability to choose one alternative action. An individual's freedom of action (which includes civil or legal rights) means his or her actual ability or opportunity to realize the chosen action

10 This non-empirical (i.e. metaphysical) feature of Kant's ethics creates some problems when applied to health care ethics, where the empirical dimension of the human being is central. Those who do not accept Kant's metaphysical assumption cannot accept his dualistic concept of the human being or the way he attempts to reconcile them. This aspect of Kant's ethics is therefore irrelevant to health care ethics today. Cf. T. Honderich (ed.) *The Oxford Companion to Philosophy*, (Oxford University Press, 1995) p. 595.

11 J.D. Rendtorff and P. Kemp, *Basic Ethical Principles in European Bioethics and Biolaw, Vol. I, Autonomy, Dignity, Integrity and Vulnerability*, (Danish Centre for Ethics and Law, 2000), pp. 33f.

12 D. D. Runes, *Dictionary of Philosophy* (Adams and Co., 1974) p. 112.

13 Dworkin, *The Theory and Practice of Autonomy*, pp. 15–20.

without external coercions, constraints or restrictions. Philosopher Harald Ofstad defines freedom of action as an individual's power to act otherwise.[14]

Freedom in these three senses may vary by individual, and in the same individual it may vary by situation. The relationship between these three forms of freedom is that freedom of will is a necessary condition for freedom of choice, which in turn is a necessary condition for freedom of action. Reason as a human capacity for thinking plays a fundamental role in the exercise of freedom in all three senses. Although all three concepts of freedom are interrelated, freedom of action is above all morally correlated to ethical right, responsibility or accountability, moral obligation or duty, praise or approval, blame, guilt and penalty.[15] Thus an individual is responsible in relation to other persons only for those deeds or omissions that presuppose freedom as liberty. Therefore, before ascribing any moral property such as responsibility or blame to a person, one should ask whether the person could have acted otherwise. If the answer is no, the person had no freedom of action; thus attributing blame or responsibility to that person is not ethically right.

Like Kant, post-Kantian humanists agree that what makes an individual a moral agent is only that he or she is human. In other words, even if an individual does not exhibit reason or free will in a given situation (e.g. due to illness), he or she is still a potentially rational and autonomous human being.[16]

Again, both Kantian and non-Kantian humanists conceive of the human being as qualitatively different from other beings. They base this view on human reason, freedom and the potentiality for goodness. On these human characteristics they base human dignity, which for them is the foundation of human rights. Likewise, both schools view dignity as a non-empirical concept with a universal value. Most important, and the most relevant difference between them in our context, is how they relate autonomy to human dignity.

---

14 Ofstad does not mention freedom of action, but talks about freedom of decision, which he includes in the former. He defines what he calls a 'stable decision' – a decision that leads to a planned result and that is 'supported by the cognitive and motivational orientation of the individual and meet no inner resistance' (H. Ofstad, *An Inquiry into the Freedom of Decision*, Norwegian University Press and George Allen and Unwin LTD, 1961) p. 17 f; H. Ofstad, *Ansvar og handling: Diskusjon av moral- og rettsfilosofiske spørsmål* [Responsibility and Action: discussion of issues within moral philosophy and philosophy of law] (Scandinavian University Press, 1980).

15 Cf. Dworkin, *The Theory and Practice of Autonomy*, p. 112; R.M. Hare, *Moral Thinking* (Oxford University Press, 1981) pp. 29–32.

16 R. Brandt (ed.), *Social Justice* (Prentice-Hall, Inc., 1962), p. 19; P. Singer 'All Animals are Equals', in P. Singer (ed.), *Applied Ethics* (Oxford University Press, 1986).

3.3. AUTONOMY IN NON-HUMANISTIC PHILOSOPHY

Kantian and post-Kantian humanists differ in the way they justify human uniqueness in relation to animals. Non-humanists, by contrast, deny human uniqueness and accept only a difference of degree between human beings and animals.[17]

Some non-humanists, like B.F. Skinner, deny the existence of both human autonomy and dignity. Others attribute autonomy in different degrees to different human individuals. For example, Nietzsche asserts that autonomy varies according to the individual. He ascribes more autonomy to the super-humans than to the average person or to a crowd. He thus assigns a higher value to the former than to the latter.[18]

Those non-humanists who believe that humans have autonomy reduce the content of that autonomy to an individual's actual freedom, feeling of moral worth, self-esteem and self-respect. As this kind of feeling and this concept of autonomy, as individual freedom, may vary by individual, the value of an individual (i.e. his or her dignity) is not constant or equal among all human beings. This view of the human being has negative consequences for social justice in democratic societies, such as the Nordic countries.

As we have seen, while humanists emphasize what all human beings have in common, non-humanists emphasize their differences. Thus, while for the humanists human autonomy is the basis of human dignity, for the non-humanists actual autonomy is the basis of an individual's dignity: 'a constructive (i.e., non-humanistic) interpretation of dignity as the result of the moral efforts and actions of the autonomous subject should not be excluded.'[19] These differences, as we shall see, have relevant consequences for ethics in general and for health care ethics in particular.

---

17 Singer, *Applied ethics*, 1986, pp. 57–85. Non-humanists, like Skinner, deny the existence of human freedom, dignity and responsibility. We can say that, for them, ethics do not exist. See B. F. Skinner, *Beyond Freedom and Dignity*, (Vintage Books, 1980).

18 F. Nietzsche, *Jenseits von Gut und Böse* [Beyond Good and Evil] (Alfred Kröner Verlag, 1976) p. 196; Friedrich Nietzsche, *Zur Genealogie der Moral* [On the Genealogy of Morality](Alfred Kröner Verlag, 1976) p. 211.

19 Rendtorff and Kemp, *Basic Ethical Principles in European Bioethics and Biolaw*, pp. 33f.

3.4. AUTONOMY AS A NORMATIVE PRINCIPLE IN HUMANISTIC HEALTH CARE ETHICS

For both humanists and non-humanists, autonomy is a defining characteristic of the human being and a basic normative principle in health care ethics. But they use the term 'autonomy' differently.

The centrality and normativity of autonomy are emphasized in health care contexts, in which informed consent is contrasted with non-justified paternalism. Informed consent can be defined as 'the expression of the priority given to the autonomy of the patient over the paternalist approaches, which might ignore the wish of the patient'.[20] The nature and function of informed consent can be described as follows:

> The principle of informed consent is a statement of the fidelity between the man who performs medical procedures and the man on whom they are performed ... The principle of informed consent is the canon of loyalty joining men together in medical practice and investigation.[21]

The value and purpose of informed consent can be stated as '(t)he purpose of requiring the patient's consent to treatment is to protect his physical and psychic integrity against unwanted invasions, and to permit the patient to act as an autonomous being'.[22]

In both definitions the 'autonomous being' is the individual patient as seen in relation to other individuals. This view differs from Kant's, for whom autonomy is the human will subjected not to laws of nature but to its own law, the 'categorical imperative', which is given and imposed by human reason or rationality.[23] Kant formulates his categorical imperative in three different but closely related ways. In essence, we should always treat other persons as ends in themselves, never only as means for achieving any other end or goal (e.g. our own interests or desires).[24]

As we have seen, Kant's concept of autonomy is abstract, general and applicable to the state of an individual as a human being. Hence, to be autonomous is to be a

---

20 The Explanatory Report to the Biomedicine Convention, para. 9. See also J. Dute, 'The Leading Principles of the Convention on Human Rights and Biomedicine', in J.K.M. Gevers et al. (eds.) *Health Law, Human Rights and the Biomedicine Convention* (Martinus Nijhoff Publishers, 2005) pp. 3–12.

21 Dworkin, *The Theory and Practice of Autonomy*, p. 102.

22 Ibid.

23 Kant, *Groundwork for the metaphysics of moral*, p. 41.

24 An 'end or goal' in itself means something with *intrinsic* value that has value in itself, whereas 'means' means something with only *extrinsic* or *instrumental* value. Implicit in this formulation of the categorical imperative is the universal principle of humanity.

rational being, a being distinctive from both non-rational living beings (e.g. animals and plants) and from non-sensible beings (e.g. stones). While Kant's concept of autonomy urges us to always be impartial in our use of ethical norms and principles, it does not guide us in concrete situations. However, post-Kantian humanists talk about individual autonomy as a person's freedom of choices and actions, protecting him or her from the will, power or coercion of other individuals. Therefore, to talk about autonomy as the individual's freedom or liberty is more useful than Kant's abstract concept of autonomy in health care ethics, especially when paternalism is an issue. Liberty is an actual ability and right that one can use to protect one's wishes, desires and interests, and 'to effectuate decisions in action'.[25]

According to Dworkin, autonomy 'claims to be at the center of the justificatory basis for informed consent'. Informed consent is 'justified in terms of privacy, self-determination, loyalty, autonomy, freedom, integrity, dignity, and benefits'.[26] A relevant definition of paternalism here is 'interference with a person's liberty of action justified by reasons referring exclusively to the welfare, good, happiness, needs, interests, or values of the person being coerced'.[27]

4. HUMAN DIGNITY IN HUMANISTIC AND NON-HUMANISTIC PHILOSOPHY

4.1. CONCEPTUAL CLARIFICATION

The word 'dignity' has been used throughout the history of ethics in different ways. In accordance with ethicists Jacob Dahl Rendtorff and Peter Kemp, I shall give seven of these before focusing on those most relevant in our context:

- In Ancient Greece and Rome 'dignity' described 'the outstanding position of a person in society. Cicero (106–43 BC) used the concept of dignity to refer to the respect due to the political master'.
- The Stoics used 'dignity' to designate 'the high value of a human being who possessed the capacity of rationality and was able to obtain insight into the cosmic order'.
- For Renaissance humanists such as Pico della Mirandola (1463–1494), 'the concept of human dignity expressed the moral superiority and responsibility

25 Dworkin, *The Theory and Practice of Autonomy*, p. 105.
26 Ibid., pp. 101 and 103.
27 Ibid., p. 121.

of human beings in relation to themselves, animals, nature and the whole universe.'

- In Christianity, which holds that the human being 'was created in the image of God, imago Dei ... every individual life is therefore of intrinsic worth and inviolable'.
- For Kant 'a human being possesses dignity as an intrinsic value because of his or her autonomous will'.[28]
- For post-Kantian humanists, human dignity is the same as human intrinsic worth, which is regarded as equal for all human beings.
- For non-humanists, dignity 'is something to be acquired by the moral effort' based on the actual freedom of each human individual.[29]

As the next section will show, all of these meanings are still relevant in different contexts, for example, in health care ethics, law and basic human rights. However, in these fields the most relevant definitions are the last three (those of the Kantians, the post-Kantians and the non-humanists).

4.2. HUMAN DIGNITY IN KANTIAN HUMANISM

Kant maintains that while everything has a given price, the human being has dignity and is otherwise priceless. In saying this, he emphasizes dignity as the most fundamental (i.e. ultimate) value of the human being, one that is unique and inestimable. As it is an 'intrinsic worth' which is 'infinitely beyond all prices', humans therefore should never be used only as a means to an end.[30] Kant also talks about the sanctity of human life, suggesting that the right attitude towards human beings is respect or reverence.[31] For Kant – as for all humanists – human dignity is inviolable, constant or unchangeable, inalienable, undeniable, unconditional and equal for all human beings. In other words, every human being has dignity unconditionally. The only condition necessary and sufficient for having dignity is that one is human.

---

28 Rendtorff and Kemp, *Basic Ethical Principles in European Bioethics and Biolaw*, p. 32. See also A. Schulman, 'Bioethics and Human Dignity', Working Paper (The President's Council on Bioethics, 2005).

29 J.D. Rendtorff and P. Kemp, *Basic Ethical Principles in European Bioethics and Biolaw*, pp. 33f.

30 Kant, *Groundwork for the metaphysics of moral*, p. 40f.

31 Ibid., p. 41; I. Kant, *Critique of Practical Reason*. (The Bobb-Merrill Company, 1956/1975) p. 95.

4.2.1. *Human dignity, the sanctity of life and their relationship*

The idea that human life is sacred occurs in many times and places, e.g. Renaissance humanism, the Judeo-Christian and Islamic ethical traditions and Kant's ethics.[32] This belief is closely related to the concept of dignity as previously described. It gives life its inalienable and intrinsic value, which is fundamental for ethics, law and human rights today. However, Renaissance humanism and the Judeo-Christian and Islamic ethical traditions justify the sanctity of life from the belief that the human being is created in God's image. But Kant's justification (i.e. how he relates the sanctity of life to autonomy and reason as necessary conditions for dignity) is not clear. What is clear, however, is that Kant sometimes uses the sanctity of life to emphasize the inviolability of human life.[33] At times Kant appears to use 'dignity' as a synonym for the 'sanctity of life', with both terms referring to the human being's intrinsic and absolute value.[34] Thus Kant holds that the right attitude to human dignity is reverence or respect.[35] From this point of view, one might assume that Kant builds his concept of dignity partly on the Renaissance humanist concept of dignity, especially as conceived by Pico della Mirandola (who, like other Renaissance humanists, grounded human dignity in the view of the human being as created in God's image.[36] However, this assumption conflicts with Kant's attempt to conceive of dignity in non-religious terms. To solve this conflict, one must deny that autonomy and reason are both necessary and sufficient conditions for dignity as Kant affirms. Instead, one should regard them as only necessary conditions, just as one should regard the sanctity of life as a necessary condition for dignity. If they can or need to be combined, then, taken together, they are necessary and sufficient conditions for dignity.[37]

32 Kant, *Groundwork for the metaphysics of moral*, p. 41.

33 Ibid.

34 Ibid., p. 35f. Kant has been criticized for having a religious and metaphysical foundation for human dignity. For a defence of Kant, see D. Birnbacher, 'Human cloning and human dignity', 10 *Reproductive BioMedicine Online* Suppl. 1 (2005), 50–55.

35 Kant, *Groundwork for the metaphysics of moral*, p. 41; Kant, *Critique of Practical Reason*, p. 95.

36 Rendtorff and Kemp, *Basic Ethical Principles in European Bioethics and Biolaw*, p. 32.

37 The humanistic concept of dignity has been criticized and rejected, e.g. by post-modern philosophers, who are non-humanists. One critique of Kant is that '[h]is exclusive focus on rational autonomy leaves Kant with a rather narrow and constricted account of our moral life, one that has precious little to say about the moral significance of a whole range of biomedical interventions that currently arouse ethical controversy ... On ... basic questions in bioethics Kant's account of human dignity does not offer clear moral guidance'. A. Schulman, 'Bioethics and Human Dignity', 1–11.

4.2.2. *The relationship between autonomy and dignity in Kant's ethics*

As we have already seen, from the viewpoint of Kant's ethics, dignity as a specific human value or moral worth is a supervening property, the existence of which presupposes the existence of autonomy and reason.[38] We have also seen that according to Kant, both autonomy and dignity have absolute value and are unchangeable and ought not to be violated. These are some of their common features. We can illustrate the relationship between the two concepts as follows:

Figure 1. Kant's view of the relationship between his concepts of autonomy and human dignity and worth

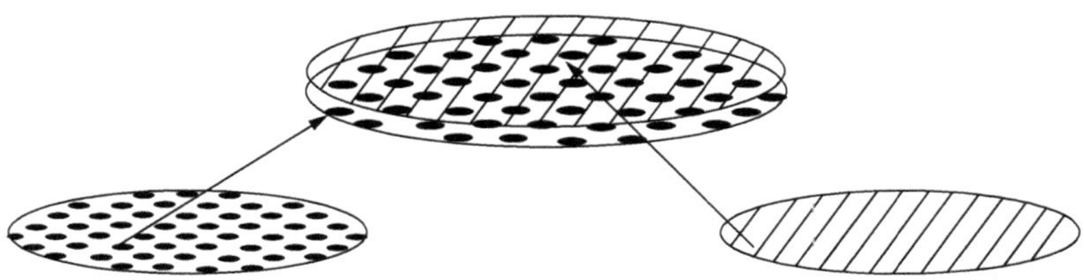

The upper circle comprises the two lower circles, which represent autonomy and dignity and worth.

Although according to Kant dignity is based on autonomy, they are closely related to each other in the following ways: autonomy is the ontological basis of dignity. Autonomy and dignity represent the same ethical value. Autonomy and dignity are complementary concepts. If dignity is violated, autonomy is also violated, and vice-versa. Both autonomy and dignity belong unconditionally to all human beings. Both autonomy and dignity give all human beings the right to 'equal treatment and treatment as equal', 'equal concern and respect', and 'equal protection'.[39] Thus autonomy and dignity cannot be separated from each other and therefore have the same normative value (fig. 1). For Kant to respect human dignity is simultaneously to respect human autonomy, because dignity is based on the autonomy and rationality of the human will.

In contemporary health care ethics, European non-Kantian humanists regard the principles of dignity and integrity – not the principle of autonomy – as the most

38 A supervening property is based on another property of a different kind. For example, mental properties like the experience of pain depend on (the consequence of) neurophysiologic properties. In ethics saying that dignity (a value property) is based on reason and human potentiality to do good (non-value properties) is the same as saying that dignity is dependent on reason and human potentiality to do what is good (cf. T.E. Horgan, 'Supervenience', in R. Audi (ed.), *Cambridge Dictionary of Philosophy,* Cambridge University Press 1995, 778–779).

39 R. Dworkin, *Taking Rights Seriously* (Duckworth, 1978).

fundamental normative principles. Rendtorff and Kemp, in their analysis of the normative principles of European bioethics today, make this view plain when they state that 'respect for human dignity seems to be the most fundamental principle ... Here dignity is put forward as that which characterises every human being. And therefore the notion of human dignity should proceed when taking account of the idea of autonomy'.[40]

This view of dignity, like the Kantian, cannot be justified either scientifically or philosophically. It appears to be a humanistic assumption, whereas autonomy, in the context of the statement just quoted, appears to be an empirical concept. Thus dignity is taken here as constant, unchangeable and equal for all human beings, whereas autonomy is taken to be changeable and variable from individual to individual.

Yet even the concept of dignity (like that of Kantian autonomy), if seen from a purely empirical point of view, will give rise to unsolvable ethical problems, for example how to scientifically, philosophically or ethically justify that all humans beings are equal in dignity.[41] Thus the non-Kantian humanistic view that all human beings are equal in dignity (but not in autonomy) is as problematic as Kant's view that all human beings are autonomous.

Some non-humanists attempt to avoid this problem by conceiving of dignity, autonomy and integrity in purely empirical terms. But this attempt creates other problems, as we shall soon see. For the non-humanists, who believe that humans have autonomy, the principle of autonomy – not the principle of dignity – is the most fundamental normative principle in health care.

The common features of Kant's view of human dignity and autonomy and their interrelationships have positive consequences for both ethics in general and for health care ethics in particular. In Western Europe today the Kantian concept of dignity as an absolute value is both basic and very relevant to health ethics, law and basic human rights.

4.3. HUMAN DIGNITY IN POST-KANTIAN HUMANISM

Post-Kantian humanists also base human dignity, among other things, on human reason, autonomy and potential for goodness. But they differ considerably from Kant's humanism by not regarding human reason as part of what Kant calls a super-sensible dimension of the human being. For them dignity is a purely

40 Rendtorff and Kemp, *Basic Ethical Principles in European Bioethics and Biolaw*, p. 20, note 11.
41 A. Schulman, 'Bioethics and Human Dignity', p. 6.

humanistic concept based on philosophical-anthropological facts.[42] In his analysis of Kant's justification of human dignity by reference to autonomy, the latter based on human reason; philosopher of law Alan Gewirth – a non-Kantian humanist – not only points out the difficulties involved in Kant's concept of autonomy but also reinterprets it:

> Kant held that ... autonomy is not an empirical characteristic, since it applies only to rational beings as things-in-themselves. This doctrine however involves all the difficulties of the distinction between phenomena and noumena, including the cognitive uncertainty of the latter. We may, however, abstract from this aspect of Kant's doctrine and reinterpret it.[43]

Gewirth gives his non-Kantian but humanistic view of autonomy as follows:

> All human rights, those of well-being as well as of freedom, have as their aim that each person have rational autonomy in the sense of being a self-controlling, self-developing agent who can relate to other persons on a basis of mutual respect and cooperation, in contrast to being a dependent, passive recipient of the agency of others.[44]

Like Kant, Gewirth sees a logical connection between autonomy and dignity: '... the connection of the [human] rights with human dignity is not merely asserted but is explicated in terms of the autonomous rational agency that grounds this dignity.'[45]

4.3.1. *The objective versus subjective concept of dignity according to humanism*

Non-Kantian humanism, like the Kantian, conceives of autonomy and dignity as fundamental characteristics of all human beings simply because they are human. This 'objective', universal and non-empirical concept of dignity should be sharply distinguished from the 'subjective' and particular concept. The following passage makes this distinction clear:

> When it is said that all human beings have dignity, what is presumably meant is not that dignity is an empirical characteristic in the way the having of interests or capacity of feeling physical pain is empirically ascertainable. The sense of 'dignity' in which all

42 See J. Kekes, *Human Nature and Moral Theories*, 28 *Inquiry. An International Journal of Philosophy* 2 (1985): 231–245; A. Barbosa da Silva and M. Ljungquist, *Vårdetik för ett mångkulturellt Sverige* [Health care ethics for a pluralistic Sweden] (Studentlitteratur, 2003) pp. 220–222.

43 A. Gewirth, *Human Rights. Essays on Justification and Applications*, (University of Chicago Press, 1982) p. 28.

44 Ibid., pp. 5 and 29.

45 Ibid., p. 5.

> humans are said to have equal dignity is not the same as that in which it may be said of some person that he lacks dignity or that he behaves without dignity, where what is meant is that he is lacking in decorum, is too raucous or obsequious or is not dignified. This kind of dignity is one that humans may concurrently exhibit, lack, or lose, whereas the dignity in which all humans are said to be equal is a characteristic that belongs permanently and inherently to every human as such.[46]

This passage offers both an objective and a subjective concept of dignity. The first is a universal, unchangeable, non-contingent and ethically normative concept of dignity. This objective concept is completely distinct from the subjective concept of dignity as changeable, empirical and descriptive, and as something that can be lost.[47] While a person's objective dignity can be violated and disrespected without the person's knowledge, this appears not to hold true for the person's subjective dignity.[48] In addition, it is the objective (and normative) concept of dignity that is now the basis of human rights and the ultimate justification of the basic principles of Western Europe's health care ethics. The non-Kantian humanistic concept of dignity – as an objective and universal concept – appears to have the same value, characteristics and function as the Kantian concept of dignity. Both are conceived as non-empirical, unchangeable, universal, normative, and inviolable.

However, non-Kantian humanists base dignity not on reason alone but also on human freedom and potential goodness as purely humanistic concepts, not metaphysical ones. Non-Kantian humanists also differ from Kantian humanists in attributing a higher value to dignity than to autonomy. This objective, non-Kantian humanistic concept of autonomy and dignity, one closely related to that of personal integrity, now dominates health care ethics. As Rendtorff and Kemp state: '[o]ur European vision of personhood goes further than a minimalistic conception of person, by not only focussing on autonomy but also looking at the concepts of integrity, dignity and vulnerability ... Thus integrity and dignity are terms which, though not identical, are closely linked'.[49]

Rendtorff also emphasizes that '(i)n bioethics and biolaw the idea of integrity (is used) as an untouchable core, the personal sphere, which should not be subject to external intervention ...'[50] Writing about bioethics, Rendtorff and Kemp state that 'respect for human dignity seems to be the most fundamental principle ...

---

46 Ibid., p. 27f.

47 M.J. Meyer, 'Dignity, Rights, and Self-Control', 99 *Ethics*, 3 (1989), 520–534.

48 Cf. B. Mitchell et al. *Biotechnology and the Human Good* (Georgetown University Press, 2007) pp. 58–60.

49 Rendtorff and Kemp, *Basic Ethical Principles in European Bioethics and Biolaw*, p. 23.

50 J.D. Rendtorff, 'Basic ethical principles in European bioethics and biolaw: Autonomy, dignity, integrity and vulnerability – Towards a foundation of bioethics and biolaw', 5 *Medicine Health Care and Philosophy* 3 (2002), 235–244.

Here dignity is put forward as that which characterises every human being. And therefore the notion of human dignity should proceed when taking account of the idea of autonomy'.[51]

When humanists prioritize dignity over autonomy by attributing a lesser value to the latter, this choice is arbitrary and unjustifiable. To state that all humans have equal dignity because they are human is no more justifiable than to assert the same about autonomy, as Kant does. Both statements express a humanistic belief, not an empirical fact or a scientific truth.[52]

4.4. HUMAN DIGNITY IN NON-HUMANISTIC PHILOSOPHY

For the concept of dignity at least two types of non-humanistic philosophy apply. One of them denies (objective) human dignity or reduces it to something else.[53] The other type, which I shall deal with here, conceives of dignity in terms of an individual's freedom of choice and action alone.

Non-humanistic philosophy talks less about human dignity than about a human individual's moral worth as an empirically dependent, actual, acquired and changeable property that varies by individual and that may disappear. Further, the non-humanists we are discussing here hold that not all human individuals have moral worth – only those who are persons. For example, philosopher Michael Tooley holds that an individual is a human person only if he or she fulfils two necessary conditions: awareness of him- or herself and awareness of possessing 'the concept of a continuing self'.[54] Tooley asserts that not all humans have a right to life – only those who are persons, i.e. who fulfil these two conditions. In contrast

---

51 Rendtorff and Kemp, *Basic Ethical Principles in European Bioethics and Biolaw*, p. 20, note 11.

52 According to A. Schulman, 'Bioethics and Human Dignity', pp. 7–11, none of the traditional universal concepts of dignity (e.g. the ones discussed in this chapter), have an acceptable justification, and none are suitable for bioethics today. Some critics of the use of dignity in bioethics have substituted dignity with 'respect for persons'. But Schulman maintains that this alternative 'does not explain why all persons are entitled to respect' (ibid., p. 7).

53 This type of non-humanism, because it denies human autonomy, also denies the possibility of ethics, since autonomy is closely related to duty and responsibility (cf. Skinner, *Beyond Freedom and Dignity*). As Kant convincingly shows, autonomy is a necessary condition for ethics. See Kant, *Critique of Practical Reason*, pp. 95 and 124–137.

54 M. Tooley, 'Abortion and Infanticide', in P. Singer (ed.), *Applied ethics* (Oxford University Press, 1986) pp. 57–85. Tooley defines the 'right to life' as follows: 'A has right to life is roughly synonymous with 'A is the sort of thing that is a subject of experiences and other mental states, A is capable of desiring X, and if A does desire X, than other are under a prima-face obligation to refrain from actions that would deprive him of it'. Tooley further declares that 'I believe that a new-born baby does not possess the concept of a continuing self, [and] infanticide during a time interval shortly after birth must be morally acceptable' (ibid., p. 83).

to humanists, Tooley suggests that being human is not a necessary condition for being a person, as he says that even a non-human animal may be a person: '... one may find himself driven to conclude that our everyday treatment of animals is morally indefensible and that we are in fact murdering innocent persons'.[55] He likewise suggests that being human is not a sufficient condition for being a person because there are human individuals who do not fulfil the two conditions just mentioned.[56]

Non-humanists also define the concept of person so that autonomy, in the sense of liberty, is a necessary condition for being a person: '[t]he phenomenological description of the concept of personhood signifies that consciousness, liberty and development of identity are conditions for personhood. The person might also be defined as 'any individual capable of valuing its [sic] own existence.'[57]

From the non-humanistic viewpoint of what a person is, discussing a person's value as something objective, absolute and inviolable in human nature as such is not appropriate, because a person acquires his or her moral worth through his or her own moral efforts, which presuppose the use of his or her actual autonomy. Rendtorff and Kemp contrast the Kantian-humanistic view of dignity, autonomy and their interrelationship with the non-humanistic view as follows:

> In contrast to the Kantian interpretation, considering dignity as a sacred feature of every human being, a constructive interpretation of dignity as the result of the moral efforts and actions of the autonomous subject should not be excluded. According to this interpretation dignity is something to be acquired by moral effort, rather than something absolute that is present in the human from its very beginning ... It supposes that dignity is what the subject achieves on a journey of self-realisation and emancipation from the realm of natural necessity.[58]

According to the non-humanistic concept of person, 'dignity' is not omnipresent and given in human nature as such and therefore equal for all human beings. An individual's actual efforts give him or her moral worth (dignity) and the right to life. Consequently, different individuals may have different moral worth or value,

---

55 Ibid., p. 85. Like Michael Tooley, Peter Singer regards 'elephant, pig, or chimpanzee' as having the same value as certain human individuals (P. Singer, *Applied ethics,* 1986, p. 228). For a critique of Tooley, see D. Føllesdal, 'The Potentiality Argument and Stem Cell Research', in L. Østnor (ed.), *Stem Cells, Human Embryos and Ethics. Interdisciplinary Perspectives* (Springer Science + Business Media, 2008) pp. 137–147.

56 Tooley declares that: '[a]n organism possesses a serious right to life only if it possesses the concept of a self as continuing subject of experiences and other mental states, and believes that it is itself such a continuing entity' (Tooley, 'Abortion and Infanticide', 1986, p. 85).

57 Rendtorff and Kemp, 1 *Basic Ethical Principles in European Bioethics and Biolaw,* p. 22.

58 Ibid., p. 33f.

which gives them the rights they deserve (which may differ significantly among them). By basing an individual's moral worth (dignity) on his or her actual freedom, non-humanists relativize the concept of dignity, because freedom so conceived will vary by individual and may in the same individual vary in different situations. Thus for non-humanists dignity is not equal for all human individuals. Because the value of a person is the basis of his or her rights, even for non-humanists, this empirically based view of a person's dignity and worth has negative consequences for social justice if it is adopted in democratic and pluralistic societies like the Nordic countries. It also has negative consequences for health care ethics.[59] A person's worth so conceived is not the same as the humanistic dignity that forms the basis of human rights.[60]

If distributive social justice must be based on an individual's relativized worth as the basis of his or her rights, it logically follows that some categories of individuals have no right to social welfare. For example, small children, individuals with disabilities and those suffering from dementia (all of whom either do not have or have lost their freedom of action) may not receive from society the necessary economic (and other) help they need, because they do not deserve such help – after all, they cannot contribute to the welfare of the society in which they live. They may be treated paternalistically, mistreated, or even subjected to non-voluntary euthanasia if they are regarded as non-persons in Tooley's sense of the term.[61] Thus in his terms only certain individuals possess human rights, e.g. the right to life.

4.5. DIGNITY AS THE BASIC NORMATIVE PRINCIPLE IN HEALTH CARE ETHICS

Human dignity, universally conceived as the inalienable or absolute human moral worth that is equal for all humans, is for all humanists the ultimate ethical justification for the obligatory character of the principles of health care ethics. The most basic and relevant of these are the following: the principle of respect for human integrity, supplied and defended by the principles of non-maleficence, beneficence, justice and human vulnerability; and the principle of autonomy,

59 An extreme form of non-humanism is implicit in Nazism. See how it adapted Social Darwinism to its political ideology, according to H. Ofstad, *Vår forakt for svakhet: en analyse av nazismens normer og vurderinger* [Our contempt for human weakness: an analysis of Nazi norms and value judgments] (Pax, 1991) pp. 36–41.

60 Article 1 in UN's Universal Declaration of Human Rights.

61 Tooley declares: 'I believe, that a new born baby does not possess the concept of a continuing self, ... infanticide during a time interval shortly after birth (before 3 months) must be morally acceptable.' Tooley "Abortion and Infanticide", in P. Singer (ed.), *Applied ethics*, p. 83.

supplied and defended by the principles of informed consent, confidentiality, privacy and liberty, personal identity, and justified or genuine paternalism.[62]

Each of these principles suggests an ethical value. Applied to health care, the ideal would be to combine all of them. But sometimes one has to choose between them. For example, when an individual's capacity for choice, informed consent, decision-making and action is limited or absent, the principles governed by respect for human integrity should receive priority, provided that one accepts as ethically normative the Kantian-humanistic tradition, the UN Universal Declaration of Human Rights, or later international treaties and conventions on human rights (all of which defend dignity as an objective, absolute, universal and unchangeable human value).

If one asks why one should obey the basic principles of a humanistic health care ethics, the answer is because a patient, as a human being, has a human dignity that gives him or her fundamental human rights. Thus according to humanistic ethics a person's right to be respected in his or her integrity, autonomy and basic rights is ultimately justified by reference to his or her dignity and worth. As professor in philosophy Knut Erik Tranøy states, the concepts of a person's autonomy, dignity and integrity are closely related to one another, so that to disrespect, harm or violate a person with regard to one of them implies disrespect or harm to the person with regard to the other values.[63] This standpoint is quite Kantian. Therefore, the Kantian concept of autonomy as the foundation of dignity cannot conflict with the patient's dignity and integrity, as they imply and complement one another. But for non-Kantian humanists, autonomy may conflict with dignity, and when this happens, one should prioritize dignity.[64] Thus dignity for both Kantian and non-Kantian humanists is the most fundamental normative principle of health care ethics.[65]

62 T.L. Beauchamp and J.F. Childress, *Principles of Biomedical Ethics* (Oxford University Press, 2001); H.R. Wulff et al. *Philosophy of medicine: an introduction* (Blackwell, 1986) p. 233f.

63 K.E. Tranøy, *Medisinsk etikk i vår tid* [Medical ethics today] (Sigma, 1991) 32–40.

64 Rendtorff and Kemp, *Basic Ethical Principles in European Bioethics and Biolaw*, Vol. I, p. 20, footnote 11.

65 A. Schulman, 'Bioethics and Human Dignity', pp. 1–11.

5. INTEGRITY FROM BOTH HUMANISTIC AND NON-HUMANISTIC PERSPECTIVES

5.1. CONCEPTUAL CLARIFICATION

The word 'integrity', which means the condition of being whole, entire or undiminished, is sometimes used as a synonym for what is 'untouchable'.[66] Humanists also use it in the sense of incorruptibility, purity, honesty, wholeness, completeness and unity. One can use all these meanings of 'integrity' to express the view that a human person should be respected as an integrated whole, i.e. what is human 'must not be hurt, damaged or altered'.[67] Four meanings in particular are relevant designations of different concepts of integrity: physical integrity (which includes genetic integrity); mental or psychic integrity and spiritual integrity; personal integrity (comprising privacy and self-determination), moral integrity (i.e. honesty), or the integrity of character and conscience.[68, 69] From a humanistic view, an individual's right to be respected because of his or her personal integrity is justified through his or her human dignity. Physical, mental and personal integrity, taken together, can be seen as an individual's objective personal integrity, to distinguish them from moral integrity, which differs considerably from the concept of personal integrity. As we shall see, the two concepts have different functions in ethics, health care ethics, law and human rights.

5.2. INTEGRITY IN THE HUMANISTIC AND THE NON-HUMANISTIC PHILOSOPHY

Kantian humanism and post-Kantian humanism appear to give the concept of integrity the same content and value. However, they differ in the way that they ultimately justify it. This section analyzes these differences, which are very relevant to the discussion at hand.

---

66 M. Andersson, *Integritet som begrepp och princip: en studie av ett vårdetiskt ideal i utveckling* [Integrity as a concept and principle: a study of an ideal of health care in development] (Åbo Academic Press, 1994) pp. 32–37.

67 Rendtorff and Kemp, *Basic Ethical Principles in European Bioethics and Biolaw*, p. 38.

68 Dworkin, *The Theory and Practice of Autonomy*, p. 102.

69 By integrity of conscience is meant that '... the individual should always do what he thinks is right'. D. Turner, *The Autonomous Man. An Essay in Personal Identity and Integrity* (The Bethany Press, 1970) p. 123.

5.2.1. *Personal integrity versus moral integrity*

Ethically speaking, a person's integrity may refer to a person's awareness of his or her sense of having moral worth (e.g. feeling that he or she deserves being treated with respect), or to his or her personal integrity, regardless of whether he or she is aware of having moral worth.[70] An awareness of moral worth or dignity will vary by individual. But according to the humanistic ethics any human individual's personal integrity (which is inherent, objective and unchangeable) is the inestimable worth that the individual shares with all human beings and that remains the same for all human individuals, unconditionally. Hence, to respect an individual's personal integrity is equivalent to respect his or her human dignity. When an individual's personal integrity is identified with his or her dignity, he or she is taken as whole and as a human being, regardless of current circumstances (e.g. being comatose).

For clarity, I shall call integrity in the psychological sense the subjective concept of integrity to distinguish it from integrity in the personal sense, which is the objective concept of integrity (i.e. personal integrity).[71] This distinction is important because one may lose subjective (and also moral) integrity but not personal integrity.[72]

According to humanistic ethics, personal integrity shares with dignity all the features associated with dignity.[73] Thus even if an individual's physical integrity may change after an amputation, respect for the individual's personal integrity nevertheless goes to the person as a whole, in the sense of 'respect for the unity of a life-story, a life context and a life-totality by which we recognise the identity of the other'.[74] Therefore, when health professionals concentrate on the patient's diseased body alone, while disregarding or violating his or her mental or spiritual integrity, they do not respect the patient's personal integrity.[75] To sum up, the right to be respected in one's personal integrity implies at least three things: First,

---

70 Cf. C. Taylor, *Sources of the Self. The Making of the Modern Identity* (Cambridge University Press, 1994) p. 15f.

71 Although integrity in the objective sense is the same as personal integrity, I prefer the term 'objective integrity' to convey the view that integrity is constant and unchangeable, regardless of how an individual experiences it. The term 'personal' can easily be associated with what is subjective, individual and private. But in the literature the term 'personal integrity' is the most common.

72 D.G. Jones, *Valuing People. Human Value in a World of Medical Technology* (Paternoster Press, 1999) p. 50f.

73 Rendtorff and Kemp, *Basic Ethical Principles in European Bioethics and Biolaw*, pp. 38–45.

74 Ibid., p. 39.

75 Ibid. An individual's spiritual integrity comprises his or her religious beliefs and existential experiences, such as a belief in God or an experience showing that suffering has a meaning.

nobody has the moral right to violate another individual's personal integrity. Thus the moral right to be respected in one's personal integrity is the same for all people. Second, a person's right to be respected in his or her personal integrity is ultimately justified by the humanistic ethics that all human beings have equal dignity. Thus in some contexts, integrity is a synonym for dignity. Third, the right to be respected in one's integrity is today a human right, based on human dignity as a humanistic concept.

We can explain the relationship between an individual's personal integrity and dignity as follows. A person's human dignity is the ethical basis for and justification of that person's right to be respected in his or her personal integrity. Although actual autonomy, physical integrity, subjective integrity and moral integrity may vary by individual, a person's dignity and personal integrity are unchangeable. First, human dignity and personal integrity are the basis of respect for people's identity. All human individuals have the same right to be respected in their different identities because, according to humanism, every individual possesses equal human dignity and integrity.[76] Second, dignity and personal integrity form the basis for the principle of respect for human vulnerability, especially within health care ethics.[77]

From the standpoint of Kant's normative ethics, the reason for respecting another person's dignity is implicit in what he calls the 'categorical imperative', as defined in section 3.4. All post-Kantian humanists accept Kant's categorical imperative, which implies that the human being has the right to be respected in his or her dignity and personal integrity as an absolute value.

Known persons with great moral integrity are few, e.g. Socrates, St. Francis of Assisi, Mahatma Gandhi, Martin Luther King and Nelson Mandela. These persons are seen as ethical models for other people. As far as humanistic ethics is concerned, moral integrity – as an individually acquired characteristic (in contrast to personal integrity) – should not be the basis for social justice or for individual basic rights, legal or otherwise. To use moral integrity as a material principle of distributive justice, e.g. in health care, would create great inequality among patients and clients in social work.

---

76 This is so solely because the person is human, according to both Kantian and Christian humanism.

77 For health care professionals, that humans are vulnerable is factored into their codes of ethics, which prescribe obedience to moral obligations for alleviating suffering, preventing sickness, promoting health and trusting the patient. They can achieve these goals by obeying the ethical principles of non-maleficence, beneficence and genuine or justified paternalism.

5.2.2. Autonomy, integrity and dignity in non-Kantian humanism

This section contrasts the non-Kantian humanistic concepts of integrity and autonomy – the latter defined as an individual's freedom, independence and liberty – and relates them to dignity in the Kantian sense in terms of health care ethics. As already indicated, post-Kantian humanists accept Kant's concept of dignity but not his concept of autonomy. Like Kant, they hold that individual dignity and personal integrity are unchangeable, inalienable, absolute, omnipresent, and equal for all human beings. But they do not attribute these properties to autonomy. Moreover, post-Kantian humanists also justify human dignity in anthropological terms, not in religious terms (as some pre-Kantian humanists do) or in metaphysical terms (as Kant does). Philosopher Peter Singer, who criticizes the humanistic concept and justification of dignity, maintains that post-Kantian humanists do not justify human dignity at all:

> Pico and other humanists based their estimate of human dignity on the idea that man possessed the central, pivotal position in the 'Great Chain of Being' that led from the lowest forms of matter to God himself; this view of the universe, in turn, goes back to both classical and Judeo-Christian doctrines. Modern philosophers have cast of these metaphysical and religious shackles and freely invoke the dignity of mankind without needing to justify the idea at all.[78]

Moral philosopher William K. Frankena defends the equality of all human beings in purely human terms when he writes 'all men are to be treated as equals, not because they are equal, in any respect, but simply because they are human ...'[79] Frankena uses not 'dignity' but 'equality', which in this context appears closely related to 'dignity', as '(o)ne's human dignity ... is a mark of one's equality on some fundamental level with other human beings'.[80]

In contrast to Kantian humanists, non-Kantian humanists relate dignity to autonomy as follows: a person's actual autonomy (ability or competence to exercise free will, free choice and action) is not equal in all human beings. Even for the same person it may change in different situations. For example, having a severe impairment or dementia, being a prisoner, or being comatose may change an individual's autonomy but not his or her dignity and worth.[81] The non-Kantian

---

78 P. Singer, 'All Animals are Equals', in P. Singer (ed.), *Applied Ethics* (Oxford University Press, 1986) pp. 227f.

79 W.K. Frankena, in R. Brandt (ed.) *Social Justice*, (Prentice-Hall, 1962) p. 19.

80 M.J. Meyer, 'Dignity, Rights, and Self-Control', 99 *Ethics*, (3) 1989, 520–534.

81 R. Dworkin, *Life's Dominion* (Harper Collins Publishers, 1993) p. 225, where he holds that a person with dementia 'has right to dignity'.

humanistic view of the relationship between an individual's dignity, integrity and autonomy can be illustrated as follows:

Figure 2. The relationship between an individual's autonomy and the individual's dignity and personal integrity in two different situations[82]

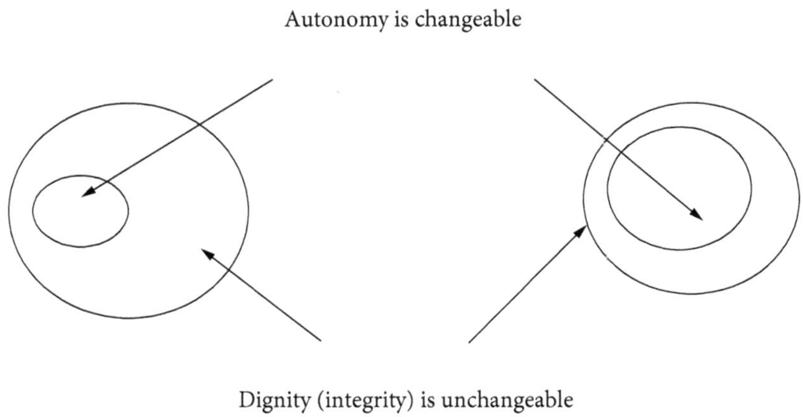

As applied to health care ethics, if a patient's or client's autonomy diminishes or disappears, his or her dignity and integrity remains unchangeable. In such a condition, he or she may not be able to give informed consent (an expression of autonomy). However, the principle of respect for the patient's informed consent[83] exists for the sake and protection of human dignity and personal integrity. As we have seen, the obligatory character of the principle of informed consent is ultimately justified by human dignity and personal integrity.[84] Therefore, in cases in which health professionals may not (or cannot) respect the patient's autonomy because it does not exist or is very diminished, they are nevertheless morally obligated to respect the patient's dignity and integrity, even when there is nobody (no proxy) to defend the patient's basic rights. As previously emphasized, in such cases the following ethical principles become prominent and deserve priority: non-maleficence, beneficence, justice, vulnerability and genuine or justified paternalism.[85] As Dworkin points out, in some situations the values defended by

82 Figure 2 is borrowed from G. S. Braut, 'Verdigrunnlaget for medisinen i kommende tider' [The value base for medicine in the future], 120 *Tidsskrift Norsk Lægeforening* (30) 2000, 37, 43–5. Reprinted with the permission of the editor.

83 This phrase also implies other ethical principles that defend, protect and promote human autonomy.

84 Dworkin, *The Theory and Practice of Autonomy*, pp. 113–115.

85 Wulff et al., *Philosophy of medicine* ..., pp. 233f.

these and other closely related principles override the principle of respect for autonomy:

> There are certainly other values that are of fundamental moral importance and of crucial significance to any person. These include dignity, health, well-being, integrity, security. It is possible that in order to promote any of these values it may be necessary to sacrifice some autonomy. It is also possible that the promotion of autonomy in the long run requires sacrificing autonomy in the short run. Finally there are cases in which a person is already in a non-autonomous state or one of diminished autonomy and the principle ceases to have application or at least its application is more problematic than in normal cases.[86]

This non-Kantian but humanistic view of the relationships among autonomy, dignity, integrity and other fundamental ethical values differs considerably from the non-humanistic view, with different consequences for health care ethics. The right to autonomy or self-determination leads to the intricate question of how autonomy can be protected in vulnerable situations so that it may not conflict with questions such as who can be trusted to care for the patient when he or she is too vulnerable and fearful to care for himself or herself, and whether physicians and/or state officials can be trusted to protect rather than abuse vulnerable people.[87]

5.3. INTEGRITY IN NON-HUMANISTIC PHILOSOPHY

To the extent that we can use integrity in the same normative sense as dignity, some non-humanists deny the existence of human integrity. For example, behavioural psychologist Burrhus F. Skinner denies that humans have dignity or autonomy.[88] Some forms of non-humanistic philosophy consider dignity a property that differs by individuals. To them it is a subjective (experienced) integrity, not an objective (personal) integrity. Non-humanists consider integrity an acquired property: '[p]ersonal integrity, as the achievement of the authentic self, comes from integrating life experiences within the narrative of self-development'.[89] This view of integrity is implicit in the non-humanistic concept

---

86 Dworkin, *The Theory and Practice of Autonomy*, p. 114.

87 R. A. Burt, 'The Suppressed Legacy of Nuremberg', in *Hasting Center Report*, September-October 1996, pp. 30–33.

88 There are non-humanists, like Skinner, who deny the existence of human freedom, dignity and responsibility. We can say that, for them, ethics in humanistic sense, does not exist (see Skinner, *Beyond Freedom and Dignity*, pp. 19f, 41f, 55 and 189f.).

89 A. Giddens, *Modernity and Self-Identity. Self and Society in the Late Modern Age*, (Stanford University Press, 1991) p. 80.

of the value of a human individual, which, as previously indicated, is based on the individual efforts, merits, or contribution to the welfare of society.

From the purely biomedical point of view, personal integrity loses its meaning, as Rendtorff and Kemp point out: '[b]ut today, when the body is considered as an object for scientific and technological interventions, and is often reduced in medical science to being merely such an object ... the concept of the integrity of the human body as analysed here disappears'.[90] Because physical integrity is an essential element of an individual's personal integrity, when the former disappears, the latter will also disappear. The problem here is that personal integrity, as opposed to autonomy and moral integrity cannot be evaluated by degree. One either has personal integrity or does not. The same can be said of dignity. This non-humanistic view of integrity has negative consequences for health care ethics (e.g. distributive social justice) in democratic countries like the Nordic ones.

6. HUMAN DIGNITY AS THE BASIS OF MODERN HUMAN RIGHTS, HEALTH CARE AND LAW

This section analyzes the humanistic concept of human dignity as the basis of modern human rights, health care ethics and law, for all of which the term 'right' is central. Law here specifically means 'a general institution ...[91] common to all societies which have even minimal legal systems'.[92]

6.1. CONCEPTUAL CLARIFICATION

The concepts of right, justice and equality are central to modern and contemporary jurisprudence, health care ethics and human rights. The term 'right' has at least 62 different meanings.[93] The two that are relevant here are morally or ethically right and right as a 'legal principle considered as an underlying cause of truth, justice, morality, or ethics'.[94] In ethics right is a property of actions. Thus an action is considered either right or wrong, as in the following examples: 'it is right (one ought) to treat people equally', 'it is right to pay one's debts', and 'it is not right (it is wrong) to harm an innocent person'.

---

90 Rendtorff and Kemp, *Basic Ethical Principles in European Bioethics and Biolaw*, p. 42.

91 R.A. Burt, *The Suppressed Legacy of Nuremberg* (Hasting Center Report, 1996) p. 32.

92 Gewirth, *Human Rights. Essays on Justification and Applications*, pp. 275f.

93 *Webster's Encyclopaedic Unabridged Dictionary of the English Language*, New Revised Edition, New York/Avenel: Gramercy Books 1996, p. 1233.

94 Ibid.

In legal contexts, when the word 'right' occurs in an expression such as 'to have a right to', it means to have an entitlement, a privilege, or a claim 'as against liberties, powers, and so forth'.[95] Sometimes the concept of moral right is used much like that of the legal right (entitlement), and they may occur in the same statement: 'it is right (morally right) that parliamentarians have (the right, i.e. entitlement to) political immunities'.[96] Sometimes the same action may be at once characterized as legally and morally right, as in 'to say that one has a right to do something (i.e. legal right) is to say merely that it is not morally wrong (i.e. it is morally right) for one to act in this way'.[97]All these uses of 'right' are indispensable in the contexts of jurisprudence, health care ethics and human rights.[98]

6.2. NATURAL LAW, HUMAN RIGHTS AND LEGAL RIGHT, AND THEIR INTERRELATIONSHIP

As previously mentioned, the concept of moral right is central to health care ethics, basic human rights and law. It is, however, a controversial issue whether morality (ethics) is the ultimate foundation of law and human rights. In other words, what is most basic – the 'legally' right or the 'morally' right? To resolve this issue, one has first to resolve another controversial issue within both moral philosophy and the philosophy of law, namely what is the ultimate justification of the obligatory character of a legally and morally right action? This question is partly about the autonomy and the foundation of law and morality, and partly about whether law and morality are either conceptually independent of each other (autonomous) or interdependent (heteronomous). The question of either the autonomy or heteronomy of law, irrespective of morality, is answered from the viewpoint of how law ultimately justifies its fundamental concepts (e.g. right and wrong, permitted and forbidden, responsible and non responsible). All these concepts are directly or indirectly related to the concept of morally or ethically right or just action.[99]

---

95 Gewirth, *Human Rights. Essays on Justification and Applications*, p. 219.

96 The term 'right' as synonymous with 'claim', 'entitlement', and 'privilege' is used here as a noun, whereas 'right' in the sense of 'just' and 'fair' is used here as an adjective.

97 C. Wellman, 'Rights', in R. Audi (ed.), *Cambridge Dictionary of Philosophy* (Cambridge University Press, 1995), p. 696.

98 Rights constitute primary a moral concept for people who belong to states that have not ratified the UN Declaration of human rights. For people who belong to states that have ratified it, rights constitute both a moral and a legal concept, e.g. obeying traffic signs is both legally and morally right.

99 B. Almond, 'Rights', in P. Singer (ed.), *A Companion to ethics*, Oxford, Blackwell Publishers Ltd. 1993, pp. 259–269 (quoted p. 261).

Here I shall primarily focus on the issue of whether law (the legally right) is conceptually dependent on morality (the morally right) by attempting to answer the question of what constitutes the ultimate foundation of the obligatory character of legal norms (legal rules and principles). Is it, for example, morality (i.e. moral value and norms) or is it some basic feature of law itself? Two primary answers to these questions exist within two mutually exclusive philosophies of law. One lies within the natural law tradition, whereas the other lies within the legal positivist tradition.[100] These two traditions, which give different answers to the question of autonomy of moral or ethical right, also exist within moral philosophy.[101]

Theories of natural law defend 'the existence of objective moral values binding upon the whole humanity'.[102] According to the natural law tradition, the ultimate foundation of law is morality.[103] Natural law theories affirm that moral obligation is imposed by human reason, which has the insight of what moral law requires of human beings and an intrinsic feeling of respect for the moral law.[104] This feeling motivates the human will to obey moral obligations imposed on them by human reason itself.[105] By contrast, legal positivist theories hold either that the ultimate justification of the obligatory character of law is inherent in the law itself or that it is wholly dependent on an external human authority such as a legislature or a court of justice.[106]

The following section discusses these two different answers in relation to five briefly described answers given from five possible logical relationships between what is legally right and what is ethically right. It then assesses and defends the plausibility of the answer from the natural law tradition.

---

100 'Natural law' is not the 'law of nature'. The former refers to the moral law that is assumed to exist in human reason or conscience, whereas the latter refers to unchangeable laws of nature, like gravity.

101 There is a humanistic answer *à la* Immanuel Kant and a theological answer *à la* Thomas Aquinas. M.P. Golding, *Philosophy of Law* (Prentice-Hall, 1975), pp. 20f and 40–42.

102 Simmonds, *Central Issues in Jurisprudence. Justice, Law and Rights*, p. 3.

103 Defenders of the natural law tradition fall into two groups, the humanist and the theological. Socrates, Plato, Aristotle and the Stoics fall in the first, and medieval theologians such as Augustine and Thomas Aquinas fall in the second. Both traditions hold that law is based on or deducible from ethics. But they differ with respect to the source of moral knowledge. For the humanists the source is human reason, whereas for the theologians it is human conscience, in which God has put the capacity for knowing what is morally right and wrong (Christian theologians refer to Rom. 2:14.).

104 Kant calls this obligation 'a command of reason', i.e. 'an imperative'. Kant, *Critique of Practical Reason*, pp. 126 and 95.

105 J.B. Schneewind, 'Kant and Natural Law Ethics', 104 *Ethics. An International Journal of Social, Political, and Legal Philosophy* (1993), 53–74.

106 Cf. Golding, *Philosophy of Law*, pp. 3, 20f and 40–42.

6.2.1. Five logically possible relationships between law and morality

In practice the criteria for assessing what is right or wrong according either to law or ethics are legal norms and ethical norms. Both types of norms consist of rules and principles based on values (e.g. life, health, liberty, justice).[107] Legal norms, which usually vary by country, not only impose legal duties and obligations on citizens but also defend these citizens' rights and privileges. By contrast, according to the natural law tradition, some fundamental ethical norms have universal and cross-cultural validity. Thus, in principle certain moral norms impose duties or moral obligations on all human beings. Examples of such norms are that one should not kill, one should help a person in need, and one should not steal. Other norms with cross-cultural validity, and which are primarily moral, are basic human rights such as the right to life, liberty, security, and right to health care.[108]

Although some legal norms may also be moral ones – e.g. not to kill – no agreement exists among scholars of jurisprudence and moral philosophy concerning the exact relationship between legal norms and ethical ones or between law and morality or ethics. The views of theorists within the natural law tradition and the legal positivist tradition do not exhaust all possible relationships between law and ethics. Indeed five possible relations exist, not merely two.

First, from the viewpoint of logic, legal norms may express exactly the same duties and obligations as ethical norms. This relationship appears in Figure 3.a.

Figure 3.a

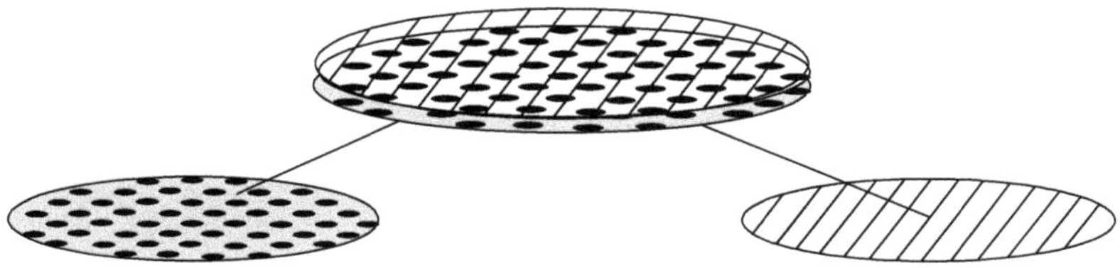

Two coincident circles representing law and ethics, showing no difference between them (i.e. all legal norms are ethical norms and vice-versa). The arrows illustrate how the contents of law and ethics overlap.[109]

---

107 See A. Barbosa da Silva (ed.), *Etikk og menneskesyn i helsetjeneste og sosialt arbeid* [Ethics and view of the human being in health care and social work] (Gyldendal Akademisk, 2006), p. 147.

108 Human rights are moral rights for all people. In addition, for citizens of states that have ratified human rights conventions, human rights are also legal rights.

109 Barbosa da Silva (ed.), *Etikk og menneskesyn i helsetjeneste og sosialt arbeid* [Ethics and view of the human being in health care and social work], pp. 189–191.

Second, from the legal viewpoint, another possible relationship is that law depends on ethics in such a way that all legal norms are necessarily ethical norms but not the opposite, i.e. there are ethical norms that are not legal norms. This possible relationship appears in Figure 3.b.

Figure 3.b

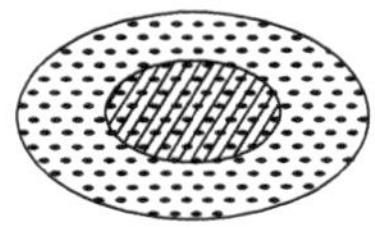

The circle in the middle represents legal norms, which are also ethical norms. The field in the bigger circle, around the little circle, represents ethical norms that are not legal norms.[110]

Third, a logically possible relationship between law and ethics is that ethics depends on law in such a way that all ethical norms are also legal norms but not the opposite, as shown by Figure 3.c.

Figure 3.c

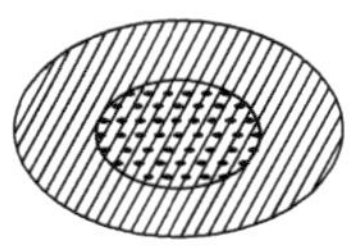

The circle in the middle contains all ethical norms. The field in the circle around the little one contains legal norms that are not ethical norms.

Fourth, a possible relationship between law and ethics is that although law and ethics share common norms, there exist specific legal norms and specific ethical norms, as Figure 3.d illustrates.

110 An example is the statement all Norwegians are Europeans but not all Europeans are Norwegians.

Figure 3.d

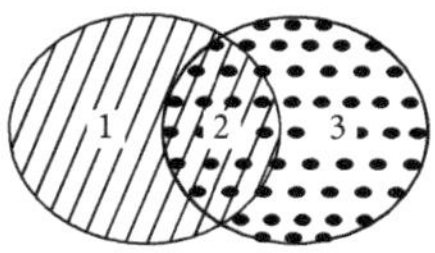

The left field (1) contains only legal norms; the right field (3) contains only ethical norms, whereas the central field (2) contains norms that are at once legal and ethical.

Fifth, a logically possible relationship is that law and ethics are autonomous realms of human experience and therefore logically independent of each other, as Figure 3.e illustrates.

Figure 3.e. The independent relation between law and ethics

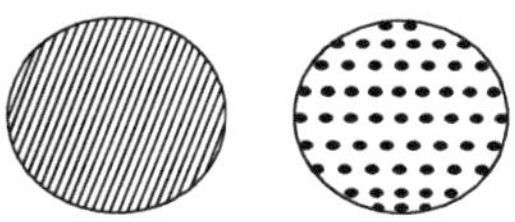

The view of natural law theorists, within both law and ethics, appears in Figure 3.b, whereas Figure 3.e illustrates the view defended by legal positivist theorists. Figure 3.d illustrates what appears to be the actual relationship between law and ethics in democratic countries like the Nordic ones. Gewirth defends the relationship in Figure 3.b when he says: '[f]or legal obligations to be determinative of what men ought to do, they, or the institution from which they derive, must be morally justified'.[111] R. Dworkin also defends a necessary connection between morality and law when he asserts that '(t)he integrity of a community's conception of justice demands that the moral principles necessary to justify the substance of its legislature's decisions be recognized in the rest of the law'.[112] He also asserts

111 Gewirth, *Human Rights. Essays on Justification and Applications*, p. 277.

112 R. Dworkin, *Law's Empire*, (The Belknap Press of Harvard University Press, 1986) p. 166. First, when Dworkin requires that legislators, judges and courts use the moral principle of integrity, he uses this principle in a way analogous to Kant's categorical imperative, i.e. as a meta-norm for the testing of all other norms (for Kant all ethical norms, whereas for Dworkin all judicial norms). Regardless of how Dworkin intentionally relates himself to either the natural law tradition or to the positivist one, it follows by logical necessity from his statements that morality is the ultimate foundation of law. Second, Dworkin's 'the integrity principle' is intended to defend integrity as a moral value higher than justice, to take priority when the two values conflict. Dworkin's position is known as the 'interpretativist view' (R. Dworkin, *Law's Empire*, pp. 45–86; K.E. Himma, *Law and Morality* (Ashgate, 2005), p. xii). I distinguish here between what Dworkin *de facto* does in his writings, and what he says he is doing, i.e. his interpretation of his own writings. By making a reasonable interpretation of Dworkin's works

that as a 'legislative principle ... integrity asks lawmakers to try to make the total set of laws morally coherent'.[113]

6.3. HUMAN DIGNITY AS THE BASIS OF MORALITY, LAW AND HUMAN RIGHTS

The conceptual dependence of the legally right on the morally right is reasonable under the following conditions: if the human being has inherent dignity (and worth) and if human dignity is the foundation of basic human rights.[114] If so, then the view of the human being determines the view of morality, which in turn determines the view of law. This relationship appears true, not only if law and morality are ultimately based on or justified by human dignity and worth but also if they are justified by reference to human fundamental values, desires, basic needs, interests and vulnerability as universally applicable human characteristics. Indeed, referring to Thomas Aquinas and to 'contemporary social scientists', Martin P. Golding points out fundamental features of natural law that make them 'a meeting ground for law and morality'[115]:

> What gives content to natural law is the rational apprehension of the essence of man and human good. Aquinas develops this along Aristotelian lines. Man is by nature a social animal: he desires to live a life in common with other men, and he satisfies his needs and wants only in cooperative enterprise with others. One, therefore, ought to cooperate with others for one's own good and as well as theirs. The first percept of natural law could, in fact, be formulated in this way. Now, social living has certain prerequisites whose fulfillment makes it possible. It requires, for example, that we should not harm our neighbors, which implies a prohibition against murder and theft ... This list could easily be extended, in the spirit of Aquinas, by following the tables of the 'basic needs' put forth by contemporary social scientists.[116]

Moral philosopher John Kekes calls the fundamental features that constitute 'the essence' of humanity: 'the facts of the body, self and social life', which are universal.[117] If Aquinas, Golding, Kekes and other humanists holding the same view are correct, then the real and true – and not only logically possible –

---

as a whole, one can assess the first without considering the second. A reasonable interpretation of a text can be made by anyone who is competent in the language in which the text is written and who knows the subject matter of the text.

113 Ibid.

114 Meyer, 'Dignity, Rights, and Self-Control', 99 *Ethics*, 3 (1989), 520–534; Gewirth, *Human Rights. Essays on Justification and Applications*, pp. 27f.

115 Golding, *Philosophy of Law*, p. 33.

116 M.P. Golding, *Philosophy of Law* (Prentice-Hall, 1975), p. 32.

117 Kekes, 'Human Nature and Moral Theories,' pp. 234f.

relationship between law and morality is that defended by the natural law tradition. According to them, basic human rights are expressions of natural ethical values and norms 'existing independently of any human action or institution. This explains how they can be used as an independent standard in terms of which to criticize the laws and politics of governments and other organizations.'[118] For example, the norms of the 1945 Nuremberg trial of prominent Nazi leaders in Germany after the World War II were basically ethical and according to the natural law tradition. From this viewpoint and that of international law, basing the natural law tradition on the necessary connection between morality and law is more plausible and fruitful than that of the legal positivist tradition. Gewirth points out that 'even a positivist such as Hans Kelsen is unable to avoid attributing to law ... a basic moral content.'[119] And even a 'prominent legal positivist' like Joseph Raz defends the necessary connection between morality and law.[120]

If there is a necessary connection between law and morality – as conceived by theorists within the natural law traditions – then professionals of ethics and law should collaborate with one another when dealing with normative concepts related to health care. The choice between the two traditions cannot be justified by either purely scientific arguments or purely philosophical ones, because it rests on two completely different views of the human being and society and their relation to reality.

6.4. AUTONOMY, DIGNITY AND INTEGRITY, AND THEIR INTERRELATIONSHIP AFTER KANT

After Kant came at least two important uses of autonomy, dignity and integrity, both of which are relevant here. One occurs in the writings of post-Kantian humanists who continue to use these terms to refer to fundamental norms in ethics and law but give them a different justification than that of Kantian humanism. They also relate them to one another differently from Kant. The other use of these uses occurs in the writings of non-humanists, e.g. the post-modernist philosophers.

118 C. Wellman, 'Rights', in R. Audi (ed.), *The Cambridge Dictionary of Philosophy*, (Cambridge University Press, 1995), p. 695f.

119 Gewirth, *Human Rights. Essays on Justification and Applications*, p. 278, footnote 17.

120 'Raz refutes the idea that positivists deny the existence of any necessary connection between law and morality and goes on to explore a number of potential connection between law and morality ... and asserts that [it] is part of law's very nature that it has the property of being morally valuable. Indeed, Raz argues that law, by its nature, is an institution with a moral task to perform' (Himma and B. Bix (eds.), *Law and Morality*, p. xiif).

6.4.1. *Autonomy, dignity, integrity and ethics in post-Kant humanism*

As a post-Kantian humanistic concept, autonomy is a person's ability or competence to exercise his or her free will, free choice and action without intervention from outside forces. Autonomy differs with the individual, for whom it may also change in different situations.

As we have already seen, while post-Kantian humanists accept Kant's concept of human dignity as an inherent human property, they do not give it the same foundation. Like Kant, they do not consider human dignity a purely empirical concept, since they attribute it equally to all human beings.

According to non-Kantian humanism the difference between an individual's dignity and his or her integrity and autonomy is that autonomy is changeable, whereas dignity and integrity are not. They view dignity as the basis of respect for a person's integrity and autonomy. When a person has lost his or her autonomy, the person should still be respected for his or her dignity and integrity, which can never be lost. If dignity conflicts with autonomy, dignity should receive priority. For example, a severe impairment, a comatose state or a serious mental illness may change an individual's autonomy but not his or her dignity and worth. Thus we can say that for post-Kantian humanists it is human dignity, not the individual's autonomy that constitutes the ultimate foundation of health care ethics, law and human rights.[121] However, it is unjustified and arbitrary for humanists to defend Kant's universal concept of dignity and attribute to it a higher value than that of autonomy, because saying that all humans have dignity because they are human is not more justifiable than saying the same about autonomy. The former expresses a humanist belief, not a scientific truth.

6.4.2. *Non-humanistic views of autonomy, dignity, integrity and health care ethics*

While both post-Kantian humanists and non-humanists today use the terms 'dignity' and 'integrity' as synonymous, they give them different contents and justification. As non-humanists base an individual's dignity and integrity on that individual's actual autonomy, for them autonomy, not dignity, is the ultimate normative principle in health care ethics.

Non-humanists hold that what gives an individual value (dignity) are his or her virtues, achievements and contributions to the welfare of society, something that

121 Rendtorff and Kemp, *Basic Ethical Principles in European Bioethics and Biolaw*, p. 20, note 11.

can be achieved only through the individual's efforts and actions by using his or her actual autonomy (free will, free choice and free decisions and actions). Therefore, the individual's actual autonomy is what gives him or her the right to be respected in his or her dignity, integrity and identity. From this viewpoint, the individual has no inalienable human rights, only acquired ones. As we have seen, for Tooley – a non-humanist by our definition – what makes an organism a person (i.e. an individual with moral worth) is some of its actual empirical properties. Therefore, for him it is wrong to talk about a person's dignity as something absolute and inviolable in human nature, because he believes that a person acquires his or her moral worth through moral efforts resulting from his or her autonomy.

Rendtorff and Kemp contrast the Kantian-humanistic view of dignity and its relationship to autonomy with the non-humanistic view as follows:

> In contrast to the Kantian interpretation, considering dignity as a sacred feature of every human being, a constructive interpretation of dignity as the result of the moral efforts and actions of the autonomous subject should not be excluded. According to this interpretation dignity is something to be acquired by moral effort, rather than something absolute that is present ...[122]

I understand the expression 'a constructive interpretation of dignity' in a non-humanistic sense. This view of human dignity as changeable and gradable has negative consequences for morality, and such a view cannot be the ultimate basis for law, human rights and health care in democratic societies, which emphasize the equality of all their citizens.

Since moral efforts presuppose free will in the threefold sense previously described, we can illustrate the relationship between an individual's actual free will and his or her actual value or moral worth as follows (fig. 4).

122 Ibid., pp. 33f.

Figure 4

a. The individual's basic rights, e.g. respect for his or her life, dignity, basic needs and identity

↑

b. The individual's moral worth or value as the ethical basis for his or her basic rights

↑

c. The individual freedom of will, freedom of choice and action as the ethical basis for his or her dignity and worth

The relationship between an individual's actual autonomy and his or her actual moral worth and rights, according to a non-humanistic point of view. The arrows should be read as affirmation (a) is based on (b), and (b) is based on (c), or (a) derives from (b), which in turn derives from (c).

According to this view, when autonomy changes, dignity will also change. The changeable character of an individual's autonomy and moral worth (dignity or integrity) and their interrelationship – according to non-humanism – can be illustrated as follows (figs. 5.a and 5.b).

Figure 5.a

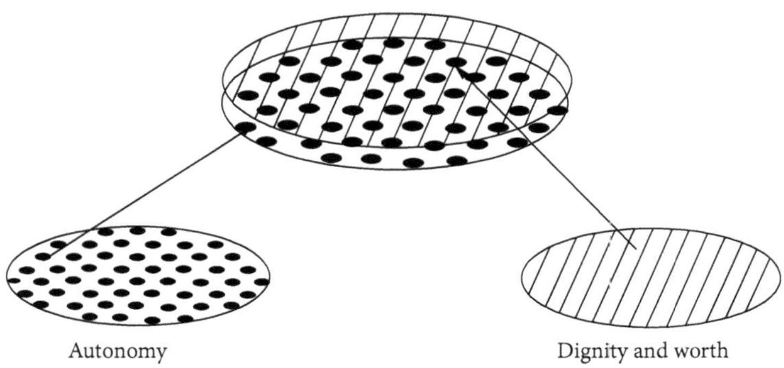

Figure 5.b

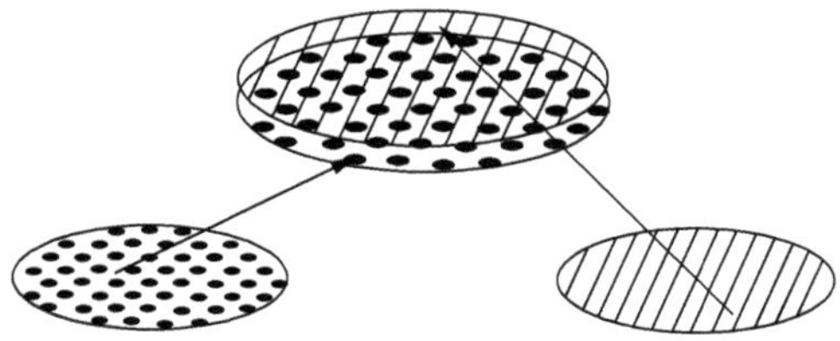

Figure 5.a and 5.b: The changeable character of both the individual's autonomy as freedom and dignity and moral worth from a non-humanistic standpoint. The arrows illustrate how the content of law and that of ethics coincide.

This relationship (5.a and 5.b) has negative consequences for health care ethics, especially with regard to distributive justice. For example, some patients or social clients may receive what they need because of their achievements, efforts and contribution to the welfare of society. Others may not get the help they need because they lack such virtue, efforts and did not contribute to the welfare of society. All humanists – whether religious or not – have reasons to regard this view of distributive justice as unjust.[123]

6.5. THE VIEW OF THE HUMAN BEING AS THE ULTIMATE BASIS FOR HUMAN DIGNITY

A fundamental question within the contexts of health care ethics, human rights and law is why one should respect a person's dignity, personal integrity, and basic human rights. As Kantian humanists, non-Kantian humanists and non-humanists give different answers to this question, we must examine the different ultimate reason or justification they give for their normative ethics, which presuppose different views of the human being, society and reality. Thus we can say that the question as to why we should respect a person's dignity, personal integrity, basic rights, etc. can be answered in different ways, depending on one's view of value and morality, of human beings, of society, of reality, and of their interrelationships.

---

123 However, both humanists and some non-humanists share the view that a person must be free in the threefold sense given earlier in order to be morally responsible, accountable for actions and omissions, and praised, blamed or considered morally responsible, accountable or guilty.

As to health care ethics, we need to distinguish between two different views of the patient: a holistic view and an ontologically reductionist view. The former implies a humanistic view of the human being, whereas the latter implies a non-humanistic view.

The holistic view conceives of the patient or client as a human being constituted by three different but closely related dimensions: the living body, the psyche, and the spirit or mind.[124] This view necessitates respect for the patient's physical integrity, psychic or mental integrity, moral integrity and spiritual integrity. The holistic view holds that the three human dimensions are causally related to two different types of fundamental needs: physiological needs (food, water, warmth, sleep, and sex), psychosocial needs, spiritual or existential needs (fellowship, security, acceptance, recognition, respect, meaning, forgiveness, and self-realization). All these needs, both primary and secondary, may have a profound impact on human health and well-being.[125]

The reductionist view of the human being (patient or client) denies the spiritual dimension, emphasizes the primary (physiological) needs, and ontologically reduces the patient to his or her disease.[126] It defines disease in purely biomedical terms as a defect or dysfunction in the physical body and it defines health as the absence of disease. The holistic view, by contrast, conceives of health as more than the absence of disease. For example, ethicist Lennart Nordenfelt, who defends the holistic view, defines health as an individual's capacity to realize his or her vital goals.[127]

These two different views of the human being presuppose different and mutually exclusive views of reality, thus giving rise to different types of ethics. The holistic view presupposes a pluralistic-holistic view of reality, whereas the reductionist view presupposes a monistic, materialistic, mechanistic, and deterministic

---

124 A. Barbosa da Silva (ed.), *Etikk og menneskesyn i helsetjeneste og sosialt arbeid* [*Ethics and view of the human being in health care and social work*], pp. 116–121.

125 T. Kolander et al., 'Existential and Spiritual Needs in Mental Health Care: An Ethical and Holistic Perspective', in 27 *Journal of Holistic Nursing* 1 (2009), pp. 34–42.

126 For the concept of ontological reductionism, see A. Barbosa da Silva, *The Phenomenology of Religion as a Philosophical Problem. An Analysis of the Theoretical Background of the Phenomenology of Religion in General, and of M. Eliade's Approach, in Particular* (CWK Gleeup, Liber, 1982) pp. 72f.

127 L. Nordenfelt, 'The concept of heath and illness revised', 10 *Medicine Health Care and Philosophy*, (2007), 5–10.

view.[128, 129] The reductionist view also denies the existence of human freedom, dignity and integrity. Consequently, those holding this view have no ethics in the humanistic sense of the term, since ethics and morality presuppose human freedom.[130] For example, B.F. Skinner expresses his reductionist view of the human being when he writes: '[a]s a science of behaviour adopts the strategy of physics and biology, the autonomous agent to which behaviour has traditionally been attributed is replaced by the environment ...'.[131] Skinner also denies that humans have dignity.[132] The consequence of this denial is that, from the reductionist viewpoint, neither humanistic ethics nor human rights exist.

The differences between the holistic and the reductionist views have different consequences for social justice and health care ethics. If health professionals endorse a reductionist view of the human being, they may not respect their patients' autonomy, dignity, integrity, vulnerability and fundamental human rights.

7. CONCLUSIONS

This chapter analyzes the concepts of autonomy, dignity and integrity, and their interrelationships with regard to their basic role in health care ethics, law and basic human rights. The analysis starts from the viewpoints of Kantian humanism, non-Kantian humanism, and the non-humanistic concept of the human being. While presenting both humanistic and non-humanistic positions, the chapter defends the humanistic, holistic view of the human being.

The analysis shows that Western European health care ethics is dominated today by two central normative concepts: dignity and autonomy. Human dignity is still used in the Kantian sense, which is the intrinsic, objective and inalienable worth of human life, which is equal for all human beings. Yet in Western European health care ethics today autonomy is used in an empirical, changeable and non-Kantian humanistic sense, that is, as changeable from individual to individual.

---

128 A pluralistic-holistic view of reality asserts that reality is constituted by different dimensions or principles, which are non-reducible to one another or to something else (K. Wilber, *Sex, Ecology, and Spirituality* (Shambhala, 1995)).

129 A monistic view of reality means one according to which reality can be explained in terms of only one principle or substance, which may be material or spiritual, or have an aspect of both (neutral monism). The view rejected here is materialism: that it is mechanistic and deterministic means that it conceives of every event, including human actions, as determined only by the laws of nature.

130 Kant, *Critique of Practical Reason,* p. 95, pp. ix and 124–139.

131 Skinner, *Beyond Freedom and Dignity,* p. 175.

132 Ibid.

When the patient's autonomy conflicts with his or her dignity in health care contexts, the respect for and protection of human dignity is given priority over autonomy. Such prioritizing suggests that health care professionals may at times refrain from respecting the patient's autonomy for the sake of respecting his or her dignity, integrity and basic rights.

The analysis also emphasizes that because the Kantian concept of dignity is universally applicable to all humans; it is the normative foundation for the contemporary human rights doctrine. This doctrine has positive consequences for ethics in general (e.g. social justice) and for health care ethics in particular (e.g. respect for the basic rights of all categories of patients), especially in democratic countries like the Nordic ones.

One area of controversy concerns whether or not a logically or conceptually necessary connection exists between ethics or morality and law. This chapter examined five different logically possible relationships between law and morality in the light of two mutually exclusive interpretative traditions, that of natural law and that of legal positivism. It concludes that ethics or morality is a necessary condition for law, a standpoint defended by the natural law tradition. Finally, the chapter pointed out that given a humanistic view of ethics, a holistic view of the human being, and a pluralistic and holistic view of reality, and their inter-relationship, morality must be seen as the foundation of law. So conceived, morality will have positive consequences for law, social justice and health care ethics.

CHAPTER 2
DIGNITY AND HUMAN RIGHTS IN THE MODERN WELFARE STATE

Henriette Sinding Aasen

1. INTRODUCTION

The modern welfare state, built on democratic and humanistic ideals and a policy of social justice, is characterized by its protection of civil and political rights, as well as of economic, social and cultural rights. It recognizes that respect for human dignity implies protection of all basic human rights, which together represent an indivisible normative unity in which the different rights are equally important, interrelated and interdependent. Although the legal protection of autonomy, private life and liberty (i.e. classical civil rights) is more developed and advanced at the international level than the protection of health, social security and an adequate standard of living (social welfare rights), the latter has a sound legal basis in national legislation in all the Nordic countries.[1] The protection of both fundamental civil rights and rights to necessary health care and social services reflects the social aim of healthy, well-functioning citizens who have both legal and *de facto* rights to enjoy their basic human rights and to participate in and contribute to society. The legal point of departure, and the main way of ensuring respect for human dignity, is respect for individual autonomy and the derivative requirement of informed consent.

All the chapters in Part II are based on the assumption that respect for autonomy is essential for the respect of human dignity, and is therefore a basic obligation not

---

1 The European Convention on Human Rights and Fundamental Freedoms (ECHR, Council of Europe, 1950) includes only civil and political rights. While Article 3 of the Convention for the Protection of Human Rights and Dignity of the Human Being with regard to the Application of Biology and Medicine. Convention on Human Rights and Biomedicine, Council of Europe, 1997) (Biomedicine Convention) includes a provision on equitable access to health care, it does not establish an individual right. As for the two general international covenants (UN, 1966), only the Covenant on Civil and Political Rights (ICCPR) has a system for individual complaint, while the Covenant on Economic, Social and Cultural Rights (ICESCR) has only a state reporting system.

only of states and public institutions but also of health personnel and providers of social services. However, when the individual does not have the legal capacity to consent to an intervention (e.g. due to dementia or mental disability), applying the principle of autonomy without putting other rights or interests at stake is not always morally acceptable. Therefore, both international and national laws specify that such situations allow exceptions from the main principle of respecting individual autonomy. Although the human rights framework does not always give a clear and non-contradictory recipe for respecting and applying individual rights in all situations, this lack of specificity does not suggest an exception from the overarching principle or obligation of respecting human dignity. When the principle of autonomy or self-determination cannot be applied, human dignity must be protected by other means.

The basic question throughout this volume is what the principle of human dignity requires in various situations where the impossibility of fulfilling informed and free consent and a clear need for protecting the human dignity of vulnerable individuals coincide. A complicating factor is that, in some situations, a strong emphasis on the protection of vulnerable individuals may imply that these individuals, or the group to which they belong, are excluded from benefits that other groups enjoy, for example the potential possibility of improved treatment based on clinical medical research.

This chapter provides a theoretical overview, a conceptual framework, and a brief description of some of the tensions between different human rights in modern welfare states. The following chapters give more details, in particular about decision-making areas involving children and the treatment of and care for individuals with mental illness, cognitive impairment and physical disabilities.

2. HUMAN DIGNITY AND THE MODERN WELFARE STATE

The modern welfare states in the Nordic countries are primarily products of social policies developed after World War II. The overall socio-political objective has been the enhancement of the quality of life for citizens in general, and the promotion of social equality as a means of preventing poverty and minimizing social instability and tension. The modern welfare state is inspired by the human rights ideals inherent in the Universal Declaration of Human Rights (UDHR), creating a normative unity of different human rights and protecting both classical civil rights and social welfare rights.[2] A look at the historical backdrop of the UDHR reveals that many of the human rights violations that took place in the concentration camps of Nazi Germany during World War II happened in the name of science, improvement of public health, and the creation of socially fit individuals (eugenics).[3] In that context, especially in the light of the post-war Nuremberg trials, where patient autonomy was made the touchstone for human subject research and patient care, Nordic policy makers chose to put strong emphasis on the protection of individual civil rights.[4]

The US (Yale) Law professor Robert A. Burt asks how the Nuremberg judges, after hearing about barbaric concentration camp experiments through months of testimony could begin their judgement with the proclamation of voluntary consent. The disturbing answer he proposes is that insisting on the importance of consent was the only imaginable criteria for the future: 'The fact was, as the 133 days of testimony clearly demonstrated, that these experiments had been approved and carried out by recognized leaders of the German medical profession ... In the face of this social reality, other more apparently plausible condemnatory criteria – in particular, the criteria subsequently set out in the tribunal's judgement that good physicians never purposefully inflict death or disabling injury on anyone – lacked convincing effective force'.[5] Therefore, as Thomas Hobbes had seen three centuries earlier in the aftermath of the English civil war, in a world of cruelty and spiritual degradation, the only predictable source of human protection was each person's solitary instinct for self-preservation.[6]

However, the UDHR acknowledges the idea that respect for human dignity depends on both social and civil rights.[7] The UDHR thus represents a more holistic approach to human rights than the two UN conventions of 1966, the International Covenant on Civil and Political Rights (ICCPR) and the International Covenant on Economic, Social and Cultural Rights (ICESCR). The two UN

---

2 UN, 1948.

3 D.B. Resnik, *The Ethics of Science. An Introduction*, London and New York: Routledge 1998, pp. 163, 169, 183f and 204, G. Broberg and N. Roll-Hansen (eds.), *Eugenics and the welfare state. Sterilization Policy in Denmark, Sweden, Norway, and Finland*, East Lansing, Mich.: Michigan State University Press 1996, J.J. Walter and T.A. Shannon, *Quality of Life. The New Medical Dilemma*, New York: Paulist Press 1990.

4 R.A. Burt, 'The Suppressed Legacy of Nuremberg', *Hastings Center Report* 26, no. 5 (1996), pp. 30–31.

5 Ibid.

6 Ibid. For an in-depth analysis of the foundations and concept of informed consent, see R. R. Faden and T. L. Beauchamp, *A History and Theory of Informed Consent*, Oxford: Oxford University Press 1986.

7 The preamble states that 'human beings shall enjoy freedom of speech and belief and freedom from fear and want'. For freedom from want, see Article 25(1): 'Everyone has the right to a standard of living adequate for the health and well-being of himself and of his family ...'.

conventions thus express the division of human rights into two separate units, symbolizing the competing ideologies of the world during the Cold War era.[8] The UDHR describes human dignity as an inherent property, belonging to all members of the human family.[9]

While the classical liberal state is characterized by its emphasis on human liberty and the individual's right to freedom from state control and interventions, the modern welfare state is also characterized by the acceptance of state interventions in individual property and freedom rights in order to promote a fair distribution of resources and other welfare policies.[10] In the Nordic welfare states, the state makes organized efforts to improve the living conditions of its citizens. An important assumption justifying these efforts is that a healthy, educated population is beneficial not only for the protection of human dignity and the basic needs of individuals but also for society as a whole. The building of public schools and hospitals, as well as social security systems (decided by constitutional parliaments and financed through the common tax system), exemplifies welfare state policies for ensuring education, health care and basic financial security as fundamental goods for everyone.[11]

Compulsory school attendance and coercive treatment of individuals with serious mental health problems are examples of paternalistic welfare policies that all welfare states have implemented and that are widely recognized as ethically and legally justified. The paternalistic principle of beneficence – even when the benevolent act violates the liberty of the person concerned – is based on a general trust in the possibility and ability of experts in different fields (doctors, psychologists) to make sound ethical and professional judgements about what is in the best interest of the patient or for society.[12] Thus a constant tension exists between the principle of individual autonomy and that of paternalistic beneficence, which are both founded in notions of protecting human dignity.

---

8 P. Cumper, 'Human Rights: History, Development and Classification', in *Human Rights. An agenda for the 21st Century* (Hegarty and Leonard eds.), London: Cavendish Publishing Limited 1999, p. 6–9.

9 Preamble.

10 H. Gustafsson, 'Taking social rights seriously (I)', *Tidsskrift for Rettsvitenskap* 4–5/2005, p. 444.

11 S. Kuhnle og L. Solheim, *Velferdsstaten – vekst og omstilling* [The welfare state – development and change], Oslo: Tano 1985, and A. Hatland, S. Kuhnle og T. I. Romøren (ed.), *Den norske velferdsstaten* [The Norwegian welfare state], Oslo: Gyldendal 2001.

12 T.L. Beauchamp and J.F. Childress, *Principles of Biomedical Ethics*, Oxford: Oxford University Press 2001, pp. 39, 176–188, 191 f, 214–222, and H. Wulff et. al., *Philosophy of medicine: an introduction*, Oxford: Blackwell 1986, p. 233 f. The distrust in the medical profession following after the Nuremberg trial did not prevent the development of a social system based on trust in the medical and other professions.

Paternalism, whether justified or not, has always been an inherent aspect of health care and other welfare policies.[13] Public institutions for treatment of persons considered to constitute a social problem (e.g. alcoholics, persons with mental illness, ethnic minorities, young criminals) and institutions for individuals with special needs (e.g. schools and homes for persons with cognitive impairments, children with behaviour problems and institutions for persons with impairments) have traditionally been an important part of Nordic welfare programmes aimed at both individual treatment and social control, protection and 'renovation'.[14] Such institutions, along with outplacement treatment programmes, have shifted responsibility from the private to the public domain. However, they involve not only the help and support of individuals and their families but also significant interference in private life and individual freedom. Public reports and research in Norway have documented and criticized serious violations of fundamental freedom rights (in several institutions) in the name of improved health and social functioning of the individuals concerned, i.e. justified by the principle of beneficence.[15]

In Norway and other Nordic countries, many of the institutions established after World War II were closed after the public scrutiny and criticism that occurred during the 1970s and 1980s. More open and transparent institutions and services have since been established, with emphasis on respect for individual autonomy and participation. However, the same basic dilemma and tension between different values and human rights – autonomy, private life and liberty versus life, health and an adequate standard of living – still prevail. Even with conscious attempts at implementing all these values and rights, in some situations complying with them all at once is simply impossible. Thus the dilemma occurs not necessarily among the values but over what to do when they cannot be realized and implemented simultaneously, because full respect for one right may seriously undermine other rights. The essential question, therefore, is how to understand, apply and implement different human rights in the interests of ensuring an ideal balance between them: how do we define and determine this ideal balance, understood as an acceptable and fair harmonization of classical civil rights and social rights in

13 See H. Wulf et al., *Philosophy of medicine: an introduction*.

14 T.S. Dahl, *Child Welfare and Social Defence*, Oslo: Norwegian University Press 1985, and T.S. Dahl, 'Statsmakt og sosial kontroll. Et bidrag til velferdsstatens historie' [State power and social control. A contribution to the history of the welfare state], in *Pene piker haiker ikke*, Oslo: Universitetsforlaget 1994, pp. 271–301.

15 Granskningskommisjonen for Reitgjerdet. Rapport om forholdene ved Reitgjerdet sykehus, 31 August 1980 (public report concerning Reitgjerdet mental hospital), H.S. Aasen, *Pasientens rett til selvbestemmelse ved medisinsk behandling* [Patient's right to self-determination], Bergen: Fagbokforlaget 2000, pp. 136–138, with further references to Dahl, Løchen, Benneche, Aubert, Eskeland, Christie, Mathiesen and Bernt, who have given valuable contributions to the Norwegian debate on coercive treatment of vulnerable groups in the Norwegian welfare state.

today's welfare state?[16] In the health care context this balancing act can be described as determining the justified paternalism versus the non-justified. A study of coercion in the mental health care system in all the Nordic countries recommends that future research should give priority to the identification of variables such as process exclusion, pressure, threats, power disparity and asymmetry, and to the operationalizing of concepts such as procedural justice, process control, fairness, equity, autonomy and dignity.[17]

Too strong an emphasis on some values, rights or goals, and lack of attention on circumstances that increase the actual and perceived coercion, may lead to human rights violations that are by definition morally unacceptable and unjustified.[18] The notion of human vulnerability is essential in determining the fair balance between paternalism and autonomy and whether an intervention is justified or not. Burt puts the crucial question thusly: 'who can be trusted to care for me when I am too vulnerable and fearful to care for myself?'[19] If doctors and health care personnel, who are educated to relieve people from illness and pain, cannot be trusted in this task, who else can be? The answer is that we probably do not have anyone else to trust, and that the real social task is to make them do as ethical a job as possible, through education, policies, legal regulation and other appropriate means.

3. HUMAN DIGNITY AND HUMAN RIGHTS

Chapter 1 has shown that we may describe human dignity from a moral philosophical perspective as the intrinsic worth of human life, which is equal for all human beings. This inherent dignity implies that human beings should not be treated only as a means to an end but also (and always) as ends in themselves. Although the concept of human dignity is rarely described in human rights sources, that the respect for human dignity is *the* core value to be protected

16 The term 'fair balance' is often used by the European Human Rights Court in cases concerning interventions in private life, e.g. the Grand Chamber decision in *Hatton and others v. UK* (2003, Application No. 36022/97, www.echr.coe.int), in which the Court stated that 'regard must be had to the fair balance that has to be struck between the competing interests of the individual and of the community as a whole' (para. 98).

17 G. Høyer et.al., 'Paternalism and autonomy: A presentation of a Nordic study on the use of coercion in the mental health care system', *International Journal of Law and Psychiatry*, vol. 25, Issue 2, March-April 2002, pp. 93–108.

18 One may question the appropriateness of the term 'right' when health care or other treatment is coercive. However, legally it is clear that a person may have a right to care and services that he or she rejects, and that society is obligated to ensure the right when the person is incapable of consenting to the service in question.

19 Burt, 'The Suppressed Legacy of Nuremberg', p. 32.

through human rights instruments is clear. The preamble to the UDHR proclaims that 'recognition of the inherent dignity and of the equal and inalienable rights of all members of the human family is the foundation of freedom, justice and peace in the world'. Article 1 stipulates that '[a]ll human beings are born free and equal in dignity and rights. They are endowed with reason and conscience and should act towards one another in a spirit of brotherhood'.

René Cassin, one of the drafters of the UDHR, compared it to the portico of a temple and identified its four pillars as human dignity, liberty, equality and brotherhood.[20] The preambles of both the International Covenant on Civil and Political Rights (ICCPR) and the International Covenant on Economic, Social and Cultural Rights (ICESCR) describe human rights as outcomes or products of the inherent human dignity in that they '... derive from the inherent dignity of the human person'.[21] Hartlev notes that Article 1 of the UDHR mentions human dignity *before* rights: 'This might be taken to indicate that dignity is in some way regarded as more fundamental within human rights thinking than individual rights and freedoms, such as, e.g. personal liberty and freedom of expression.'[22] Indeed, the drafters of the UDHR recognized the historical evidence that people, left to their own free will, do not always behave rationally or well, and that human dignity – if left to the principles of autonomy and liberty only – may be in danger.

Unlike the UDHR and the UN human rights conventions, the European Convention on Human Rights and Fundamental Freedoms (ECHR) does not explicitly mention 'dignity'. However, the practice of the European Court of Human Rights (ECtHR) clearly confirms the notion of human dignity as the core idea of human rights thinking. In *Pretty v UK*, followed by *Goodwin v UK* the same year, the ECtHR stated that '[t]he very essence of the Convention is respect for human dignity and human freedom'.[23] Again, human dignity and human freedom are reflected as two separate and different entities, despite the court is pointing out the close relationship between them.

The concept of human dignity is included in other Council of Europe legal instruments, such as the Biomedicine Convention. In Article 1, the State Parties agree to 'protect the dignity ... of all human beings'. The preamble, which mentions the developments in medicine and biology and indicates the need to use them for

20 M.R. Ishay, *The History of Human Rights*, Los Angeles: University of California Press 2004, p. 3.

21 UN, both covenants from 1966.

22 Chapter 6, sec. 2.2.

23 *Pretty v. UK*. Application No. 2346/02, para. 65, and *Goodwin v. UK*, Application No. 28957/95, para. 90 (both at www.echr.coe.int).

the benefit of present and future generations, proclaims 'the need to respect the human being both as an individual and as a member of the human species', and 'the importance of ensuring the dignity of the human being'. It points out that 'the misuse of biology and medicine may lead to acts endangering human dignity' and that the ratifying states resolve 'to take such measures as are necessary to safeguard human dignity and the fundamental rights and freedoms of the individual with regard to the application of biology and medicine'.[24] The Explanatory Report of the Biomedicine Convention states that the 'concept of human dignity ... constitutes the essential value to be upheld', and that it 'is at the basis of most of the values emphasised in the Convention'.[25]

This book considers the understanding of the relationship between human dignity and rights, namely that human dignity is 'the essential value to be upheld' through all the human rights instruments and that it is ultimately 'at the basis' of human rights. Throughout this book, the assumption is that *human dignity* is the most fundamental value, an assumption fully in line with the Kantian humanistic tradition that human beings, as opposed to other objects (all of which have a price), are 'priceless' beings with dignity, which requires respect or reverence.

Furthermore, human dignity is not to be identified with the capacity of autonomous decision-making, since doing so would suggest that those who are not able to exercise their autonomy do not have human dignity. Such an interpretation would be unacceptable from a humanistic perspective. Rather, human dignity is the underlying basic value inherent in, but not identical to, one particular human right – the protection of each human being as someone unique and ethically special, who deserves unconditional respect and whose basic human needs and rights must not be violated. In a medical context, dignity refers to the overall well-being of the person, not only in the short term but also in the longer term, e.g. in situations of life-saving treatment in health care. Furthermore, human dignity refers to the ability to lead 'a dignified life', e.g. in terms of being able to study, work and participate in common social activities. In addition, human dignity underlies not only the requirement of respect for the needs of the individuals themselves but also the obligation of society to uphold respect for human life, even if the person does not see the value of his or her own life and wishes to end it.

---

24 Here we also see the distinction between human dignity and 'fundamental rights and freedoms'.

25 Council of Europe. Explanatory Report to the Convention on Human Rights and Biomedicine (Strasbourg, May 1997), para. 9.

In essence, respect for human dignity as an inherent property of each human being requires respect for all human rights, since all of them reflect basic (though different) individual and societal needs and interests, such as respect for life, health, liberty, security, integrity and private life. Human dignity may be violated not only through breach of civil liberties, such as confinement in institutions where personal liberty and freedom of movement is restricted, but also in situations where access to adequate care, food, housing, education, work or necessary health care and social services are denied, ignored or neglected. Human dignity may also be violated if individual needs and particular circumstances are not recognized and taken into account.

4. THE UNITY AND INTERDEPENDENCE OF HUMAN RIGHTS

The human rights framework represents a normative unity in which the different rights are to be considered equally important, interrelated and interdependent. The Vienna Declaration and Programme of Action states in paragraph 5 that all human rights are 'universal, indivisible and interdependent and interrelated'.[26] If one right is taken away, a basic condition for human well-being will be missing, and other rights will suffer as well. For example, if a state denies its citizens the right to health care, education and basic social services, not only social rights but also civil and political ones will be undermined. If an individual is sick, has no access to health care or food, and has no education or work, he or she will find it hard to live, to realize his or her human potential, or to participate meaningfully in society. In such a situation, even though the individual is not locked up in an institution and no one is directly bothering him or her, to assert that he or she is enjoying his or her personal liberty, with his or her human dignity upheld and respected, would be a distortion of the truth. When the state does not protect basic human needs, human dignity will be in danger of violation or disrespect. Thus the common distinctions between 'negative' and 'positive' rights, between 'first and second generation' human rights, and between 'civil' and 'social' rights should not be overestimated. To protect human dignity, which is the basic aim of all human rights, we must take seriously not only the 'negative' civil and political rights but also the 'positive' ones, the second generation human rights and the social human rights.[27]

'Negative rights', a term closely related to 'first generation' human rights, mean the individual right to be free from intervention in liberty, private life, physical

[26] UN, adopted by the World Conference on Human Rights on 25 June 1993.
[27] Gustafsson, 'Taking social rights seriously'.

integrity, etc. 'Positive rights', a term related to 'second generation' human rights, mean entitlement rights of individuals to health care and social services. These are called 'social' human rights because they give rights to certain goods and services that society provides. These rights are products of a political ideology in which society takes on the responsibility for the creation of good life conditions for everyone. In practice, the rigid classification and distinction between civil and political rights on the one hand, and social, economic and cultural rights on the other has not been easily maintained. There have always been exceptions to the rule that obligations imposed by civil and political rights were only 'negative' (e.g. *not* to kill or torture), while economic, social and cultural rights placed the state under a positive duty to take positive measures (e.g. providing health care and social services).[28] After all, as the British legal scholar Cumper points out, 'a civil and political right, such as the right to fair trial, ensures that the State must set up and finance a legal system by providing, among other things, court buildings, trained judges, legal aid for those who cannot afford a lawyer, and interpreters for those who do not understand the language being spoken in court'.[29] Therefore, there has been a growing recognition that the full realization of civil and political rights is impossible without the enjoyment of economic, social and cultural human rights. The Vienna Declaration and Programme of Action states in paragraph 5 that the international community 'must treat human rights globally in a fair and equal manner, on the same footing, and with the same emphasis ... it is the duty of States, regardless of their political, economic and cultural systems, to promote and protect all human rights and fundamental freedoms'.

An important aspect of the unity of the human rights framework is that we not interpret the rights concerned in such a way that they infringe upon other rights. This view is expressed in General Comment No. 28 of the UN Human Rights Committee (2000) on the equality of rights between men and women, which states that state parties are obligated to 'ensure that traditional, historical, religious or cultural attitudes are not used to justify violations of women's right to equality before the law and to equal enjoyment of all Covenant rights.[30] In other words, the right to enjoy cultural rights must not infringe on women's rights.

Similarly, a strong one-sided and unconditioned protection of one right (e.g. the right to health care) may lead to severe violations of other human rights (e.g. the right to personal liberty, freedom of movement and private life). Thus, for the human rights framework to be a coherent unity, the rights must be harmonized,

28 Cumper, 'Human Rights: History, Development and Classification', p. 7.

29 Ibid., p. 7.

30 Human Rights Committee, *Equality of rights between men and women* (on the International Covenant on Civil and Political Rights, Art. 3) para. 5. See also paras. 21, 24, 25, 26, 32.

balanced against and working in the light of one another, because they are logically and normatively interdependent and interrelated.

However, in some situations giving full protection of one right without violating other rights is impossible. An example is the violation of the personal autonomy and private life of a person to protect his or her right to life or health in emergency situations, a situation typically occurring when consent to treatment cannot be obtained because the person is unconscious. In such situations it is ethically and legally justifiable to give preference to the protection of life and health at the expense of autonomy and private life – and such a prioritization will also follow from state legislation. For example, the Norwegian Health Personnel Act of 2 July 1999, No. 64, section 7, states that when health care is urgent in medical emergency, health personnel are obligated to give treatment even if the patient is not able to give valid consent and even if the patient objects. The Finnish Act on the Status and Rights of Patients 1992, No. 785, section 8, states that emergency treatment must be given even if the will of the patient cannot be assessed. However, according to the Finnish act, if the patient has earlier steadfastly and competently expressed his or her will concerning treatment, he or she must not be given a treatment in contradiction to that expressed will.

This prioritization suggests a form of 'ranking' the values and rights involved, in situations where they cannot all be fulfilled simultaneously. However, situations may occur in which a need arises for discussing whether a strong protection of life violates human dignity, for example where patients are kept alive in a vegetative state for years by mechanical means. This was the question in the well-known US *Quinlan* case involving an unconscious young woman in a persistent vegetative state. When the father of the 22-year-old woman was allowed to act on her behalf, he demanded that her respirator treatment be terminated. The Supreme Court of New Jersey accepted his claim based on the right to private life.[31]

A similar but perhaps more problematic balancing of conflicting rights is explicitly mentioned in the ECHR, Article 5, on the protection of personal liberty and security. It states that no one shall be deprived of his or her liberty, 'save in the following cases and in accordance with a procedure prescribed by law'. It mentions 'the lawful detention … of persons of unsound mind, alcoholics or drug addicts or vagrants'.[32] Similarly, but with stricter wording, the Biomedicine Convention, Article 7, states that individuals with 'a mental disorder of a serious nature' may be subjected to an intervention aimed at treatment even without their consent. These provisions reflect a long tradition of the involuntary treatment of psychiatric

31 *In re Quinlan*, 70 N J 10, 355 A, 2d 647 (1976).

32 Practice of the ECtHR has narrowed the scope of this provision.

patients, constituting a wide exception from the general rule of self-determination and informed consent. This exception is normally explained with reference to the view that psychiatric patients, because of their mental disorder, are not capable of making sound decisions about proposed treatment.[33]

However, to balance human rights, one must consider each right separately, and in relation to other rights, in the light of the particular circumstances and individual situation of the person whose human rights are being infringed upon. The question then is whether a violation of the right to autonomy and private life is justified in a particular case. Are the overall well-being and dignity of the person concerned (or the well-being and dignity of vulnerable individuals in similar situations) better served by non-consensual, involuntary or coercive treatment or by the withholding of treatment?[34] Both the state and health care professionals must evaluate several factors related to the individual situation before reaching a conclusion. Examples of such considerations appear in chapters 3, 5 and 6, showing that the overall aim is the protection of human dignity at both the individual and the societal levels.

5. AUTONOMY AND CONSENT AS THE LEGAL STARTING POINT

5.1. AN OVERVIEW

Respect for personal liberty, autonomy or self-determination (referred to here mainly in terms of autonomy or self-determination) is one important aspect of protecting human dignity. It represents both a core value and a basic principle in democratic societies founded on fundamental freedoms and human rights. Respecting the human being as an individual with inherent dignity and integrity implies a duty to respect his or her personal autonomy as far as possible. Thus the legal point of departure is always that competent human beings have the right to make their own decisions in matters concerning themselves.[35]

---

33 Explanatory Report (para. 50).

34 In *Pretty v. UK*, which involved the British ban on assisted suicide, the ECtHR recognized that the law in question 'was designed to safeguard life by protecting the weak and vulnerable and especially those who are not in a condition to take informed decisions against acts intended to end life or to assist in ending life' (para. 74). The ECtHR stated that it was primarily up to States to assess the risk and likely incidence of abuse if the general prohibition on assisted suicide were relaxed.

35 Faden and Beauchamp, pioneers in the field of informed consent, write, '[t]o respect an autonomous agent is to recognize with due appreciation that person's capacities and perspective, including his or her right to hold certain views, to make certain choices, and to take certain

This right applies to all aspects of human life involving decisions, such as those about education, work, where to live, how to live (within certain social limits), memberships, etc. Naturally, the right of autonomous decision-making also applies to health care, although the paternalistic and doctor-centred medical tradition has been long and enduring, representing a contradiction to the generally accepted Western value of individual self-determination.[36] The following section explores in greater detail the legal starting point of self-determination in both health care and in other areas of welfare state interventions, and looks briefly at some of the exceptions.

5.2. FREE INFORMED CONSENT AS A BASIC PATIENT RIGHT

Today the main rule of free 'informed consent' to medical treatment is established as a legal norm in the health care legislation of most Western civil law and common law countries, as well as laid down in international law.[37] Among the Nordic countries, Norway, Denmark and Iceland have ratified the Biomedicine Convention, while Finland and Sweden have signed but not ratified it. The Biomedicine Convention sets forth the most important principles of the application of biology and medicine, including the principle and requirement of informed consent: '[a]n intervention in the health field may only be carried out after the person concerned has given free and informed consent to it. This person shall beforehand be given appropriate information as to the purpose and nature of the intervention as well as on its consequences and risks'.[38] The provision is applicable for any 'intervention in the health field', giving it a wide range. The Biomedicine Convention covers all medical and biological applications for human beings, including preventive, diagnostic, therapeutic and research applications.[39]

In countries like Finland and Norway, the principle of informed consent is put forward in specific patient rights legislation, covering all important patient

---

actions based on personal values and beliefs' (*A History and Theory of Informed Consent*, p. 8).

36 J. Katz, *The Silent World of Doctor and Patient*, Baltimore: John Hopkins University Press 1984 (2002). See also Dieter Giesen, 'From Paternalism to Self-Determination to Shared Decision Making in the Field of Medical Law and Ethics', in Westerhäll and Phillips (eds.), *Patient's Rights*, Stockholm: Nerenius and Santérus Publishers 1994, pp. 19–39, and Aasen, *Pasientens rett til selvbestemmelse ved medisinsk behandling*, [Patient's Right to Self-Determination] p. 83 f.

37 See the comparative study of Giesen, 'From Paternalism to Self-Determination to Shared Decision Making in the Field of Medical Law and Ethics', pp. 19–39.

38 Art. 5, secs. 1 and 2.

39 Explanatory Report (para. 10).

rights.[40] The Norwegian Patient Rights Act states in section 4–1 that health care may be given only on the basis of the consent of the patient, unless a particular law or other legal basis provides an exemption. For the consent to be valid, the patient must receive necessary information about his or her condition and about the content of the proposed medical procedures. These conditions ensure that the consent of the patient is based on proper understanding of his or her situation and of the proposed medical intervention. The consent must be voluntary and valid, not the result of coercion, fraud, incompetence or other invalidating circumstances. The patient may withdraw his or her consent at any time, with no negative consequences. However, the provider of health care is then obligated to provide necessary information about the consequences or implications of not accepting treatment. Similar provisions appear in Swedish, Danish, Finnish and Icelandic law.

The most common exception to the main rule of free informed consent to treatment is medical emergencies, in which the decisions of health care personnel are decisive. Other exceptions are made for children, where the parents have the right to consent on behalf of the patient, in situations of legal and other incompetence, and in cases of serious mental illness. These situations, all of which are covered by the Biomedicine Convention, Articles 6–8, will be discussed in detail in Chapters 3, 5 and 6.

However, this rather black-and-white description of situations in which the capacity for consent either exists or does not is somewhat misleading, as there is a growing legal recognition of the duty of hearing and even respecting, as far as possible, the opinions of children and adults who, due to mental disability or serious mental illness, do not have the capacity to give legally valid consent. This recognition is expressed in several ways in international and national law. The principles of self-determination and participation have gradually been expanded to include more individuals, as a way of ensuring respect for human dignity.

5.3. AUTONOMY AND CONSENT IN SOCIAL SERVICES

The principle of informed consent is a pillar of modern medical law, aiming at the protection of individual autonomy and human dignity in the medical field. However, recognizing that the principle of self-determination is general is important, because the doctrine of informed consent is a particular application of this general principle, i.e. individual autonomy and self-determination apply to

[40] In Finland, the Act on the Status and Rights of Patients No. 785 was enacted on 17 August 1992, and the Norwegian Patient Rights Act on 2 July 1999, No. 63.

all situations of social intervention in private life. The ECHR, Article 8, as well as the ICCPR, Article 17, protects the right of everyone to respect for his or her private and family life, home and correspondence (the principle of privacy). These articles prohibit arbitrary interference by the state or its agents in the private individual sphere. These provisions are open-ended, covering a range of issues, including involuntary treatment of any kind, matters of personal integrity and access to personal records. The state and its agents must not only refrain from interference in the rights protected but must also take appropriate measures to protect these rights from violation by others.[41]

We need to bear in mind the right to private and family life in relation to the range of social services that are part of the welfare state policies, especially with regard to the various forms of treatment of individual and socially related problems. Examples are different kinds of child protection, voluntary and non-voluntary treatment of alcohol or drug addiction, assistance and support of individuals with physical impairments, care for the elderly, and care for individuals with cognitive impairments. The principle of autonomy and self-determination, as part of the broader and more general principle of respect for private life, applies to all these kinds of services. All interventions in private life require individual consent or other legal bases to be ethically and legally justifiable.

6. CONCLUSIONS

The modern welfare state is a beneficent state based not only on 'negative' freedoms and civil rights but also on 'positive' social entitlement rights. Although the principle of self-determination is fundamental, the welfare state is to some extent paternalistic, as it does not leave individuals completely to their own destiny but takes responsibility for their survival and well-being. The paternalistic aspect of the welfare state is a problem mainly in the case of coercive interventions in the private sphere of individuals, such as coercive or non-voluntary treatment and care for health purposes. The term 'health' in this context not only refers to the absence of disease and illness but also includes individual well-being and social functioning (one of the main objectives of the welfare state). The human rights framework, including civil and social human rights – with human dignity as the core value – is the overarching normative guideline for the implementation of social policies in modern welfare states. However, the inherent tensions between various human rights need thorough and constant analysis and discussion, separately and in relation to other rights. The balancing of human rights is an

---

41 See Jacobs and White, *The European Convention on Human Rights*, Oxford: Oxford University Press 2006, Fourth edition, pp. 241–300.

ongoing normative process that will continue along with social, scientific and normative developments at both national and international levels. Nation states are obligated to formulate laws for the more precise normative balancing of these tensions in their respective jurisdictions. In addition, to ensure a life of dignity for everyone, nation states are obligated to combat exclusion and discrimination as experienced by vulnerable social groups.

PART II
PROTECTION OF VULNERABLE INDIVIDUALS IN HEALTH CARE, MEDICAL RESEARCH AND SOCIAL SERVICES

CHAPTER 3
CHILDREN'S RIGHT TO PARTICIPATE IN HEALTH CARE DECISIONS

Kirsten SANDBERG

1. INTRODUCTION

The central international document on children's rights is the UN Convention on the Rights of the Child (CRC), making it a natural starting point for a discussion of children's rights in any connection. The UN Committee on the Rights of the Child, supervising the implementation of the CRC, has pointed to four of the articles as general principles, among them Article 12, which states the right of the child to be heard. This right is part of the participation rights of the convention, 'participation' being used here in relation to both individual decisions and the wider democratic right to have a say in society. The first application of participation is the focus of this chapter: the individual child's right to be heard in decisions concerning his or her own health.

Of the other three general principles – the right to life and development in Article 6, the best interests principle in Article 3, and the right to non-discrimination in Article 2 – only the first two are relevant to the discussion in this chapter. Life and development are closely linked with health, and the wide, general right of Article 6 is spelled out in Article 24, which states that the child has the right to the highest attainable standard of health and to facilities for the treatment of illness and rehabilitation of health. In addition, state parties must strive to ensure that no child is deprived of his or her right of access to such health care services. This chapter will discuss the relationship between this 'no deprivation' statement and the parents' right of refusal. According to Article 3, the best interests of the child shall be a primary consideration in all actions concerning children, including both individual decisions and legislation.

Underlying the CRC is a tension between the autonomy of the child and the protection of the child. While the problem of balancing the two is not new, with the CRC explicitly confirming the child as a right-holder, it has garnered renewed interest. To what extent should a child have the right to decide for him- or herself, even if the decision, in the eyes of the parents, the health personnel, etc. may not be the best for the child? If the decision the child wants to make has harmful consequences or implies the risk thereof, should the scope of the child's own decision-making be narrowed? The CRC does not give the child the right to self-determination, since Article 12 states only that the child should have the right to express his or her own views freely and that those views should be given due weight. Thus the final decision still rests with someone else, who also has the discretion of deciding what weight to give to the opinion of the child. One question is whether this solution is desirable; another is what to do if one or both parents do not agree with the child, whether the child wants treatment or not.

The CRC obtained a special position under Norwegian law in 2003, when it was incorporated into the Human Rights Act of 1999 – which also contains the European Convention on Human Rights and Fundamental Freedoms (ECHR) and the two general UN Covenants on Civil and Political Rights and Economic, Social and Cultural Rights. These conventions are thus considered as Norwegian legislation under section 2 of the Act. The Act provides them with an even stronger legal position than national legislation, as section 3 states that in any conflict between the two, the conventions have priority.

This chapter discusses the right of the child to participate in health decisions concerning him- or herself, according to the CRC and within Norwegian law. Section 2 presents the contents of Article 12. Sections 3, 4 and 5 describe the rules for consent, participation and information in the Norwegian legislation, and sections 6 and 7 discuss the vital questions of lack of parental consent and parents' disagreeing with each other. Sections 8 and 9 examine whether the Norwegian health legislation sufficiently provides for the autonomy of the child.

2. CONVENTION ON THE RIGHTS OF THE CHILD, ARTICLE 12

2.1. THE CHILD'S RIGHT TO BE HEARD

As the right of the child to be heard under Article 12 applies to 'all matters affecting the child', the provision has quite a wide scope, including matters of physical and mental health. However, the term 'affecting the child' may also imply the child's right to be heard in matters primarily concerning the health of a parent or other close person, e.g. whether the father or mother should have a long hospital stay. Nevertheless, even if the child has a right to state his or her opinion, that opinion has less weight than where the child's own health is concerned.

The prerequisite for the child's right to be heard is that he or she is capable of forming his or her own views. Thus the child must be able to form views on the matter in question, so that he or she has an interest in taking part in the decision. The child, however, need not have definitely made up his or her mind, e.g. whether to undergo major surgery or choose a certain treatment. The child may have something to say about going to the hospital or not, or whether to do something about, say, stomach pain. Furthermore, the right to be heard is not limited to whether the child's views are well-founded, nor can anyone require the child's views to be formed independently of parents or others, even though Article 12 says his or her own' views. While the objections on these grounds are relevant in judging the weight of the opinion, the opinion of the child cannot be *a priori* excluded on these grounds.

Although the use of the word own' cannot be interpreted as a limitation, it indicates that the child should be encouraged to make up his or her own mind, not merely follow that of parents or doctors. Thus Article 12 requires that the child have the opportunity to express his or her views 'freely'. The circumstances in which the child expresses his or her views should be adjusted to the child, so that he or she can feel comfortable and speak without constraint. For instance, the health personnel may need to talk to the child without the parents present if they have any reason to believe that the child will otherwise say merely what he or she thinks the parents want to hear.

Although Article 12 does not impose a clear duty on health personnel themselves to hear the child, paragraph 1 stipulates that the child has the right to express his or her views freely but not to whom. Paragraph 2, while more specific in its requirements, concerns 'judicial or administrative proceedings', which hardly cover the question of medical treatment. The UN Committee on the Rights of the Child has adopted a General Comment on adolescent health and development, pointing to the parents' duty to hear the child before they give their consent, but it does not mention health personnel in this connection.[1] As to Article 12 in particular, the General Comment contains only a more general statement about the importance of public authorities, parents and other adults working with or for children to 'create an environment based on trust, information-sharing, the capacity to listen and sound guidance that is conducive for adolescents' participating equally including in decision-making processes'.[2] The General

1 General Comment No. 4, 2003, CRC/GC/2003/4, para. 32.
2 Ibid, para. 8.

Comment also mentions the significance of consent, which I shall return to shortly.

As the ability to form one's own views is not dependent on age, Article 12 states no age limit. When the question of whether age limits in national legislation are still acceptable was put to the chair of the UN Committee on the Rights of the Child during the Committee's General Day of Discussion in September 2006 (I was present), the answer was that in an ideal world there would be no need for age limits. But as the world is not ideal, an age limit may serve at least to secure the right to be heard for children above that age. However, for compliance with the requirements of Article 12, an age limit must be combined with a rule saying that younger children also share the right in so far as they are capable of forming their own views.

To be able to form views, the child needs information about the matter in question. For children and adults alike, properly making up one's mind with insufficient knowledge about the case is impossible. The right to the necessary information must consequently follow from the right to be heard and to participate in the decision-making process. This consequence holds true for medical decisions in which the requirement of *informed consent* is crucial. Even if Article 12 does not deal with consent, the vital role of information remains the same. Such information must cover all relevant circumstances regarding the seriousness of the disease or injury and the consequences of the alternative solutions, which may include different treatments or no treatment at all. However, with children both the scope and the form of information need adjusting to the individual child's capacity for understanding.

2.2. THE WEIGHT GIVEN TO THE CHILD'S OWN VIEWS

According to Article 12, the views of the child should be given 'due weight. Whereas some factors about the views have to be considered, others concern the balancing of the child's view against other relevant arguments. As to the child's views, Article 12 states that the weight should be in accordance with the age and maturity of the child, e.g. while age may be an indication, it should be subordinate to maturity. Maturity is more difficult to ascertain. However, it is much more indicative of whether the child has understood the situation and has been able to consider it on the right premises. Indeed the child's understanding and ability to judge the situation must be central factors in considering the weight. The more complex the matter, the more difficult it may be for the child to judge the situation wisely.

If the opinion of the child is firm and stable, the weight should be greater than if the opinion wavers. However, if the child has changed his or her mind and can give good reasons for doing so, this change of mind is not a negative factor. On the whole, well-founded views receive greater weight. As previously mentioned, whether the views are the child's own or strongly influenced by the parents or others is another factor. Still, even if the child is under pressure to state certain views, or states them out of loyalty to the parents, he or she may identify with the views and feel that they are his or her own. The child may then experience any setting aside of those views as an infringement of his or her autonomy or rights. This is but one of the dilemmas of hearing the child and deciding what weight to give his or her views.

In each case, the child's opinion must also be balanced against other considerations, primarily the medical importance or necessity of the treatment and the seriousness of an intervention and the risk it represents. Both considerations may be placed on a sliding scale. The more important a particular treatment is for the child's health, and the less of an intervention, the easier it is to follow the child's wishes. But if the child does not want to undergo the treatment in question, the decision depends on the necessity and degree of serious medical intervention as compared with other possible treatments, balanced against the strength and foundation of the child's objections.

3. THE RIGHT TO CONSENT TO OR REJECT TREATMENT – WHAT HAPPENS IN NORWAY?

In Norway, while the age of legal majority is 18 years, the age of medical majority – at which a young person normally has the right to consent in medical matters – is 16 (Patient Rights Act, sec. 4–3 b). Below age 16, the right to consent is placed with the parents (sec. 4–4). If the parents have joint parental responsibility, they have to agree, which means that both have to consent to the medical treatment. What happens if they do not agree will be discussed in section 4.7.

3.1. THE RIGHTS OF CHILDREN ABOVE THE AGE OF 16

One may ask why 16 was chosen as the age of medical majority. First, that age has a long tradition in Norwegian medicine. Second, the reason for not setting a higher age could be that the decisions are closely connected with a person's own physical integrity. For a 16- or 17-year-old, for somebody else to decide what medicines to take, whether to undergo surgery, or whether to have physio- or psychotherapy, may feel like a violation of personal integrity.

Still, 16 years is not an absolute limit. Some matters are specifically regulated in other acts, such as organ transplants, where the age of consent is 18 (Transplantation Act, sec. 1), and sterilization, where the age of consent is 25 (Sterilization Act, sec. 2). In addition, even without such special provisions, a judgement on the type of medical intervention may change the age of consent to 18 (Patients Rights Act, sec. 4–3 b), e.g. participating in experimental treatment or having plastic surgery.[3] A factor common to these interventions is that they are not medically necessary. (Were lobotomy still a remedy for psychiatric disorders, its seriousness and attendant risks would have raised the age of consent to 18.) A third exception is grounded in the seriousness of refusing medical help. For example, a politically motivated adult on a hunger strike has the right to refuse food, and a patient with serious religious convictions has the right to refuse a blood transfusion – but not someone below the age of 18 (Patient Rights Act, sec. 4–9, last paragraph). The reason most likely lies in an assumption that, in addition to the very serious consequences, a younger person's convictions are not fully developed.

Finally, one exception applies to all persons, age notwithstanding: competence to consent may be suspended totally or in part if the patient, as a result of mental or physical disorders or mental disability, is obviously incapable of understanding the meaning of the consent (Patient Rights Act, sec. 4–3, second paragraph). Competence in such instances is to be judged case by case or at least by type of treatment; nobody can be deprived of the general right to consent in medical matters without being legally declared to be without mental capacity.[4] Whereas the former exceptions are grounded in the intervention itself, this one primarily focuses on the person and his or her capabilities, even if the type of treatment also factors into the overall judgement.

3.2. THE RIGHTS OF CHILDREN BELOW THE AGE OF 16

One may also ask why the Patient Rights Act does not set an age lower than 16. As the Child Protection Act has the lower age of 15 for the child's right to consent to being placed in an institution for children with serious behavioural problems, the same age was proposed for the Patient Rights Act. However, the age met with

3 Ot.prp. No.12 (1998–1999) on the Patient Rights Act, para. 6.7.2.1 p. 83–84.

4 A. Syse, *Pasientrettighetsloven med kommentarer* [commentaries to the Patient Rights Act], 2nd ed., Gyldendal Akademisk, Oslo, 2004, p. 272.

objections from the Norwegian Children's Ombudsman during the written hearing, and the Ministry of Social Affairs and Health accepted them. The grounds for sticking to age 16 were the seriousness of these decisions, the potential for the negative or even irreversible effects of making a wrong decision, and the assumption that assessing and balancing both need and effects demand maturity and a critical sense. The Ministry found that younger children should be protected from the responsibility of making such difficult decisions.[5]

However, why general medical decisions are more difficult for a young person to make than one about being placed in a residential institution is hard to understand. Perhaps the real reason for the age difference is that children with serious behavioural problems often have had family difficulties and a more complex relationship with their parents. Consequently, the lower age limit may result from the state having less trust in the parents in such cases, as opposed to greater trust in the young persons. Whatever the reason, this discussion illustrates that the matter of choosing an age of consent is difficult at best, leaving us with the question of whether stipulating such an age is a good idea at all. This chapter will continue this particular discussion later.

While coercive psychiatric treatment is regulated in a separate act, the consent of the child is regulated by the same rules in the Patient Rights Act. One difference, however, is that if a child older than 12 does not agree to the psychiatric treatment, the control commission of the hospital makes the decision. Thus instead of the parents making the final decision, it is left to an outside body deemed particularly competent to make such decisions. This difference from somatic treatment probably stems from a combination of the difficulty of giving this kind of treatment to a person who does not want it, and coercive psychiatric treatment's being an extremely harsh invasion of a person's autonomy.

According to the Patient Rights Act, 16 years is an absolute age limit, in that younger children may not consent to medical treatment. An exception, however, may be allowed for very personal issues such as contraception.[6] A doctor has a certain right not to inform the parents when the patient is between 12 and 16 if the young person has legitimate reasons for not wanting the parents to be involved (Patient Rights Act, sec. 3–4). The reasoning is that if the young person cannot trust the doctor's confidentiality, he or she will not seek medical advice and perhaps end up having unprotected sex. Thus to obtain consistency in the legislation and ensure that young people get proper advice and treatment, the

5 Ot.prp. nr. 12 (1998–1999) on the Patient Rights Act, para. 6.7.2.1, p. 83.

6 Syse, *Pasientrettighetsloven med kommentarer* [commentaries to the Patient Rights Act], p. 274.

consent of the parents to the medical measure cannot be required in such situations.[7] The exception may also be applied in cases of strong disagreement between the young person and his or her parents, where the young person fears severe parental punishment.

As previously mentioned, there is an exception in section 4–3, first paragraph b, stating that a judgement on the type of medical intervention may lead to a higher age of consent. The committee reviewing the Children and Parents Act in the spring of 2008 interprets this stipulation to allow even younger children to consent to medical treatment to a certain extent if they are able to take care of their own interests in a sensible way, and if the behaviour and attitudes of the parents are not necessarily in the child's best interest.[8] But defending this interpretation is difficult because the exception is placed in a provision dealing with minors *older* than 16.

Another question is whether a child's right to refuse treatment should be more far-reaching than his or her right to consent to treatment. However, while a coercive intervention is a greater infringement on the child's integrity, if refusal puts the child's life in danger, going through with the treatment may still be the right decision.[9] As always, the solution must depend on the circumstances.

4. THE CHILD'S RIGHT TO PARTICIPATION – NORWAY

The Children and Parents Act, section 31, gives the child the right to be heard in personal matters from the age of seven. Younger children also have that right if they are capable of forming their own views, i.e. the same wording as in the CRC, Article 12. The weight given to those views under section 31 depends not only on the age and maturity of the child but also (and necessarily) on the nature of the decision and the other factors that Article 12 mentions. One difference between the Norwegian provision and Article 12 of the CRC is that when the child is older than 12, the Norwegian provision gives his or her opinion 'great weight' instead of 'due weight'.

---

7 Ibid.

8 NOU 2008: 9 Med barnet i fokus (Focusing on the child), section 7.3.1, re: guidelines IS-12/2004.

9 For a discussion of this issue, see U. Kilkelly, *Children's Rights in Ireland: Law, Policy and Practice*, Tottel Publishing 2008, pp. 60–61.

The reason that Norway has the age limit of seven years is partly that before the CRC was incorporated into the Human Rights Act, Norway gave all children of 12 years and above an automatic right to be heard. Had that limit simply been removed, then older children would have lost their automatic rights and might have been in a worse position than before. In addition, in practice it had turned out that 12 also functioned as a negative limit, so that younger children were not sufficiently heard. The state found children between the ages of 7 and 12 generally capable of contributing to decisions that concerned them, and wanted to ensure that those children were actually heard. Although Norway still runs the same risk – that the younger children are not heard – now a smaller number are involved. Legally, however, even the younger children have the right to be heard if they can form and articulate a view.

In medical matters the absolute right to be heard starts only at age 12 (Patient Rights Act, sec. 4–4). Younger children have the right to be heard provided that they are able to form their own views. Thus children younger than 12 are not heard automatically. One might ask if the seven-year limit should not also apply to these cases. However, the preparatory documents of the amendment to the Children and Parents Act, section 31, state that for public authorities in different areas, the specific acts should decide the age limit for the duty of hearing children.[10] Although health personnel are not necessarily public authorities, the main point here is that age may depend on the kind of issue in question. As the Patient Rights Act explicitly sets its own limit, that rule must be followed in medical issues, even if the act is older than the amendment in section 31. According to the Patient Rights Act, the weight of the child's views should increase with age and maturity, with no specific requirement of 'great weight' above 12 years as in the Children and Parents Act.

The problem with the Patient Rights Act is that only the parents are required to listen to the child, not health personnel (sec. 4–4, last paragraph). This requirement is to some extent understandable, because the parents have the competence for consent. Nevertheless, the requirement is problematic for children with parents who are not interested in hearing their views, particularly when the parents will not consent to a medically indicated treatment that the child wants. I shall return to this discussion shortly.

The Patient Rights Act also gives the patient the right to participate in decisions on how to carry out the treatment – the next stage of medical decision-making. The patient has to consent to the treatment in general, whereas the details for how it is carried out are left to the doctor, with the patient's right to influence the

10 Ot.prp. No. 29 (2002–2003) on amendments to the Children and Parents Act, sec. 10.5.

decision. If the patient is not competent to consent, e.g. because he or she is below 16, the next of kin has the right to participate with the patient in the decision-making process (sec. 3–1, second paragraph). This provision gives the child a right to communicate with the doctor directly at this stage, rather than through his or her parents.

5. THE RIGHT TO INFORMATION

The patient's general right to information is regulated in the Patient Rights Act, section 3–2. For a young person or a child, a separate provision in section 3–4 applies the age limit of 16. Above that age a young person generally has an exclusive right to information – with two exceptions. One gives the parents the right to information that is necessary for fulfilling the parental responsibility, e.g. in cases of more serious mental disorders, drug abuse or major physical injury resulting from criminal acts.[11] The other exception, which applies to anybody above 16, is connected to an exception from consent, where the patient is obviously incapable of taking care of his or her interests due to a physical or mental disorder or mental disability. In that case the next of kin has the right to all information necessary for deciding whether to consent. This next-of-kin right does not deprive the patient of the right to information: both have that right, as the patient should normally not be left totally out of the decision-making (Patient Rights Act, sec. 3–1).

Below the age of 16, both the child and the parents have the right to information. However, an exception applies if a child between 12 and 16 does not want information to be given to the parents for reasons that should be respected (sec. 3–4, second paragraph), e.g. information dealing with parental abuse or a serious difference of convictions with a direct bearing on the medical matter. The choice is then left to the health personnel. Advice about sexuality and contraception is also to be given without informing the parents if the young person does not want his or her parents to be told.[12]

6. LACK OF PARENTAL CONSENT

The question here is what possibilities exist if the parents do not consent to a medically indicated treatment for a child younger than 16. Certainly in a medical emergency situation health personnel have a duty to give treatment without

[11] Ot.prp. No.12 (1998–99) on the Patient Rights Act, chap. 12, comments to sec. 3–4.
[12] Syse, *Pasientrettighetsloven med kommentarer* [commentaries to the Patient Rights Act], p. 227.

consent (Health Personnel Act, sec. 7). This section, however, deals with non-emergency situations.

In a presumed conflict of interests, e.g. a suspicion that the child is being abused by the parents, the public guardian's office may appoint a substitute guardian under the Guardianship Act, section 15, to make the decision.

Other situations call for specific legal grounds for setting aside a lack of parental consent. The Norwegian Child Protection Act, section 4–10, contains a relevant provision for examination and treatment when the child suffers from a life-threatening or other serious disease or injury. It is a rather demanding criterion, applicable to cancer, diabetes, serious arthritis, serious digestive diseases and serious infections. The evidential requirement for the disease or injury is 'reason to believe', which is not as strong as the ordinary probability requirement. The reason is that when the parents are not willing to consent, medical personnel may not even have the opportunity to examine the child. Since the application of this provision represents a form of coercion, the County Board on Social Matters, an independent administrative body with an adversarial and thorough procedure, makes the decision. The Board is also the competent body for other interventions, such as taking children into protective custody.

But what if the situation is not as serious as this provision requires? Law professor Aslak Syse maintains that a precondition for the parents' right to make decisions is that they use their authority in the best interest of the child. If they do not, he argues that their decisions are not valid.[13] While Norwegian law requires parents to act in the child's interests and needs (Children and Parents Act, sec. 30), such action is not a condition for validity: the duty is imposed on the parents, and others do not have the right to set parental decision aside. Indeed, parental authority is considered legally strong. Parental decisions cannot be overruled by whoever finds the child's interest to be different from what the parents think.

If one wants to set aside the decisions of the parents in matters in which they have the competence to decide, one needs a statutory provision or other valid law, such as that covering a medical emergency. Syse gives the example of blood transfusion in life-threatening situations, something that parents cannot refuse even if it is contrary to their religious beliefs. The legal ground for this provision is the medical emergency endangering the child's health or life, not a case of applying the general 'best interests' principle. The Child Protection Act, section 4–10, shows how far the legislature has been willing to go, and the existence of this provision underlines the common view within child law. Before this provision

13 Ibid., p. 274.

was added to the Act in 1992, parental responsibility had to be temporarily removed from unwilling parents before health personnel could give a child the necessary medical treatment.

It follows from the wording of the CRC, Article 3, and the preparatory works that the best interests principle does not apply to parents. Under Article 18, which recognizes the parents' primary responsibility for rearing the child, the parents are still supposed to have the best interests of the child as their basic concern. However, whether they do is difficult to ascertain, and the CRC does not solve the question of the consequences should parents not act in their child's best interests.

One may criticize section 4–10 for setting conditions that are too strict. In other words, giving children necessary medical treatment without parental consent ought to be possible even if the medical problem is not as serious as the provision requires, especially if the treatment is uncontroversial and the child has a well-founded wish to undergo it.

7. PARENTS DISAGREEING WITH EACH OTHER

A common occurrence in cases of joint parental responsibility is that one parent wants the child to undergo a medically indicated treatment, while the other one does not. The reasons for the difference may be religious beliefs, disagreement with health care personnel, or even a desire for revenge against the other parent. In some cases one parent is abroad or in other ways difficult to contact.

If the child lives with only one of the parents, that parent has the power to decide in matters concerning daily care (Children and Parents Act, sec. 37); thus ordinary doctor visits for a fever or other minor reasons do not need the other parent's consent. The same applies to ordinary medication for acute diseases, allergies, etc.[14]

The daily care provision does not cover treatments that are risky, controversial, far-reaching or for other reasons debatable.[15] The consent of both parents is thus needed for serious medical intervention such as surgery[16], including minor

14 Syse, *Pasientrettighetsloven med kommentarer* [commentaries to the Patient Rights Act], p. 274.

15 Aasen, Henriette Sinding (2000), *Pasientens rett til selvbestemmelse ved medisinsk behandling* (The patient's right to self-determination in medical treatment), Bergen: Fagbokforlaget, p. 574.

16 Ot.prp. No. 12 (1998–99) on the Patient Rights Act, pp. 133–34.

operations on a finger or a toe. Treatments (whether medication or psychotherapy) for mental problems also require the consent of both. Some people have a certain reluctance to acknowledge that mental problems or disorders may also be a medical problem requiring medical or psychological treatment; such reluctance, combined with a distrust in psychologists and a reluctance to admit that their child might need such help, may cause some parents to withhold their consent. It has long been a problem in practice that some children do not get the medical treatment they need because one of the parents refuses to consent. If the conditions of section 4–10 of the Child Protection Act are met, they can be applied to these cases as well. But, as we have seen, the conditions are very strict, and the provision cannot be used for diseases of a less serious nature. Thus a gap exists between the ordinary illnesses or injuries covered by daily care, and the rather serious ones covered by section 4–10. The Children's Ombudsman has pointed out that lack of consent is a particular problem in treatment for mental problems[17] and that in many of these cases section 4–10 cannot be applied.

One might ask whether the law might be interpreted so as to make the rule less strict. Law professor Henriette Sinding Aasen maintains that the doctor may presume consent to ordinary treatment for an ordinary medical condition, i.e. where the other parent also would likely have taken the child to the doctor had the child been with him or her. If, on the other hand, the mother tells the doctor that the father (or vice-versa) does not want the child to have treatment, the doctor cannot presume consent. Then the doctor's competence for giving necessary, ordinary treatment depends on whether the viewpoint of the unwilling parent is compatible with a reasonable execution of parental responsibility. If it is not, Aasen says that the doctor may treat the child. However, if the unwilling parent's view is compatible with a parental responsibility to reject treatment (e.g. because of medical doubt about the treatment's being the right one), the doctor cannot treat the child. Either way, the treatment must not be controversial, risky or dubious, neither in general nor for the child in question.[18]

I disagree with this line of reasoning, because the Children and Parents Act does not leave room for presumed consent in cases other than those already covered by the daily care provision. Furthermore, presumed consent is an unfamiliar notion for parental responsibility when the parents do not live together. Presuming consent in a situation of potential conflict between the parents is difficult at best. Either the consent of the other parent is necessary – in which case it should be an

17 NOU 2008: 9 Med barnet i fokus (Focusing on the child), section 7.3.1, with reference to a letter from the Children's Ombudsman 1st Dec. 2006.

18 Aasen, *Pasientens rett til selvbestemmelse ved medisinsk behandling* (The patient's right to self-determination in medical treatment), p. 574.

expressed consent, not a presumed one – or it is not. Clear-cut rules promote peace between the parents, one of the most important aspects of protecting the child's best interest. Presumed consent may be seen as an offence to the other parent, if it concerns a matter where his or her consent is needed, and such a presumption may worsen the relationship between the parents. From a child law point of view, leaving it to the custodial parent to choose whether to tell the doctor that the other parent is opposed to the treatment does not make sense.

Aasen discusses in more detail the consideration of whether both parents need to consent. She deals with it as a total assessment, where several factors have to be taken into consideration: the type of intervention, its extensiveness, the possible consequences and risks, and the child's medical state. Major surgery, transplants, etc. may clearly not be carried out without the consent of both parents. As for minor surgery such as removing a mole that *might* lead to cancer, the consent of one parent would be enough. When it comes to larger interventions involving general anaesthesia, such as removing tonsils or putting a drain in the ear of a child with chronic ear inflammation, whether the consent of one parent is enough is uncertain. If the medical condition causes trouble for the child or may in the long run have more harmful consequences (e.g. reduced hearing), Aasen argues that parental responsibility implies a duty to provide the child with medical treatment and therefore the consent of one parent is enough.[19]

Law professor Marit Halvorsen reaches a similar conclusion based on the responsibility of the doctor to give medical treatment.[20] By contrast, Aasen maintains that the doctor may give treatment if it is the only defensible solution and doubtlessly in the interest of the child, concluding that the more risky or uncertain the treatment, the more the parent who is opposed to the treatment should be listened to.[21]

Good arguments exist in favour of making it legally possible to treat a child with the consent of one parent alone, if the treatment is medically indicated and uncontroversial. But again, I find it hard to defend such a position in light of the current legislation. While the Patient Rights Act, section 4–4, does not cover conflicts between the parents, it follows from the preparatory documents of the Children and Parents Act, section 37, that decisions regarding medical treatment outside the scope of 'daily care' fall under joint parental responsibility.[22] Since the

---

19 Ibid, p. 575.

20 Halvorsen, Marit (1998), *Rettslig grunnlag for medisinsk behandling (Legal grounds for medical treatment)*, Fagbokforlaget, p. 99.

21 Aasen, *Pasientens rett til selvbestemmelse ved medisinsk behandling (The patient's right to self-determination in medical treatment)*, p. 576.

22 Ot.prp. No. 56 (1996–1997) on amendments to the Children and Parents Act, p. 56.

legal concept of parental responsibility is strong, the law has to be amended if it is to cater to the need for a more flexible solution. With the current legislation the legal remedy is for the 'reasonable' parent to bring the question of parental responsibility to court and require sole responsibility on the grounds that the other parent is unreasonable and not acting in the best interests of the child. If the matter is urgent, that parent may ask for a temporary decision, which the court is obligated to deal with speedily. This is the system that the Norwegian legislature has chosen for dealing with conflicts between the parents.

Even if according to Article 24 of the CRC the child has a right of access to health care services, the article does not solve the matter of parental conflicts. As previously mentioned, while Article 18 provides that the parents should act in the child's best interests, the CRC does not deal with disagreements between the parents.

The question of consent from one or both parents in Norway may soon be solved by a legal amendment proposed by the committee reviewing the Children and Parents Act in the spring of 2008. The committee criticizes the current law for being based on parental rights, not children's rights: it allows one parent the right to deny the child medical treatment, whether such a denial is in the child's best interest or not.[23] The committee has proposed a provision in both the Children and Parents Act, section 30, and the Patient Rights Act, section 4–4, saying that even if the parents have joint parental responsibility, the consent of only one is sufficient to give necessary medical treatment to the child. According to the committee's comments to the proposed amendment, the child can receive treatment on medical grounds if health personnel find it in his or her best interests, with no requirement that the need for treatment be urgent. If the other parent objects to the treatment, he or she may demand a court decision.

If the proposed amendment is enacted, it will create an unnecessary difference between the cases in which the child has one parent on his or her side (in wanting treatment), and those cases in which both parents object. Consequently, the legislature should also consider to allow doctors to set aside both parents' refusal to consent to treatment in cases where a child under 16 years has a well-founded wish to undergo necessary treatment.

23 NOU 2008: 9 Med barnet i fokus (Focusing on the child), sec. 7.3.3.

8. THE CHILD'S PARTICIPATION AND AUTONOMY

Given the problems that some children have with making their parents listen to them and take them seriously, that the Patient Rights Act leaves it to the parents alone to hear the child in medical cases is surprising. If there were a duty for health personnel to hear the child directly (at least one older than 12), the doctor or nurse would have a better basis for discussing the matter with the parents and maybe even changing their minds. An obligation for the doctor to hear the child may in some instances be deduced from the CRC, Article 12, if the doctor is in doubt as to whether the child has been properly heard by the parents. Nevertheless, the position of the child would be stronger if such a duty were introduced into the Act.

However, nothing prevents health personnel from talking to the child and discussing the matter with him or her. When the treatment is to be carried out, a duty to inform and talk to the child follows from the Patient Rights Act, section 31, which gives the patient the right to participate in the treatment. Even if the parents are supposed to hear the child before they consent or refuse to do so, health personnel (to make a sound medical decision) should also talk to the child beforehand, not only at the time of the actual treatment. They may have a duty to do so as part of good medical practice under the Health Personnel Act, section 4, which requires them to give help in a professional and considerate manner. If so, the legislature should make clear the child's right to be heard in relation to the parents' consent to or refusal of treatment.

What if a child under the age of 16 refuses a treatment that both the doctor and the parents find necessary? In this case, the law leaves all formal decision-making to the parents. If the child has a life-threatening disease or injury and the treatment offers good chances of recovery or at least of preventing death, the child can probably be treated against his or her will – unless he or she is so unwilling that going through with the treatment becomes impossible. Where the medical state of the child is less dramatic, more weight should be placed on the child's view, especially when the child is approaching 16 and his or her choice is well-founded. The interventional character of the treatment is yet another factor for the parents to consider before giving their consent, and for the doctor to consider when deciding whether to go through with the treatment.

A separate question is whether using physical force to treat a child is acceptable. With a small child, holding him or her while giving injections, for example, may be necessary. Doing so is fully acceptable as long as the treatment is necessary and the 'holding' does not extend beyond than what is necessary. With older children, the parents and the medical personnel should first talk to the child and try to convince him or her of the necessity of the treatment in question. If the child knows that the final decision is left with the parents and the doctor, in many cases that is enough to make him or her yield. However, if the child still objects, there is no legal basis for using physical force except in medical emergencies.[24] The parental responsibility provision does not authorize the parents to use physical force; on the contrary, the Child Protection Act, section 30, forbids parents from using any kind of violence against the child, with no exception for medical cases. The law thus implies that health personnel do not have any more extensive right to use force against older children than against adults.

9. CONCLUSIONS

The rule giving the final say to the parents is debatable, because it sets aside the autonomy of the child in order to promote the child's best interests: what is in his or her best interests is left to the parents to decide. The rule thus makes very visible the distinction between the child as an acting subject and the child as an object to be protected. For a small child there is no problem accepting that he or she must be protected, even against his or her own wishes. A child of 14 or 15 years, however, can have quite strong and well-founded views, and may find it an infringement of his or her autonomy and integrity not to be allowed to decide in such crucial matters.

In child law theory an ongoing discussion focuses on how to promote the child's autonomy without going too far. Law professor John Eekelaar has launched the notion of 'dynamic self-determinism', suggesting that the child's opinion should be the starting point for deciding what is in the child's best interest, as opposed to the common practice of starting with what is 'objectively' found to be the 'best interest'. He discusses the three main objections to self-determination: unlimited freedom for the individual, promotion of impulsive acts, and the danger of self-destructive decisions, the latter being relevant in our context. He says that both children and adults may have wishes that are contrary to their true self-interest in a long life of good physical and mental health. If self-determination may in this

24 H.S. Aasen, 'Barns rett til selvbestemmelse og medbestemmelse i beslutninger om helsehjelp' [The right of the child to self-determination and co-determination in health care decisions], *Tidsskrift for familierett, arverett og barnevernrettslige spørsmål* (Journal of family law, inheritance law and child protection law) 2008 No. 1, pp. 23–24 is more willing to accept physical force in order to give a child treatment.

way be self-destructive to the child, one should disregard the principle of self-determination.[25]

Following this line of reasoning, one may well accept the legal solution that the parents and the doctor may set aside the views of a child who does not want life-saving treatment. Support for this position also appears in the CRC, Article 6, which places on the state an obligation to ensure 'to the maximum extent possible' the survival and development of the child. On the other hand, it also follows that if the child's refusal of treatment only exposes him or her to greater pain but does not have long-term negative consequences, the child should have the right to refuse. In other words, the weight placed on the views of the child should be greater when the possible consequences are less harmful. This position takes the child's own views as a clearer starting point than what the CRC, Article 12, requires.

Another question is that of age limits. Although they are easy to apply, they may be questionable in the light of the gradually developing child or his or her 'evolving capacities', as the CRC, Article 5, states in connection with respect for parents' direction and guidance in the child's exercise of his or her rights in the CRC. There are good arguments in favour of a gradually developing self-determination. In its General Comment on adolescent health and development, the UN Committee on the Rights of the Child states that if the adolescent is of sufficient maturity, *informed consent* shall be obtained from the adolescent her- or himself, while informing the parents whether that choice is in his or her best interests.[26] The comment leaves it to the ratifying states to decide whether to set a certain age limit or to refer to the evolving capacities of the child.[27] Thus, while an age limit is not in conflict with the CRC, referring to the evolving capacities is in better agreement with the CRC, Article 5, which specifically uses that term. If a child aged 14–15 years and of normal maturity wants to undergo a doctor-recommended treatment, one that is uncontroversial and does not involve a great risk, then it is hard to see why the child should not be able to consent on his or her own. While the consent of at least one of the parents would be preferable, if they object without reasonable grounds, the decision should be left to the child. Strict age limits in some cases run contrary to both the autonomy and the best interests of the child.

---

25 J. Eekelaar, 'The interests of the child and the child's wishes: The role of dynamic self-determinism', in Ph. Alston (ed.), *The best interests of the child: Reconciling culture and human rights*, Oxford: Clarendon Press, p. 42–61.

26 General Comment No. 4, 2003, CRC/GC/2003/4, para. 32.

27 Ibid, para. 33.

CHAPTER 4
CHILDREN'S PARTICIPATION IN THE CHILD WELFARE SYSTEM

Marit SKIVENES

1. INTRODUCTION

This chapter identifies reasons for involving children in decision-making processes and institutional and individual obstacles that hamper a successful fulfilment of children's right to participation.[1] It then analyzes the way in which Norwegian child welfare workers perceive children's rights to freedom of speech and to participate in decisions that affect their lives. With the increasing influence of the 1989 United Nations Convention on the Rights of the Child (CRC), children's participation in welfare decisions has become an important issue in legislation, in policy making, and among the general public in Norway and other Western countries. The rights in the CRC are built on three pillars: protection, provision and participation. According to Article 12 'States' Parties shall assure to the child who is capable of forming his or her own views the right to express those views freely in all matters affecting the child, the views of the child being given due weight in accordance with the age and maturity of the child'.

The right to participate was highly contested when the CRC was written, and research shows that children often do not participate in political or administrative cases as Article 12 prescribes. In Norway, while politicians have strongly advocated service users' participation in decision-making, child welfare cases still show a discrepancy between ideal participation and day-to-day practices in local child welfare agencies. Research shows that the most important service user in child welfare cases, the child, is often not involved in decision-making at all.[2] When

1 This chapter was made possible by funding from the Research Council of Norway to a research project on how child welfare workers in England and Norway reason in child welfare cases. The author owes many thanks to the child care workers who participated in the project.

2 A. Amundsen, 'Yngre barn som deltagere i barnevernet' ['Younger Children as Service Users in the Child Welfare System'], MA thesis (University of Bergen, 2007); J. Nybom, 'Visibility and "child view" in the assessment process of social work: cross-national comparisons', *International Journal of Social Welfare*, 14 (2005), 315–325.

children do not participate in decisions that affect their lives, then the adults in the process – politicians, social workers, lawyers, psychologists, managers, administrators, etc. – have failed to uphold the CRC participation pillar. This chapter sheds some light on challenges to children's participation in the child welfare system, first by briefly examining what participation for children might suggest for child welfare cases; second, by giving an outline of arguments for and against children's participation in child welfare cases; and third, by analyzing testimonies from 28 experienced child welfare workers in Norway, focusing on their reflections about children's participation and on ways of giving children's views due weight in welfare decisions.[3]

2. DECISION-MAKING IN CHILD WELFARE CASES

Child welfare cases are about children and families in need, and child welfare authorities are responsible for helping children with particular needs. If a satisfactory solution cannot be found for the child with his or her biological parents, child welfare authorities can propose an out-of-home placement, and the court makes the decision. In Norway, children aged seven years or older have a right to be heard: 'A child that is seven years of age, and younger children who are capable of forming their own views, shall be informed and given the opportunity to express those views freely before decisions are made in cases affecting the child. The views of the child shall be given due weight in accordance with the age and maturity of the child'.[4]

When children participate in administrative decision-making processes, we can categorize them as *service users*, a term much used in health and welfare services in Norway and other countries.[5] Service-user involvement has been on the political agenda in Norway since the 1970s, and public service clients have the legal right to take part in decision-making processes that concern them, e.g. child welfare services.[6] A service user is someone who receives one or several services

3 The interviewees had an average of 6.8 years of experience in the child welfare system.

4 Child Welfare Act [1992]. 6–3. The second part of article 6–3 says: 'A child may appear as a party in a case and bring to bear his or her rights as a party if he or she has reached the age of 15 and understands the subject matter of the case. The county social welfare board may grant a child of less than 15 years of age rights as a party in special cases. In a case concerning measures for children with behavioural problems, the child shall invariably be regarded as a party'.

5 A. Hatland, 'Lokalt skjønn i gammel og ny sosialpolitikk' ['Local Discretion in Old and New Social Policy'], in E. Benum et al. (eds.) *Den mangfoldige velferden. Festskrift til Anne Lise Seip* [The Pluralistic Welfare. Festschrift to Anne-Lise Seip] (Gyldendal Akademisk, 2003).

6 E.O. Eriksen and J. Weigård, 'Fra statsborger til kunde' ['From Citizen to Costumer'], 9 *Norsk Statvitenskapelig Tidsskrift* 2 (1993); M. Skivenes, 'Forvaltning og politikk – om den nødvendige forbindelsen mellom brukermedvirkning og borgermedvirkning' ['Administration and Politics – on the necessary relationship between user involvement and citizen involvement'],

from public authorities, and the user's involvement in the process is an important part of the concept.[7] For example, Norwegian political scientists Erik Oddvar Eriksen and Jarle Weigård argue that a service user is involved in decisions regarding how, when, and which measures or services he or she will receive.[8] Service-user involvement at this level suggests a more democratic administration of services, as service users are invited to take part in the implementation of political decisions and goals that often are vague. Ideally, being involved in the decision-making process means that service users can formulate and present their opinions, interests and goals, in a deliberative process where all possible options and outcomes are explored and where probabilities for success for the different options are known, so that the outcome is the alternative that best suits the service users' needs.[9]

Decision-making in child welfare cases is complex. Child welfare workers must usually consider normative issues such as what is 'in the best interest of a child', a question not easily agreed upon, and try to determine what the child's future will be. While doing so is hard enough in ordinary family situations, it is extremely difficult when the child's parents do not take proper care of the child, and welfare workers must intervene in the family to find adequate compensatory services. The decisions they make must be in accordance with legal requirements, taking into account the uniqueness of each child and his or her situation. Predicting the consequences of welfare decisions is also challenging. Indeed, the complexity of the decision-making process in child welfare cases has been used as an argument against children's participation, on the grounds that they do not have sufficient experience and rational judgement. However, we need to clearly distinguish between participation understood as children making decisions themselves and

in Willumsen (ed.) Brukernes medvirkning! [User Participation!] (Scandinavian University Press, 2005); K. Humerfelt, [Begrepene brukermedvirkning og brukerperspektiv – honnørord med lavt presisjonsnivå] 'The Concepts of User Participation and User Perspective', in Willumsen (ed.) Brukernes medvirkning! [User Participation!] (Scandinavian University Press, 2005).

7 T. Alm Andreassen, 'Brukermedvirkning, politikk og velferdsstat' ['User Participation, Politics and Welfare State'], Report 13 (AFI-WRI Work Research Institute, 2004); S. Seim, 'Brukermedvirkning – et fremmedord for barn og ungdom i barnevernet' ['User Participation – Not Heard of in the Child Welfare System'], in S. Seim and T. Slettebø (eds), Brukermedvirkning i barnevernet [*User Participation in the Child Welfare System]* (Scandinavian University Press, 2007).

8 E.O. Eriksen, and J. Weigård, *Kommunikativ handling og deliberativt demokrati* [Communicative Action and Deliberative Democracy] (Fagbokforlaget, 1999).

9 J. Elster, *Solomonic Judgements, Studies in the Limitations of Rationality* (Cambridge University Press, 1989), sec. III: 'Solomonic Judgements: Against the Best Interests of the Child'.

participation as involvement in a decision-making process in which the formal and final decision-making authority lies with the child welfare authorities.[10]

In child welfare cases in particular, service users do not make decisions alone. While they can choose between alternatives or choose not to participate, the overall issue here is involvement with public officials in the decision-making process. Thus a service user's participation clearly implies co-determination in decisions about which services the welfare system can provide. In a child welfare case, the authorities must act in the best interest of the child. Article 3 (1) of the CRC states that the best interest of the child shall be a primary consideration, and the state intervenes in the private sphere on the grounds of protecting those interests. Several parties are thus involved in the decision, which is made not only on behalf of a particular person's interests and needs but also on behalf of the state's interests and obligations. Co-determination is clearly what the CRC and Norwegian lawmakers had in mind when they gave children the right to participate. They believe that all children capable of forming an opinion should have the opportunity to express it, and that this view should carry weight according to the age and maturity of the child.

An increasing body of literature concerns approaches to children's involvement in decision-making, and several researchers have used a procedural approach in which the process of reaching a decision or an outcome is the core point for ensuring the quality of the decisions.[11] Drawing on theories of communicative rationality, I propose a communicative, open-minded, and exploratory approach to involving the service user in the process of finding solutions that are in his or her best interests.[12] In this approach, decision-makers would assess all relevant arguments, empirical facts, social norms and legal regulations, ensuring that the result is fair and can stand up to public scrutiny. All persons concerned with the case, including the child, would be allowed to present their arguments and

10 D. Shemmings, 'Professionals' attitudes to children's participation in decision-making: dichotomous accounts and doctrinal contests', 5 *Child and Family Social Work*, 2000, 235–243; H. Brighouse, 'How Should Children Be Heard?', *Arizona Law Review*, Autumn 2003, 692–693.

11 H. Wade and B. Badham, 'Hear by Right: Standard for the active involvement of young people', The National Youth Agency/ Local Government Association, 2003; H. Shier, 'Pathways to Participation: Openings, Opportunities and Obligations', *Children and Society*, 2001, Vol. 15, 107–117; E.O. Eriksen and M. Skivenes, 'Om å fatte riktige beslutninger i barnevernet', [On making the right decisions in the child welfare authorities], *Tidsskrift for Samfunnsforskning*, Vol 3, 1998; M. Skivenes and A. Strandbu, 'Barn og familieråd' ['Children and Family Conferences'], *Tidsskrift for Velferdsforskning*, 4 (2004); D. Archard and M. Skivenes, 'Balancing a Child's Best Interest and a Child's Views', *International Journal of Children's Rights*, Vol 17. 2009, 1–21.

12 As outlined by J. Habermas, *Between Facts and Norms* (MIT Press, 1996).

opinions. The basic premise is that without the child, making a decision about what is in his or her best interests is very difficult.

All in all, children's participation in child welfare cases refers to their involvement in decisions about their present and future. Although children must be recognized as an important part in a deliberative decision-making process, we should not confuse participation with self-determination. The child's involvement as a service user in child welfare cases is necessary for ensuring that all relevant information and arguments are part of the process that determines his or her future. The following sections present reasons for involving or not involving children in the process.

3. WHY SHOULD CHILDREN BE INVOLVED IN DECISIONS CONCERNING THEMSELVES?

While the idea of involving children in child welfare decision making is rather new, it is gaining strength in many modern democratic societies through the ratification and implementation of the CRC in national legislation. This section offers six main arguments for children's involvement in decisions about their lives and futures.

First, including the child in decisions about his or her life shows *respect,* thereby preserving the child's integrity. After all, the child's best interest is at stake. The opportunity to be part of the process as an equal partner democratizes the child's status both in the private sphere and in society.[13] Second, children possess important *information* about their situation and life, information that is critical to the decision-making process. To make a sensible and just decision, one must gather all relevant information. Thus in a child welfare case, which decides what services are best for the child and the family, information from the child is an important consideration.[14]

Third, children's participation makes the implementation of services more *efficient* because their involvement allows them to see and understand the process, i.e. the different considerations involved in solving their case or problem. Fourth, the dimension of *learning and trust* is added to the decision-making process. The child experiences the process first-hand, learning what will happen each step of the way, thus potentially feeling safer in the situation. Furthermore, one can hope

13 D. Archard and M. Skivenes, 'Hearing the Child', in *Child and Family Social Work,* forthcoming.

14 R.A. Warshak, 'Payoffs and Pitfalls of Listening to Children', 52 *Family Relations,* 2003, 373–384.

for long-term learning effects, making the child a more competent citizen and skilled member of society.

Fifth, a *rational and legitimate* decision-making process is more likely to be achieved by involving the child. As individuals are unique, applying a general rule about what is in someone's best interest without actually involving that person is not regarded as legitimate. Legitimacy is achieved only when the child that is able to form an opinion has the opportunity to participate and can, in principle, give his or her approval to the process and its outcome. Sixth, as children have the *legal right* to participate in matters concerning them, states are obligated to fulfil such rights. For example, Norwegian law very clearly states that children from the age of seven have the right to participate in decisions about their lives.

These are six well-reasoned arguments for letting children participate in their child welfare cases, the most important of which is respect for the individual:

> [W]e are obliged to hear the expression of the child's views because they come from someone who has views. If it is a child's right to express her views then their expression must be an ineliminable feature of any process in which children and adults together determine what should be done for the child. Their expression is not only of instrumental value in helping adults work out what is best.[15]

These arguments, while more or less known by lawmakers, professionals, social workers, and adults in general, clearly establish the importance of including children in decision-making processes. However, critics of children's participation (and of their status as service users in child welfare cases) have presented arguments as to why children should not participate in these processes, and their view still appears to dominate the field.

The next section will discuss the most common obstacles, as they might occur at individual and institutional levels, to children's participation.

4. OBSTACLES TO CHILDREN'S PARTICIPATION

Before we consider possible barriers to children's participation, we must distinguish between those who know about the child's right to participate (and who consciously exclude children from the process) and those who are unaware of the law. Obviously, the latter group has no incentive or reason for involving children in child welfare decision-making processes. Here, *ignorance* of the legal requirements is the reason that children do not participate. Another obvious

15 Archard and Skivenes, 'Balancing a Child's Best Interest ...', 2009, p. 18.

reason for non-participation is that the child is unable to, perhaps because he or she is too young or has a mental disability. A child might also simply choose not to participate. In addition to ignorance and incapacity, I present four institutional and five individual reasons that might explain why children do not participate in child welfare cases and in other situations where their interests are at stake.

There are at least four types of organizational obstacles to children's participation. First, an organization may lack *formal procedures* and guidelines instructing child welfare workers to speak with the child to make sure that her or his views are included. Second, social workers often have heavy caseloads, lacking *enough time or resources* for including the child. Third, social workers may lack the appropriate *space or facilities* for meeting with children and therefore do not speak with them. Fourth, child welfare workers may not be sufficiently *trained* in eliciting children's participation. In such cases the child welfare system is responsible for developing employees communication and social skills.[16]

On the individual level, at least five reasons exist for adults in general, and child welfare workers in particular, not allowing children to participate (two of these reasons overlap with those listed as organizational barriers). First, *protection* of the child is often cited as a reason for not including children in decision-making processes, especially in child welfare cases. Adults and case workers who want to protect children believe that they should be allowed to experience childhood as an innocent, happy period, and thus do not want to burden them with decisions and responsibilities.[17] In child welfare cases, as the child is obviously facing difficulties, the reasoning is that the child does not need yet another worry or burden. Adults and child welfare workers may also be concerned about loss of control and protection of their own feelings. Adults who include children in the decision-making process lose control, because they have to share power with the child and let the child's opinion carry some weight.

In addition, in child welfare cases children may have experienced extreme abuse and neglect from their carers. Child welfare workers, knowing that they cannot repair the damage inflicted on the child and that they may not be able to provide all the help the child needs, might exclude the child from the decision-making process to avoid raising his or her hopes, and to protect themselves emotionally by limiting their knowledge of the child's hurtful experiences.

Second, some adults might see themselves as *parental figures* in a decision-making situation and thus entitled to act *in loco parentis*. Such a perception masks the

16 P. Parkinson et al., 'Parents' and children's views on talking to judges in parenting disputes in Australia', 21 *International Journal of Law, Policy and the Family*, 1 (2007): 84–107.

17 D. Archard, *Children: Rights and Childhood* (Routledge, 2004).

child's individuality and hinders a necessary recognition of the child's right and ability to participate in decisions about his or her life. While parents have a special responsibility for raising their own children (including setting norms and social standards for behaviour and thereby influencing the children's perceptions of what is good for them), that responsibility does not give other adults the right to teach those children how to behave and think.

Third, adults may think children *lack the competencies*, intellect, and experience to have a say in the process.[18] The extreme version of this argument is that children are not fit to be participants. A more nuanced version of the competency argument suggests that children are less developed and less mature than adults. Thus their capacities for making decisions, thinking ahead and calculating consequences are reduced, and they are less able to formulate their needs and articulate their interests.

Fourth, *efficiency* considerations might play a role when an adult considers whether a child should be allowed to participate. From a short-term perspective speaking with the child and letting him or her participate in other ways takes more time than simply excluding the child from the process. From a long-term perspective, however, speaking with the child may make the process of identifying the child's best interests and reaching his or her goals more efficient. Fifth, *adults' abilities* to speak with children, and their confidence in those abilities, will influence whether children are included as participants. If child welfare workers feel that they lack the ability or experience to speak with children, that belief will naturally lead to the non-involvement of children.

Although this list of exclusionary reasons is not exhaustive, it covers the most common ones. Which of these explanations has the greatest explanatory force in empirical research remains to be seen. Nonetheless, as I will show, some of these reasons are better than others. Removing the four organizational obstacles should be rather easy. While doing so will take time and resources, as long as the laws and the political system favour participation, child welfare agencies have a duty to find the time and resources to include children in decisions about their lives. Likewise, three of the five individual reasons can be eliminated through the careful training of personnel.

Two arguments, however, rest on well-reasoned grounds: the argument that children do not have the same competencies as adults to make decisions, and the argument that they need protection. These arguments call for assessments of each child and his or her situation, as all children are unique, each with an individual

18 Warshak, 'Payoffs and Pitfalls ...', 2003.

history, personality, and perception of life. Thus all children cannot participate in the same way, to the same degree, and in the same situations. Sometimes, protecting a child by not letting him or her take part in the decision-making process is wise and proper, as shown in a 2004 Norwegian Supreme Court decision in which the Court found it to be the best interest of the children not to participate in their custody case.[19]

This case is about two children (ages 7 and 12) who were neither heard nor asked for their opinion in a custody dispute case. The issue for the Court to decide was a procedural fault. Although the Court heard the appeal after new regulations about children's participation were in force, the original case had been heard before those regulations applied. However, as children also had had rights of participation before 2004, the changes were not so drastic that a totally different interpretation was necessary. Of interest here is that the Court said that whether a child should participate depends on the best interests of the child (section 47). While the court did not doubt that the 12-year-old should have been heard, in light of other factors and the implications of ruling in favour on procedural grounds, the Court decided that participation was not in the child's best interest.

In sum, only a couple of the objections against children's participation are well grounded. Thus a child's right to participate must not be rejected by undocumented and poorly reasoned beliefs but rather be informed by judgements of the child's competencies and his or her need for protection. In child welfare cases, such judgements are made by the child welfare workers. The next section explores how they handle children's opinions when making decisions.

5. THE ROLE OF CHILDREN'S VIEWS IN CHILD WELFARE CASES

5.1. DATA SOURCES

To understand how children are heard and involved in child welfare cases, I have studied child welfare workers' perceptions of children's participation. In 2008 I conducted in-depth and semi-structured interviews with 28 experienced front-line child welfare workers in two Norwegian child welfare agencies. The analysis is based on the following open-ended questions: what is your understanding of children's participation in child welfare cases? Why is it useful to let children

19 Norwegian Supreme Court Ruling 2004–811.

participate in decision-making? How do you give the opinion of the child due weight in accordance with the age and maturity of the child?

One reason for focusing on this group of child welfare workers is that they are all obligated to hear the views of the child when assessing the case, as well as professionally obligated by the terms of their job to conduct assessments of and make decisions for the children with whom they work. The rest of this section presents findings from the analysis.[20]

5.2. REASONS FOR ADVOCATING CHILDREN'S PARTICIPATION

More than half of the 28 interviewees commented that respect for the child is an important reason for advocating children's participation. For example, one explained why children should participate by simply stating, '[i]t is all about respect,' whilst another said, '[i]t's all about them'. These workers show an understanding of the core reason for children's participation, and a large majority made it clear that gathering information is an important reason for speaking with the child. As one said, '[o]ften, they can tell us about their life situation, a situation that we can't see. They often have other things to tell us than their parents do. If they dare to be honest, that is'. Interestingly, many of the child welfare workers mentioned that giving information to the child is also very important, a topic to which I will return. Only one third of them referred to the Norwegian Child Welfare Act of 1992 or to children's legal rights to participate. For instance, one said, '[c]hildren have a right to be heard,' and another explained that 'the legislation has changed. We shall hear children at the age of seven years old. And seven-year-olds have many opinions about many issues'.

About one third expressed the view that letting children participate is efficient, as it makes it easier to reach the goals that the child welfare worker have for the children and their caregivers. One explained why she thinks it important for children to participate: '[i]t is [children] that will receive a service, and if they do not understand why they will have this service, they cannot tell us if it works for them or not – if it's good or bad'. Another said, '[i]t is much easier to find feasible services … that [children] wish to receive, and in my opinion, if they express what they want, it gives a much better chance to find the right service'.

20 For additional information see part three in K. Kriz and M. Skivenes, 'Lost in Translation', *British Journal of Social Work*, forthcoming.

Few child welfare workers mentioned learning or legitimacy as arguments for letting children participate in decision-making processes. Of those mentioning learning as an issue, they meant that *they* had learned something about the child, not the other way round. Only one child welfare worker explicitly made a link between the quality of the decisions and children's participation.

One argument that many of these professionals made is the importance of informing the child about how the child welfare system works and what the welfare worker plans to do. Many child welfare workers apparently believe that much of the value in participation lies in informing the child about what is going to happen. As one said, 'It creates predictability … the more a child is informed and the more predictable the situation is for the child, the easier it is for them to understand what is happening'. Another comment was that 'we want to make [the children] confident about who we are and why we are there – to establish a good relation is important. It is as important to have a good relation to [the children] as it is to their parents'. The emphasis on both informing and instructing the child shows that child welfare workers are concerned about establishing a relationship with the child. This emphasis might also indicate that child welfare workers view children as service users, because an important dimension in service-user involvement is to make sure that users are fully informed about the system and its legislation and its practices. This instructive attitude among the child welfare workers was also evident in their communications with and approaches to ethnic minority families.

We thus see that although child welfare workers give several reasons for why children should participate in decision-making processes, they primarily regard participation as a way of collecting information. This focus is not surprising, as it is an important part of child welfare work to obtain information and document any abuse or neglect. However, I find it somewhat worrisome that about half the interviewees do not even mention the most important reason for children's participation – the moral argument that children should participate because their lives and their futures are at stake. This finding now brings us to the issue of weighing a child's view.

5.3. GIVING THE CHILD'S VIEW DUE WEIGHT

When we asked child welfare workers how they give children's opinions due weight according to their age and maturity, many of the social workers straightforwardly said that they found it difficult to answer the question. This response is probably not exclusive to social workers, as similar findings resulted from an analysis of children's participation and best interest assessments in court decisions in Norway and England.[21] That analysis of written court decisions showed in several cases how little weight children's views carried, a finding partly explained by the judges' not having a clear opinion as to how to weigh a child's view.

The child welfare workers that articulated fairly clear answers to the question of due weight fall in three categories. First, a few mentioned age as a decisive factor in weighing children's views. One very clearly expressed the importance of age in relation to the weight a child's opinion should carry: 'The child welfare act states that from the age of 12 a child has a strong right to express his or her view ... If you are over 16 years old then you have a right to access documents, copies of letters and agree to decisions'. Even though few mentioned age as an important indicator of how to weigh a child's view, many commented that giving older children's views weight in the decision-making process is easier. These beliefs likely stem from the rights children receive as 12- and 15-year-olds.[22]

Second, many child welfare workers said they have to make a concrete assessment of the child and his or her maturity. While few explained what this meant, one said, 'I think it's important that children are involved ... but no more than what our assessment of the situation justifies, the child's maturity must stand in relation to the information given. They must be able to understand the information given to them – otherwise they will be overridden'. This welfare worker also said that a child's level of understanding is an important indicator of maturity, and the information given to the child depends on this assessment. This somewhat vague procedure for assessing a child's maturity corresponds to a finding in a study of 86 English child welfare workers and non-social workers, who were asked what they thought about children's participating in child welfare decisions. Although several commented that they would have to make an assessment of the child's maturity, they did not clarify what that assessment involves.[23]

Third, those few child welfare workers who gave clear, informative answers about how to give a child's view due weight said that they basically consider three issues: the reasons given for a view, the strength of the view, and a holistic consideration. One explained not only how she emphasizes the reasons given for an opinion but

21 D. Archard and M. Skivenes, 'Balancing a Child's Best Interest', 2009.

22 According to the Child Welfare Act, 15 is the minimum age for being considered a legal party in a case.

23 Shemmings, 'Professionals' attitudes to children's participation ...', 2000.

also how she contextualizes the view and interprets the meaning of the child's words:

> When I speak with a child I guess I try to understand, why does the child say this? What are the reasons underneath the spoken words? If the child displays an immature way of thinking, for instance a lack of understanding of important things as when a young person at 15 tells me that he or she has quarrelled with his or her parents and wants to move for him- or herself – and at the same time the young person is not doing well at school, hangs out with 'bad' friends, and in general is not doing well and is developing in the wrong direction – then it is not difficult for me to think that [the young person finds it] alluring to move for him or herself to be released from adult control and interference … This young person will be heard, but his or her views will not be followed.

This child welfare worker conveys the message that one needs to communicate with a young person about the situation from different angles, because 'maturity and motivation or insight into the reasons for the expressions the child and young persons give matters a lot'. Much the same reasoning comes from another professional: 'I think it is about the maturity of the child and which arguments he or she uses. It is about a review of the reason for their meaning'. Yet another shows how consistency in holding a wish or view is important:

> Yes, [in] the two examples [about a 15-year-old girl and an 11-year-old boy that she had previously described in the interview] … she is very mature as she can express herself very clearly – I can hardly misinterpret her opinion – as I have spoken with her several times, she displays what she thinks about what is said and her opinions are smart. The younger one … will say different things to me and to others … want to stay there, then another place …

One welfare worker offers important insight into the situation for children in the child welfare system: '[o]ne must look into maturity even if they have the required age … It is a professional assessment of their [children's] functioning, seen in relation to the situation they are in and whether they can understand the consequences of the issues at stake'. The same person also shows us that a neglected or abused child might be difficult: 'Many children who experience neglect or have problems at home, display a very high maturity on some issues … but on other issues they are far behind what could be expected. It is a difficult assessment … You must hear their views but make a decision about how much weight they should carry'.

These child welfare workers had fairly informed views about what it means to include a child's view in the decision-making process. An analysis of eight Norwegian Supreme Court rulings about custody and child welfare cases in 2005–2007 revealed five features for the weighing of the child's view: the child's age, the child's reasons for the view given and consistency in holding that view, the child's understanding of the consequences if his or her view should be decisive, respect for the child's view as a separate consideration, and the way in which the child had formed his or her opinion.[24]

To sum up, child welfare workers do not have precise, well thought out, or articulate answers about how they give children's views due weight. This finding is critical, as it shows that child welfare workers do not know which considerations are important in assessing the child's competency and weighing the child's view. Instead they take multiple approaches, based on the individual child welfare worker's discretion about how to weigh a view. Yet, in assessing a child's maturity or competencies, they should clearly apply two important considerations: first, the assessment of a child's maturity must be a separate process, not one conflated with assessments of the child's view. These should be two separate assessments, as the child's competencies might be devalued when his or her view does not match what the child welfare worker thinks is in his or her best interest. Second, an equity principle must prevail, so that a child's competency is not measured against a standard that most adults would fail. The standard for children must be reasonable and relevant for the specific child involved.

6. CONCLUSIONS

Children are the most important service users in child welfare cases because the child welfare system is making decisions about their interests: their childhood, their health, their present and future situation. To protect and provide for the basic human dignity, integrity and right of the child, the system must allow any child capable of forming a view to be heard. That is what the CRC requires. This chapter has demonstrated that there are other reasons for including children in decisions about their future: information, efficiency, learning, legitimacy and their legal rights.

The analysis of interviews with experienced Norwegian child welfare workers showed that many gave information as the most important reason for involving

[24] In several cases, the court did not assess the child's maturity or the quality of the child's opinion. See part three in D. Archard and M. Skivenes, 'Balancing a Child's Best Interest …', 2009.

children, with half concerned with respect for the child and about one-third giving legal rights or efficiency as reasons. Perhaps expecting all child welfare workers to acknowledge the importance of putting the child in the centre of decision-making (and to emphasize that these decisions are about the child's life) is too optimistic. Nonetheless, that about half of the interviewees were conscious of respecting and preserving the dignity of the child is encouraging – especially seen in light of existing research in the area. Although well-reasoned arguments exist for making careful considerations about how children should be involved, there are also many obstacles to children's participation, obstacles that need attention at that both systemic and individual levels. It is therefore promising that a large majority of welfare workers perceived the child as an important source of information, as this perception might lead to the realization that the child's direct involvement is a necessary condition for legitimate child welfare decisions.

The study also demonstrates that the process of giving a child's view due weight in accordance with age and maturity (something child welfare workers must do almost daily) was difficult for most child welfare workers to explain. Those few who had a clear answer considered the quality of the child's reasons for a view and the consistency of these views to be important, especially in relation to the whole case. That many child welfare workers could not articulate how they go about weighing a child's view is troubling. If their answers are representative of the Norwegian child welfare system and of other systems where a child's view should be weighed, this finding warrants immediate attention.

In light of research that shows that children do not participate in child welfare decisions in accordance with their legal rights, the findings presented here may point to a new era: they suggest that children in Norway are increasingly seen as service users and are involved in decision-making. However, merely talking to children and hearing their opinions, to gather information about their situation, is not enough. Their views must be given due weight in the decision-making process. It is clear that improvements in the child welfare system are needed when it comes to understanding why a child has a right to participate in decisions affecting his or her future life, and how the views expressed by children should be weighed in the decision-making process.

CHAPTER 5
AUTONOMY, HUMAN DIGNITY AND TREATMENT OF INDIVIDUALS WITH COGNITIVE IMPAIRMENT

Henriette Sinding Aasen

1. INTRODUCTION

As patient rights are a reflection of human rights, over the last four decades the rights of patients have received increasing attention throughout Europe. Improved legal status and rights in health care legislation, as well as the adoption of patient rights acts, are common legal developments in a number of countries (e.g. Denmark, Finland, Hungary, Iceland, the Netherlands). The right of giving *informed consent* to treatment is one essential patient right, derived from the general principle of autonomy or self-determination. The right to individual autonomy, however, is problematic when the person concerned lacks or has reduced capacity for giving legally valid consent. This problem occurs not only in situations concerning invasive medical treatment but also in everyday health care, including decisions related to meals, personal hygiene, physical activities and security. The right to autonomy is especially challenged with regard to coercive measures, such as moving the person to a special institution or unit.

Characteristic in these situations is that the conflict of interests is often related to the same person, as opposed to conflicts of interests between the person concerned and society (e.g. prevention and punishment of criminal behaviour) or between the person and other persons (e.g. confinement of a violent person in order to protect the life and health of specific individuals).[1]

This chapter examines some situations in which the conflict of interests occurs in relation to the treatment of adult persons with cognitive impairments in a way

---

1 E. Rynning, 'Rättssäkerhet och rättsskydd i vården av icke beslutskompetenta vuxna' [Legal safeguards and protection of adults who do not have the capacity to consent to medical care and treatment], in Westerhäll (ed.), *Rättssäkerhetsfrågor inom socialrätten*, Stockholm: Norstedts Juridik AB 2002, pp. 267-268.

that the right of autonomy needs balancing against other rights, such as the right to life and the right to necessary health care. It examines under which conditions medical treatment may or should be carried out when the patient is unable to defend his or her own interests, due to either temporary cognitive impairment (e.g. from an accident) or permanent cognitive impairment (e.g. from developmental disabilities or dementia).

The tension between the right to autonomy, life and health constitutes a constant dilemma in the provision of many welfare services. Some individuals in obvious need of medical treatment or care may not be able to give full and valid consent to proposed interventions, because of either age (minors) or mental disability. If a person with serious dementia clearly does not understand the implications of a particular treatment or of no treatment at all, but smiles and says 'yes' or repeatedly says 'no' to everything, determining his or her wishes is very difficult. Thus, an appeal to respect for 'autonomy' and the requirement of 'informed consent' clearly will not sufficiently safeguard the person's interests or dignity.[2] This lack of protection is especially clear if the person repeats his or her refusals of treatment while being in obvious need of a particular treatment, e.g. diabetes medication. Clearly, in such a situation refraining from treatment and care is not necessarily a good solution, even when the patient constantly says 'no' or physically rejects the proposed intervention. The reason is that other rights of the person – such as the right to health, and sometimes even the right to life – will suffer.

Because these individuals are not able to fully protect themselves, neither through the exercise of informed consent nor through the assertion of the right to proper treatment, ensuring a fair balance between the rights in tension with additional legal safeguards is especially important. Such safeguards are necessary for protecting the dignity of the person concerned. In particular, the human dignity of the person must be secured by the protection of what appear to be the most basic needs of the person under the circumstances, even though doing so entails not (fully) respecting other rights. However, to protect vulnerable individuals from neglect and abuse, one must specify the conditions under which interventions may or should take place without the person's consent.

This chapter briefly considers the rights at stake in situations where the person's capacity for consenting to medical treatment is reduced or absent due to cognitive impairment. Then it will examine how international and national laws protect the

2 The requirement of informed consent is never a sufficient safeguard, not even when the patient is fully competent. Health care personnel are also obligated to provide due care as an independent professional duty. However, when the patient has a serious mental disability, the requirement of informed consent may become almost meaningless.

dignity and rights of individuals in these situations, including the balancing of the basic rights in conflict.

2. HUMAN DIGNITY AND THE RIGHTS AT STAKE

2.1. HUMAN DIGNITY AS THE BASIC VALUE

Human dignity is the essential value to be upheld and protected through the human rights instruments in general and the Convention on Human Rights and Biomedicine (Biomedicine Convention) in particular.[3] In medical treatment, the requirement of informed consent from the patient and the duty of health personnel to provide due care according to professional standards are the main instruments for protecting the interests of patients, including their human dignity. From a humanistic perspective, however, human dignity is not to be identified with the actual capacity of autonomous decision-making, since doing so would imply that persons who are not able to exercise their autonomy and give valid consent to proposed treatment do not have human dignity. To the contrary, persons who due to age or mental disability are not capable of giving valid consent to a particular intervention have the same inherent human dignity as every other person.

Therefore, according to the humanistic perspective, the main question when a person cannot give valid consent is how to protect his or her human dignity in the particular situation. The human dignity of a person must be preserved through the balancing of the conflicting values and interests at stake. From a human rights perspective, this is a question of balancing different human rights that may be in tension or conflict, so that not all of them can be (fully) protected at the same time.

To determine how to balance the rights at stake and thereby protect the most important interests of the person, we must first identify those rights and interests, and then determine which are the most important to protect under the particular circumstances. The following section provides a brief overview of the human rights and interests at stake, including examples of how human rights monitoring bodies and other authorities in the field have understood them.

3 Convention for the protection of human rights and dignity of the human being with regard to the application of biology and medicine. Convention on Human Rights and Biomedicine, Council of Europe, 4 April 1997.

2.2. THE RIGHTS AT STAKE: AN OVERVIEW

2.2.1. The right to health care

Modern welfare states, in general, provide their citizens with a certain level of health care and related services, including care for the elderly, for persons with disabilities, and for individuals with cognitive impairment. Article 3 of the Biomedicine Convention prescribes that state parties, 'taking into account health needs and available resources, shall take appropriate measures with a view to providing, within their jurisdiction, equitable access to health care of appropriate quality.'[4] The provision contains two main obligations: That of providing equitable access to health care (non-discrimination) and that of providing health care of appropriate quality. The non-discrimination aspect of the provision implies the human rights perspective that services must be equally provided and equally accessible to everyone. As observed by human rights scholar Brigit Toebes, 'a state may violate the right to health if it structurally fails to offer adequate health services to certain segments of society.[5]

Various treaty monitoring bodies have on several occasions, referring to the International Covenant on Economic, Social and Cultural Rights (ICESCR), Article 12, the Convention on the Elimination of All Forms of Discrimination against Women (CEDAW), Article 12, and the Convention on the Rights of the Child (CRC), Article 24, urged states to ensure that vulnerable groups in the population have sufficient access to available health services.[6] The same requirement must apply under the Biomedicine Convention. The Explanatory Report to the Biomedicine Convention says that access to health care must be 'equitable', which in this context means the absence of unjustified discrimination. The report specifies that while this requirement is not identical with absolute equality, equitable access implies 'effectively obtaining a satisfactory degree of care'.[7]

The aim of Article 3 is clearly to ensure access to health care in accordance with the needs of individuals. The term 'health care' includes services offering diagnostic, preventive, therapeutic and rehabilitative interventions, designed to maintain or improve a person's state of health or to alleviate suffering. The health

---

4 See also the state obligation of providing 'the highest attainable standard of health' according to Article 12 of the International Covenant on Economic, Social and Cultural Rights (UN, 1966).

5 B. Toebes, 'The Right to Health', in Eide, Krause and Rosas (eds.), *Economic, Social and Cultural Rights*, Dordrecht: Martinus Nijhoff Publishers 2001, p. 181.

6 Ibid., with further references.

7 Council of Europe, 1997. Explanatory Report to the Biomedicine Convention, para. 25.

care must be of a 'fitting standard' in light of scientific progress and be subject to a continuous quality assessment.[8] The Explanatory Report specifies that Article 3 does not create an individual right to health care but rather prompts the state 'to adopt the requisite measures as part of its social policy in order to ensure equitable access to health care'.[9] Such measures may take many different forms 'and a wide variety of methods may be employed to this end'.[10]

As for health care for patients with various forms of cognitive impairment, the quality of the care must be of a fitting standard for individual needs. When determining individual needs in a situation where valid consent to treatment cannot be obtained, and where the patient is unable to express his or her needs, one must rely heavily on the professional standards of health personnel, psychologists, social workers and other professionals. It follows from Article 4 of the Biomedicine Convention that any intervention in the health field 'must be carried out in accordance with relevant professional obligations and standards'. In general, 'while current medical practices determine the professional standards and skills expected of health care professionals, the content of professional standards, obligations and rules of conduct may vary slightly from one society to another. Nonetheless, the fundamental principles of medical practice are applicable in all countries.[11] These principles require that professionals act with care and competence 'and pay careful attention to the needs of each patient'.[12] The Explanatory Report specifies that the essential task of doctors is not only to heal patients 'but also to take the proper steps to promote health and relieve pain, taking into account the psychological well-being of the patient'.[13] Such requirements would also follow from the overall requirement of treating everyone with dignity.

2.2.2. The right to private life, self-determination and liberty

Giving health care without valid consent or with coercion violates the right of the patient to private life and self-determination. The general rule of informed consent follows from the Biomedicine Convention, Article 5, which states that an intervention in the health field may be carried out only after the person concerned has given free and informed consent to it. Both the European Convention for the Protection of Human Rights and Fundamental Freedoms (ECHR), Article 8(1), and the International Covenant on Civil and Political Rights (ICCPR), Article 17,

---

8 Ibid., paras. 24 and 25.
9 Ibid. (para. 25).
10 Ibid.
11 Ibid. (paras. 31-32).
12 Ibid. (para. 31).
13 Ibid. (para. 32).

protect the right of everyone to respect for his or her private and family life, home, and correspondence.[14] These open-ended articles protect the general right to be left alone and to enjoy a certain personal space with reference to one's physical body, property and personal relationships, as well as the right to make personal choices such as where to live, whom to associate with, or whether to undertake a particular treatment. The right to personal autonomy and human dignity requires that individuals must be allowed to make such choices without undue interference by the state or others.[15] The state and its agents must not only refrain from interference in the rights protected but must also take appropriate measures to protect these rights from violation by others.[16] An important part of this protection is the right to privacy in terms of the protection of private information such as health-related and other personal data. (However, in this and other chapters, the main focus is on the protection of the physical and personal integrity of individuals in the context of proposed treatment, rather than on the issue of confidentiality and protection of personal data.)[17]

A non-voluntary physical intervention in a person's body, such as imposed medical treatment, is a clear violation of private life according to the ECHR, Article 8(1).[18] However, if the non-voluntary medical treatment is in accordance with national law and is also considered necessary in a democratic society in order to protect someone's health or the rights of others, it is justified under the ECHR, Article 8(2). This chapter will particularly examine examples of national legislation on the issue of non-consensual treatment of individuals who, as a result of mental impairment or disability, lack the legal capacity for giving valid informed consent.

Article 5(1) of the ECHR guarantees the right of everyone to individual liberty and security, with the primary focus on protection from deprivation of liberty.[19] Confinement in locked institutions without valid consent or another sufficient legal basis is clearly an infringement of personal liberty. This principle was clearly

---

14 UN, 1966.

15 S. Foster, *Human Rights and Civil Liberties*, London: Pearson Education Limited 2008, Second edition, p. 559.

16 Jacobs and White, *The European Convention on Human Rights*, Oxford: Oxford University Press, Fourth edition 2006, p. 243.

17 Article 10 of the Biomedicine Convention protects private life in terms of privacy of information via paragraph 1, that everyone 'has the right to respect for private life in relation to information about his or her health'. It follows from both the wording of the provision and the comments given in the Explanatory Report (para. 63) that this provision does not protect the physical integrity of persons but only concerns the right to privacy of information in the health field.

18 Jacobs and White, *The European Convention on Human Right*, pp. 269-270, re: *Glass v. UK* (2004).

19 Ibid., *The European Convention on Human Rights*, p. 123, re: *Bozano v. France* (1986).

expressed in *H L v. United Kingdom* (2004), where the applicant was autistic, was unable to speak, and had a limited level of understanding.[20] He (or his legal representative) alleged that he had been detained in a psychiatric institution as an 'informal patient' in violation of ECHR, Article 5(1). Frequently agitated, with a history of self-harming behaviour, he was considered to lack the ability to either consent or object to medical treatment.

However, since March 1994 he had resided with paid carers, while the hospital remained responsible for his care and treatment. From 1995 onwards, he attended a local day care centre. While at the centre on 22 July 1997, he became particularly agitated and started to hit himself on the head with his fists and bang his head against the wall. Although the local doctor gave him a sedative, the man remained agitated and was taken to hospital. He was finally transported to the intensive behaviour unit as an 'informal patient', where he stayed for three months. On 29 October 1997 he was admitted for treatment as an involuntary patient according to provisions in the national law, until he was discharged in the care of the paid carers in December 1997. During the time of the 'informal' hospital stay, he was under continuous supervision and control and not free to leave.

Although the applicant was 'quite compliant', had 'not attempted to run away', was calm, complied with all care needs, and accepted the change without problem, the European Court of Human Rights (ECtHR) stated that 'the right to liberty is too important in a democratic society for a person to lose the benefit of Convention protection for the single reason that he may have given himself up to be taken into detention ... especially when it is not disputed that that person is legally incapable of consenting to, or disagreeing with, the proposed action'. The ECtHR 'found that the key factor in the case was that the health care professionals who treated and managed the applicant 'exercised complete and effective control over his care and movements' from 22 July 1997, when he presented acute behavioural problems, to 29 October 1997, when he was forcibly detained. The applicant had been sedated before he was brought to hospital, and the responsible medical officer clearly indicated that had the applicant resisted admission or subsequently tried to leave, she would have prevented him from doing so and would have considered his committal involuntary under the law.[21]

This case shows that a mere a lack of protest or 'consent' from an incompetent person is not a sufficient legal basis for keeping a person under continued confinement. It also demonstrates, however, the difficulty of balancing the interests and rights involved: the need and right of the person to be taken care of,

---

20 Application No. 45508/99 (www.echr.coe.int).
21 Ibid. (paras. 90 and 91).

and the right to be respected as an autonomous person as far as possible, not to be locked up without the following of appropriate procedures under national law. An important task for state parties is to establish proper legislation for regulating the conditions under which public authorities may take care of individuals who do not have the legal capacity to make decisions about interventions in their private lives.

2.2.3. The right to life

Article 2(1) of the ECHR provides that everyone's right to life shall be protected by law. It is an absolute right that cannot be abrogated, not even in times of war and other public crisis, except for the exceptions in Article 2(2).[22] This article not only prohibits intentional killing by the state but also puts forward the positive obligation to protect life.[23] In *Kilinc v. Turkey* (2005), the ECtHR found a violation of Article 2 when the applicant, who had serious mental health problems, had committed suicide while carrying out military service.[24] The ECtHR stated that the authorities had not taken appropriate measures to prevent the risk of suicide.[25] *Keenan v. UK* (2001) concerns a young man with mental health problems who committed suicide in prison.[26] The ECtHR stated that 'persons in custody are in a vulnerable position and that the authorities are under a duty to protect them'.[27]

In the *Keenan* case, the Court examined 'whether the authorities "knew or ought to have known that Mark Keenan posed a real and immediate risk of suicide and, if so, whether they did all that could reasonably have been expected of them to prevent that risk'.[28] The ECtHR found that the authorities had responded to the risk in a reasonable way, and that there was no violation of Article 2 of the ECHR. The prison authorities had monitored the prisoner carefully in light of his condition (placing him in hospital care and under watch when he showed suicidal tendencies, providing daily medical supervision, etc).[29]

In *Öneryildiz v. Turkey* (2004)[30], concerning an accident-related death at the Ümraniye municipal rubbish dump, the Grand Chamber of the ECtHR held that

---

22 Deaths resulting from lawful acts of war are not prohibited (Foster, *Human Rights and Civil Liberties*, p. 166).

23 Jacobs and White, *The European Convention on Human Rights*, p. 62, with reference to *LCH v. United Kingdom*, Application No. 23413/94 (www.echr.coe.int).

24 Application No. 40145/98 (www.echr.coe.int).

25 Foster, *Human Rights and Civil Liberties*, pp. 167-168.

26 Application No. 27229/95 (www.echr.coe.int).

27 Ibid., para. 91.

28 Ibid., para. 93.

29 See para. 95-102.

30 Application No. 48939/99 (www.echr.coe.int).

the 'positive obligation to take all appropriate steps to safeguard life ... entails above all a primary duty on the State to put in place a legislative and administrative framework designed to provide effective deterrence against threats to the right to life', and that the positive duty of the State 'must be construed as applying in the context of *any activity*, whether public or not, in which the right to life may be at stake ...'[31]

Practice from the ECtHR shows that the state is obligated to provide an effective system of regulation, supervision and control when the risk to life arises from inherently dangerous or risky but basically lawful activities (e.g. military tests, polluting industries, sites for waste disposal, or confinement of individuals). These duties arise whether the activities are carried out by either public or private enterprises.[32] Thus 'any activity' in which the right to life may be at stake must be regulated and managed according to the level and nature of the risks. As for medical institutions that take care of individuals with mental disabilities, they are under the constant obligation of taking all appropriate measures to protect the lives of patients or inmates. The implication of this duty is, for example, that the person be given life-saving treatment when needed or be prevented from putting him- or herself into acute danger (e.g. jumping out of a window or consuming too much medication).

2.2.4. The right to freedom from torture, inhuman or degrading treatment

Article 3 of the ECHR provides that no one shall be subjected to 'torture or to inhuman or degrading treatment or punishment'. This is an absolute right that cannot be abrogated. As it has no qualifications or exceptions, there are no restrictions or limitations to the rights guaranteed. Thus the prohibition in Article 3 is absolute, even in times of crisis such as war and public emergency.[33]

For a particular conduct to fall under Article 3, it must, according to ECtHR practice, 'attain a minimum level of severity'.[34] Trivial complaints and even acts considered undesirable or illegal will not fall within the scope of Article 3 unless they cause 'sufficiently serious suffering or humiliation to the victim'.[35] The scope of the article is general, covering ill-treatment of political or other prisoners, acts committed during arrest and police detention, and conditions of detention in

31 Ibid., paras. 89 and 71.
32 Jacobs and White, *The European Convention on Human Rights*, p. 64.
33 See Article 15(2).
34 See *Ireland v. United Kingdom* (1978). Jacobs and White, *The European Convention on Human Rights*, pp. 74-75.
35 Jacobs and White, *The European Convention on Human Rights*, p. 75.

prisons or health institutions.[36] Of interest here are statements in *Price v. UK* (2001)[37] where the applicant (a four-limb-deficient thalidomide victim with numerous health problems, including defective kidneys) was committed to prison for seven days and was found to have been subjected to degrading treatment. The ECtHR stated that ill treatment must attain a minimum level of severity if it is to fall within the scope of Article 3, and that the assessment of this minimum level of severity is relative: it depends on all the circumstances of the case, 'such as the duration of the treatment, its physical and mental effects and, in some cases, the sex, age and state of health of the victim'.[38]

In this case, the ECtHR found that the treatment of this severely disabled woman amounted to degrading treatment, considering that in detention she was dangerously cold, risked developing sores because her bed was too hard or unreachable, and was unable to get to the toilet or keep clean without the greatest of difficulty.[39]

Several cases have questioned the use of solitary confinement, and both the Human Rights Commission and the ECtHR have stated that this procedure may violate Article 3, depending on the particular conditions, the stringency of the measure, its duration, the objective pursued, and its effect on the person concerned. The ECtHR has accepted that complete sensory isolation coupled with complete social isolation can ultimately destroy the personality, and that such involuntary isolation thus constitutes a form of inhuman treatment that the requirements of security or any other reason cannot justify.[40]

In *Herczegfalvy v. Austria* (1992) the Commission found a violation of Article 3 (degrading treatment). The applicant, who had been diagnosed as suffering from mental illness, was forcibly administered food and neuroleptics, isolated, and attached with handcuffs to his security bed for several weeks. The Commission concluded that the treatment went beyond the strictly necessary, and that it extended beyond the period necessary to serve its purpose (e.g. the week he was handcuffed to his bed despite being unconscious). However, the ECtHR came to the opposite conclusion. It affirmed that although mental patients are protected by Article 3, the 'established principles of medicine are ... decisive in such cases; as a general rule, a measure which is therapeutic cannot be regarded as inhuman or degrading'.[41] This statement is in itself problematic, as the purpose of medical

36 Ibid., pp. 92-99.
37 Application No. 33394/96 (www.echr.coe.int).
38 Ibid., para. 24.
39 Ibid., para. 30.
40 Jacobs and White, *The European Convention on Human Rights*, p. 95.
41 Para. 82 of the judgement.

treatment – without any consideration of the means – is not necessarily a guarantee against the violation of human rights. This decision has been criticized in the legal literature.[42]

2.3. SUMMARY

This brief presentation of the human rights that may be at stake in various situations of treatment demonstrates that human rights may be unintentionally violated. Vulnerable individuals in particular, who are dependent upon help from and decisions made by others, are at risk of human rights violations. In addition, what particular actions constitute unjustified violations or which violations are justified in protecting other rights is not always clear. Especially when the person is not able to give valid consent, the question arises as to what kind of actions or measures may be taken or invoked to protect the person's vital interests, such as life and health. The following section thus looks into the legal regulation of these issues, especially the regulation of the Biomedicine Convention.

3. LEGAL PROTECTION OF PERSONS WITH COGNITIVE IMPAIRMENT

3.1. THE INTERNATIONAL LEGAL DEVELOPMENT AND REQUIREMENTS: A BRIEF INTRODUCTION

Not only have the rights of patients in general received increased attention in international and national law, but also the protection and rights of patients who lack the mental capacity of giving valid informed consent. This section examines how both international as well as national law respond to a situation in which a patient with cognitive impairment is not able to give valid consent to proposed treatment or care. What is the design of the legal protection in these situations? At the international level has the Model Declaration of Patient Rights, proclaimed by the World Health Organization (WHO, 1994), served as an inspiration and guideline for the development of national legislation in the field (while not legally binding). Instruments approved by the Council of Europe, especially the Biomedicine Convention, the Explanatory Report to the Biomedicine Convention,

42 Hartlev (chap. 6). See also A. Syse, 'Det menneskerettslige vernet mot frihetsberøvelse og tvang i behandlingsøyemed innenfor psykiatrien' [Human rights protection against involuntary detention and coercive treatment in mental health care], *Nordic Journal of Human Rights* Vol. 24, No. 4/2006, pp. 329-330; Jacobs and White, *The European Convention on Human Right*, p. 99.

and Recommendation No. R (99)4 on principles concerning the legal protection of incapable adults. These instruments developed by the Council of Europe should be regarded partly as special regulation and applications within the general framework of human rights and fundamental freedoms protected by the ECHR.[43] The rest of this chapter will focus on the Biomedicine Convention (and its Explanatory Report), because it is a legally binding document for the ratifying member states of the European Council.[44]

Of interest here is that all the international instruments require the development of national legal regulations based on a system with *representative decision-making* in cases of incapacity. Furthermore, a basic requirement in the ECHR, Article 8(2), is that non-voluntary and coercive measures are regulated by *national law*. A typical situation for many countries is that special legal regulation is in place for coercive treatment of persons with serious mental illness, while such regulation is absent for other groups that are also subject to non-consensual or coercive measures, e.g. institutionalized persons with dementia and persons with other forms of cognitive impairment.[45] In this situation, where special legislation is not in place, general provisions of the criminal law on emergencies and the prohibition of coercion and non-consensual physical interventions are to be applied. However, these regulations will often be insufficient, because they do not cover the particular problems and circumstances characteristic of the situation of persons who have mental incapacity and are in obvious need of health care and other services.

Furthermore, a basic requirement in the Biomedicine Convention, Article 6(1), is that an intervention may be carried out only on a person who does not have the capacity to consent when it is for his or her *direct benefit*. Another requirement, in Article 6(3), is that the intervention may be carried out only with the authorization of a representative of the person concerned ('proxy consent'). The following section examines the legal requirements in the Biomedicine Convention in more detail, as well as regulation in four Nordic countries.

3.2. THE REQUIREMENT OF INCAPACITY DUE TO SPECIFIED RELEVANT REASONS

The main general rule in Article 5 of the Biomedicine Convention is that an intervention in the health field may be carried out only after the person has given

43 Rynning, 'Rättssäkerhet och rättsskydd i vården av icke beslutskompetenta vuxna', p. 273.

44 Denmark, Iceland and Norway have signed and ratified it, while Finland and Sweden have signed but not ratified it.

45 Rynning, 'Rättssäkerhet och rättsskydd i vården av icke beslutskompetenta vuxna', p. 272.

free and informed consent to it. Hence people cannot be deprived of their right to consent without specific and qualifying reasons in accordance with law and in their best interest. Article 6(3) specifies the reasons or criteria that national legislation should use when determining whether a person is capable of consenting to a proposed intervention: an intervention may be carried out where, 'according to law, an adult does not have the capacity to consent to an intervention because of a mental disability, a disease or for similar reasons ...'[46] The phrase 'because of a mental disability, a disease or for similar reasons' indicates the causes for the incapacity, and the aim of this specification is to protect the fundamental rights of the individual, and in particular to avoid the application of discriminatory criteria.[47] This provision includes persons with dementia or other forms of cognitive impairment ('mental disability'), as well as comas in which the person is unable to communicate or formulate his or her wishes ('similar reasons').[48] However, an adult who has been declared incapable but who later recovers from the temporary illness or condition and regains the capacity to consent, has the right, according to Article 5, to give consent in person.[49]

The phrase 'according to law' shows that domestic law in each country, within the framework of the Biomedicine Convention, must determine the more specific qualifications as to when depriving individuals of their capacity for autonomous decision-making is lawful.[50] The criteria in Article 6(3) give some flexibility for application and implementation. It is also up to each country, within the framework of the Biomedicine Convention, to decide in more detail which procedures that should be followed for the protection of the interests of the person concerned.

The Norwegian Patient Rights Act states in section 4-3, paragraph 2, that a person may be partly or fully deprived of the right to consent if he or she – due to physical or psychological disturbances, dementia or mental retardation – is obviously not able to understand the implications of consent.[51] The Finnish Act on the Status and Rights of Patients has a similar provision about the reason for incapacity (mental disturbance or mental disability or for other reason cannot decide on the treatment).[52] These criteria in both the Norwegian and Finnish provisions are in accordance with the Biomedicine Convention, Article 6(3), i.e. 'mental disability', 'disease' or 'similar reasons'.

---

46 This is only one of the criteria.
47 Council of Europe, Explanatory Report, para. 43.
48 Ibid.
49 Ibid.
50 Ibid., para. 42.
51 Act of 2 July 1999, No. 63.
52 Act No. 785, 1992, sec. 6, para. 2.

The Norwegian provision also clearly expresses the basic requirement with regard to incapacity, namely that the person concerned is *obviously not able to understand* the implications of giving consent. This is a strict requirement, applying to serious lack of ability to understand.[53] Thus ability to understand must be related only to the particular treatment for which consent is needed. Each proposed intervention must be subject to a particular consideration concerning the patient's ability of understanding. What is important here is that not being *able to* understand is not the equivalent of *understanding*. The Patient Rights Act, section 4–3, paragraph 3 (cf. section 3–5), specifies that health personnel are obligated, in the best possible way, to adjust the information and communication to the individual capacity and circumstances of the patient (age, mental state, maturity, experience). The purpose is to enable the patient to understand the content and consequences of proposed treatment and thereby be able to participate and give consent on his or her own terms. Only after such efforts are taken may a decision on the patient's ability to understand be made. What makes the person vulnerable is the lack of ability to understand important aspects of a proposed treatment, and this vulnerability makes him or her in need of additional legal safeguards protecting and upholding his or her human dignity.

3.3. DECISIONS ABOUT INCAPACITY

As the Biomedicine Convention does not regulate the question of who decides whether a person lacks the capacity to give consent, national law must be specific. In Norway, for example, the decision as to whether a person is competent is to be made by the person providing the health care (Norwegian Patient Rights Act, section 4–3, para. 3). While the Finnish Act on the Status and Rights of Patients does not give a clear answer to the question, this question is apparently to be decided by health personnel. Section 6, paragraph 2, states that the legal representative or a family member or other person close to the patient has to be heard 'before making an important decision concerning treatment'. Although nothing is stated about the authority to make decisions on incapacity, this decision is also likely to be made by health personnel. The same guidelines hold in Swedish and Danish law.[54]

---

53 A minor cognitive impairment or dementia is not sufficient. Preparatory documents to the act: Ot. Prp. No. 64 (2005-2006), pp. 20-21.

54 While the Swedish Act on Healthcare of 1982, No. 763, does not have particular regulation for these cases, see Rynning, 'Rättssäkerhet och rättsskydd i vården av icke beslutskompetenta vuxna', p. 270. As for Denmark, see the Danish Act on Healthcare sec. 18 and sec. 17, para. 2.

3.4. THE REQUIREMENTS OF PROPORTIONALITY AND DIRECT BENEFIT

Article 8(1) of the ECHR protects the right of everyone to private life, including physical integrity and self-determination. Thus medical treatment given without a valid consent or under coercion is a violation of the right of the patient to private life.[55] However, it follows from the ECHR, Article 8(2), that if the non-voluntary medical treatment is in accordance with national law and is also 'necessary in a democratic society' to protect health and the rights of others, it may be justified. It equally follows from ECtHR practice that in order for an intervention in private life to fulfil the requirement of necessity, the interference must 'correspond to a pressing social need, and, in particular that it is proportionate to the legitimate aim pursued'.[56] Thus the requirement is – theoretically – twofold: a pressing social need and proportionality between the intervention and the pursued objective. In practice, the basic question to be asked in each case is this: was the intervention necessary under the particular circumstances of the case?[57] The requirement of proportionality suggests the necessity of a fair balance between the intervention and the pursued objectives.[58] Thus invasive measures such as coercive or non-consensual treatment are acceptable only if strong needs justify them. If a particular intervention may successfully be replaced by other less intrusive alternatives, the requirements of necessity and proportionality are not fulfilled.

Although the requirement of proportionality is not explicitly mentioned in the Biomedicine Convention, it follows from the requirement of 'direct benefit', which is stricter than that of proportionality. When a person is not capable of giving valid consent, Article 6(1) of the Biomedicine Convention states that 'an intervention may only be carried out on a person who does not have the capacity to consent, for his or her direct benefit'. The requirement of direct benefit implies that the proposed intervention is also proportional, meaning that it is necessary and that the medical aim cannot be reached by other, less intrusive means. However, the requirement of direct benefit goes further in that the intervention must also be considered in the best interest of the person, meaning that the benefit of the intervention clearly outweighs the expected or possible harms.

The requirement of 'direct benefit' is a specific expression of the overall principle of primacy of the human being, i.e. Article 2 of the Biomedicine Convention, which is clearly inspired by Kantian humanism. It follows from Article 6(1) that

55 See sec. 2.2.2.

56 *Olsson v. Sweden* (1988), para. 67, quoted in J. Aall, *Rettsstat og menneskerettigheter*[Rule of law and human rights], Bergen: Fagbokforlaget, Second edition 2007, p. 127.

57 Aall, *Rettsstat og menneskerettigheter*, p. 128 and p. 132, re: *Hatton v. UK* (2003).

58 Ibid., p. 132 with reference to *Hatton v. UK* (2003).

deviation from the rule of direct benefit is possible in only two cases that the Articles 17 and 20 specify and that concern medical research and the removal of regenerative tissue.[59] The requirement of 'direct benefit' when the person is not able to consent is not further elaborated in the Explanatory Report to the Biomedicine Convention. However, similar to the requirement of necessity and proportionality, "direct benefit" implies an evaluation of the situation of the concerned for determining whether a treatment will be beneficial for the patient. 'Direct' means that the person himself or herself must benefit from the treatment, not other persons or future patients. The wording indicates that the proposed treatment must be expected to be clearly beneficial for the patient when compared with other alternatives.

In Norwegian law, as well as in the domestic law of other Nordic and European countries, the requirement of direct benefit in patient treatment follows from the general principle of due care. According to the Norwegian Health personnel Act, section 4, paragraph 1, health personnel are obligated to perform their profession in accordance with professional standards and out of careful consideration for the particular patient. Thus proposing medical treatment not considered of direct benefit, or with such a potential, for the particular patient would be illegal. In the same way, when a patient cannot give valid consent, careful considerations must be made for ensuring that the treatment is in the best interest of the patient. In so far as relatives or other representatives give consent on behalf of the patient, health personnel are obligated to ensure that the treatment is in the patient's best interests.[60] Thus in cases of disagreement between the patient's representative and the providers of health care, what health personnel consider in the patient's best interests will prevail.

3.5. PROXY CONSENT

3.5.1. The requirement of consent from a representative

It follows from the Biomedicine Convention, Article 6(3), that where, 'according to law, an adult does not have the capacity to consent to an intervention because of a mental disability, a disease or for similar reasons, the intervention may only

59 See also Council of Europe, Explanatory Report, para. 44.

60 The overall duty of protecting the patient's best interests is clearly expressed in the Norwegian Patient Rights Act, sec. 4-6, and the Finnish Act on the Status and Rights of Patients, sec. 6, para. 3. The Danish Healthcare Act, sec. 18, states that in situations where the decision of relatives will clearly damage the patient or the outcome of the treatment, the provider of health care may treat the patient if the Board of Health approves. Thus Danish law makes it more difficult for health personnel to overrule the decisions of relatives.

be carried out with the authorisation of his or her representative or an authority or a person or body provided for by law'. This provision establishes the lawfulness of proxy consent in situations where the person him- or herself is not capable of giving valid consent. Thus the provision gives the right to self-determination a form of protection in the sense that it requires valid and informed consent from someone representing the patient.

A diversity of legal approaches exists in Europe on the subject of legal representation. In some countries the capacity of the patient to consent must be verified for each intervention (e.g. Norway), while other countries have a system based on the institution of legal incapacitation, whereby a person may be declared incapable of consenting to one or several types of acts (e.g. signing contracts, giving costly presents, making decisions about medical treatment). The purpose of the Biomedicine Convention is not to introduce a single system for the whole of Europe but to ensure a basic protection of persons incapable of giving valid consent.[61] The most basic requirement is that individuals should be legally deprived of their capacity to consent only when doing so is necessary in the best interests of the person.[62]

Finnish legislation states that, in situations of the incapacity to give consent, 'the patient's legal representatives, a close relative, or other person closely connected with the patient, must give their consent to the treatment' (Act on the Status and Rights of Patients, sec. 6, para. 3). Danish law establishes that in the case of permanent incapacity, the nearest relatives of the patient, or the guardian if the patient is under guardianship, may give consent (sec. 18, para. 1, Healthcare Act). Only if the patient does not have close relatives or a guardian whose competence includes health care decisions may health personnel make decisions concerning treatment.[63] These provisions are fully in line with that in the Article 6(3) of the Biomedicine Convention, in that some sort of legal representation must be established once the patient himself or herself is not able to give valid consent. Swedish legislation does not provide clear regulation of these issues.[64]

By contrast, the Norwegian Patient Rights Act is more problematic, since it gives the authority to the providers of health care to make decisions on behalf on patients who are not able to give valid consent (sec. 4–6, para. 2). After a legal change that took effect 1 May 2008 (Resolution of 4 April 2008, No. 323) health care personnel may make decisions on both scope and duration for both serious

61 Council of Europe, Explanatory Report, para. 42.

62 Ibid.

63 See sec. 18, paras. 2 and 3 of the Danish Healthcare Act. If the intervention is not of a minor nature, an independent health care provider with relevant professional competence has to be consulted.

64 Rynning, 'Rättssäkerhet och rättsskydd i vården av icke beslutskompetenta vuxna', p. 270.

and less serious interventions.[65] This scope is problematic given Article 6(3) of the Biomedicine Convention, which states that in case of incapacity due to the specified circumstances, the intervention 'may only be carried out' with the authorization of the representative, authority or the body or person provided for by law. Implicit here is that health personnel may not act as the representative of the patient in relation to health care that they or other personnel in the same health care department or unit propose.[66]

The Norwegian Patient Rights Act, section 4–6, paragraph 2, requires that, when possible, information from relatives about the wishes of the patient must be obtained. Furthermore, a presumed consent from the patient for the particular intervention is needed.[67] In addition, other health personnel must be consulted before the decision is made. The reasoning behind these provisions is that although seeking information from relatives is important, relatives should not be burdened with the responsibility of decision-making about patient treatment.[68]

The preceding discussion illustrates the difficult considerations that characterize this issue: on the one hand is the protection of the vulnerable individual, and on the other is the protection of relatives from making difficult decisions on behalf of their close ones. However, the solution in Norwegian law – giving health personnel the ultimate authority to make decisions even in serious cases – is questionable from the perspective of both the patient and his or her relatives. While health personnel are capable of using only their professional judgment – since they normally do not know the patient very well – close relatives know the patient and are therefore in a better position to make decisions based on his or her needs and interests. However, since the health personnel are obligated when possible to obtain such information from the relatives and must also act in accordance with what is believed to be the patient's wishes, this objection is partly met by the Norwegian law. Nevertheless the Norwegian regulation differs from those of the other Nordic countries in this respect, and it deviates from what appears to be the requirement of the Biomedicine Convention.

3.5.2. The rights and duties of the patient's representative

The overall purpose of the Biomedicine Convention, as stated in Article 1, is to 'protect the dignity and identity of all human beings and guarantee everyone, without discrimination, respect for their integrity and other rights and

65 This authority, however, cannot be used in cases where the patient rejects the treatment, unless otherwise is decided by law (sec. 4-6, para. 3).

66 This implication appears to be the assumption in the Explanatory Report, see para. 45.

67 The provision requires that it must be probable that the patient would have given his or her consent to the intervention had he or she been able to consent.

68 Ot. Prp. No. 64 (2005-2006), p. 17.

fundamental freedoms'. Moreover, the purpose of having legal representation is that the representative can protect the interests of, and act on behalf of, the patient, and therefore must act in his or her best interest. More concretely, the representative must as far as possible ensure that only interventions for the direct benefit of the patient are carried out. For this purpose, Article 6(4) states that the representative shall be given, under the same conditions, the same information as is required according to Article 5 (the general rule of informed consent).

In addition, it follows from Article 6(5) of the Biomedicine Convention that the authorization of the patient's representative may be withdrawn at any time in the best interests of the person concerned. This provision stems from the obligation of the doctor to always act in the patient's best interests and to protect patients against representative's decisions that are contrary to those interests: 'While a person capable of giving consent to an intervention has the right to withdraw that consent freely, even if this appears to be contrary to the person's interest, the same right must not apply to an authorisation given for an intervention on another person, which should be retractable only if this is in the interest of that third party person'.[69]

Likewise, it follows from Article 9 that wishes relating to a medical intervention, as previously expressed by a patient who is not at the time of the intervention in a state to express his or her wishes, 'shall be taken into account'. If a representative knows of such wishes, he or she must give the necessary information. This provision covers not only emergency situations but also those in which individuals have foreseen that they might be unable to give their valid consent, for example, in case of dementia or coma.[70] However, taking previously expressed wishes into account does not necessarily mean that they should always be followed. If they were expressed a very long time earlier, and medical science has greatly progressed since then, the doctor must confirm that the earlier wishes of the patient apply to the present situation and are still valid.[71]

3.6. PATIENT PARTICIPATION

It follows from the Biomedicine Convention, Article 6(3), that a person with mental impairment, as far as possible, shall take part 'in the authorisation procedure', meaning that the person must be involved in the decision-making

69 Council of Europe, Explanatory Report, para. 48.
70 Ibid. (para. 61).
71 Ibid. According to the Finnish Act on the Status and Rights of Patients, the representative (including a close relative or other person closely connected with the patient), in giving consent, 'must respect the patient's previously expressed wishes or, if no wishes had been expressed, the patient's well-being' (sec. 6, para. 3).

process. The phrase "authorisation procedure" is somewhat confusing, as it could be interpreted as covering the authorization of the representative on his or her behalf – but this is clearly not the intention. The Explanatory Report to the Biomedicine Convention states in paragraph 46 that the participation of adults not able to consent in decisions 'must not be totally ruled out'. Thus, for the purpose of empowerment, explaining to the person "the significance and circumstances of the intervention and then obtain their opinion" is necessary.[72]

In addition, according to Article 6(4) of the Biomedicine Convention, the representative, authority, person or body representing the incapacitated person shall be given the same information, under the same conditions, as referred to in the main rule in Article 5. The Norwegian Patient Rights Act, section 3–1, has a particular provision on patient participation: paragraph 2 states that patients who are not able to give consent themselves still have the right to participate in the treatment – but the participation has to take place together with his or her close relatives.

4. COGNITIVE IMPAIRMENT AND THE USE OF COERCION

There is an ongoing international debate as to whether the use of coercive measures for health purposes towards individuals who are not able to give valid consent should be regulated by law. While some states are reluctant to do so, because of the possibility of increased coercion directed at vulnerable groups, other are more positive. They emphasize that legal regulation would be an acknowledgment of the use of coercive measures, thereby leading to more visibility, which in turn may lead to a reduction of their use.[73] This is the position of Norway, the only Nordic country that by law has approved the use of coercion towards various groups of individuals who are not able to give valid consent to proposed and necessary health care.

As we have already seen, coercive interventions for health purposes must be in accordance with national law and be necessary and proportional to be justifiable (ECHR, Article 8(2)). This section examines the developments in Norwegian legislation on the use of coercion towards individuals who are not able to give valid consent for therapeutic purposes. A new chapter (4A) in the Norwegian Patient Rights Act[74] provides the legal basis for the use of coercive treatment

72 Ibid.

73 Ot. Prp. No. 64 (2005-2006), p. 67.

74 The new provisions were adopted in Act of December 22, 2006, No. 99.

outside emergency situations for patients (over 16 years old) who do not have the capacity to consent and who reject proposed treatment. This regulation, which applies to all kinds of coercive health care except psychiatric treatment (which is covered by a separate law[75]) does not have a counterpart in the other Nordic countries. The objective of the new provisions in the Norwegian Patient Rights Act is to provide necessary health care for preventing significant health damage and to prevent and limit the use of coercion (sec. 4A-1, para. 1).

An important background for these new provisions is the documentation of widespread use of coercive measures in Norway, especially towards elderly persons with dementia.[76] However, the provisions may also be used towards persons with other forms of cognitive impairment, and also towards persons who lack the competence to consent because of drug- or alcohol abuse.[77] As for elderly persons with dementia, the hiding of medicine in food or drinks, the forced holding of hands, feet or head during care, bed guard, and forced washing, bathing or showering are among the most common coercive measures in practice. These measures are used most frequently with persons with serious dementia, and they are used regularly (from once a week to three times a day). The arguments used in favour of such measures are the need for a minimum level of care, to prevent the patient from falling or to provide necessary medical treatment, including medication. The report of the National Competence Centre for Dementia concludes that loss of cognitive skills, ability to manage one's own daily life and behavioural changes are those factors most determining for the implementation of coercive measures.[78]

The Norwegian Patient Rights Act specifies that health care, which must be provided by health personnel, shall be provided with respect for individual physical and psychological integrity and *as far as possible* be in accordance with the autonomy of the patient. Furthermore, coercive health care may only be given when 'necessary' for preventing *serious* health damage (sec. 4A-1 and sec. 4A-3, para. 2). These provisions are assumed to be in accordance with the requirement of direct benefit in Article 6 of the Biomedicine Convention.[79] Among the coercive measures allowable for providing necessary treatment is detention in health institutions and the use of technical alarm systems and other measures for controlling movement (belts etc.) (sec. 4A-4). However, the coercive measures must not only be constantly monitored and but also stopped once the legal

75 Act of 2 July 1999, No. 62.
76 Ot. Prp. No. 64 (2005-2006) p. 22 , re: a report by the National Competence Centre for Dementia (2002), pp. 25-26.
77 Ibid., pp. 25-26.
78 Ibid.
79 Ibid, p. 67.

requirements are no longer fulfilled. Special consideration must be given to whether the measures have positive effects, or whether they have unexpected negative consequences (sec. 4A-4, last para.).

Other alternatives must be tried before coercive measures may be used (sec. 4A-3, para. 1). If the patient persistently rejects treatment or the health personnel know with a high degree of certainty that the person will maintain his or her resistance, a decision concerning health care may be taken on certain conditions listed in section 4A-3, paragraph 2: non-treatment may lead to significant health damage for the patient, the health care measure is considered necessary, and the measures are proportional to the need for health care.

An additional requirement follows from section 4A-3, paragraph 3, which states that even if these conditions are fulfilled, health care may be given only if it is clearly the best solution for the patient.[80] Health personnel must consider both the degree of resistance and the probability that the patient will soon regain his or her capacity to consent. Only if these conditions are fulfilled may the treatment be given with coercion or other measures for avoiding patient resistance (sec. 4A-4, para. 1). The phrase 'other measures' suggests that the patient may also be deceived into taking medication as a means of avoiding direct confrontation and thereby the potential use of coercion.

The Norwegian government has considered the human rights implications of these provisions and finds them fully compatible with both the ECHR and the Biomedicine Convention.[81] It believes that in a society based on the rule of law, basing the use of coercion on legislation (the principle of legality) is essential. Its reference point is *H L v.UK*, in which the ECtHR points out the task of states to establish proper legislation for regulating the conditions under which individuals not able to give valid consent may be cared for.[82]

5. CONCLUSIONS

Human dignity is the essential value to be protected among all human rights. The requirement of informed consent, as put forward in several human rights instruments and national legislation, is not only an essential right of every patient but also the main legal way of securing respect for human autonomy and dignity.

---

80 These requirements are similar to those for coercive treatment of patients with serious mental illness (Act of 2 July 1999, No. 62, sec. 3-3).

81 Ot. Prp. No. 64 (2005-2006), pp. 66-70 (sec. 4.7).

82 Ibid., p. 68. The case *H L v. UK* is also discussed in sec. 2.2.2.

However, this chapter has shown that the main rule of informed consent may be deviated from in cases of cognitive impairment. The reason is that protection and exercise of individual autonomy in situations where the patient is not able to understand the implications of consenting to proposed treatment may lead to serious, even fatal, consequences for the patient. Therefore, to protect the best interests of the person concerned – and thereby human dignity – the human rights perspective requires a balancing of the rights at stake, taking into consideration which right or rights most urgently need protection in a situation where they cannot all be upheld simultaneously.

The Biomedicine Convention is the most important European legal instrument for the protection of vulnerable individuals with regard to health interventions. It establishes a common standard for protecting the human dignity of persons not able to consent, especially for the specification of relevant criteria for establishing incapacity, and the requirements of proper procedures, direct benefit and proxy consent, and proper national regulation. These requirements ensure basic protection for individuals who are not able to exercise meaningful autonomy in situations where issues concerning their vital health interests are at stake.

With regard to the requirement of proxy consent, while the Biomedicine Convention does not impose a single European system, it provides basic requirements. The Norwegian regulation appears in conflict with the Biomedicine Convention as it ultimately leaves even decisions about serious interventions to health personnel, despite the Biomedicine Convention's requiring authorization from the patient's representative. Norway is also the only Nordic country that legislated coercive treatment of individuals over the age of 16 who are not able to consent and who reject (non-psychiatric) treatment. In so doing, Norway has taken a step forward in terms of providing more detailed regulation of the conditions under which vulnerable individuals may be cared for. However, it is too early to conclude whether this open acceptance of the use of coercion is indeed the most proper way of regulating these difficult situations.

CHAPTER 6
COERCIVE TREATMENT AND HUMAN DIGNITY

Mette Hartlev

1. INTRODUCTION

Respect for personal liberty is one of the most widely acknowledged political rights, recognized and protected within both international human rights law and national constitutions. It serves as the foundation for more specific rights to freedom of expression, freedom of association, and privacy. Curtailments of personal liberty are normally justifiable only in extraordinary situations in which a society has a substantial countervailing interest. The use of coercion in connection with psychiatric care implies both an infringement of personal liberty and a violation of a person's right to privacy and physical and mental integrity. Consequently, compulsory care needs justification with reference either to the substantial interests of society or to the more specific interests of the person concerned.

The conflict between the right to personal liberty and coercive treatment is plain enough. However, how coercion relates to *human dignity* is less clear. Where persons with mental disorders are concerned, living conditions that lack such dignity may easily arise – either because the relevant individuals are left alone, with the attendant risk of being exploited by others, or because they are institutionalized under very poor conditions. Nevertheless, clarifying the role that coercion might justifiably play in this regard, either as promoting or inhibiting respect for psychiatric patients' dignity, is no simple task.

The concept of human dignity plays an important role within both moral philosophy and law. Yet, with no consensus on its definition, we need to clarify the implications of dignity in the present context and analyze the way in which it relates to coercive treatment. The significance of human dignity within law has grown as international human rights law has become increasingly integrated into legal thinking. Developments in biotechnology have also led to increased awareness of the importance of respect for human dignity. This chapter explores the concept of dignity in both moral philosophy and law, and discusses the relationship between various conceptions of human dignity and the use of coercion in psychiatric care. The legal analysis will concentrate on human rights law, in which human dignity has a central role.

2. THE CONCEPT OF DIGNITY

2.1. MORAL PHILOSOPHY

The concept of dignity attracts a good deal of attention in moral philosophy. It is often associated with the philosophy of Immanuel Kant and in particular with the distinction, in Kantian thinking, between *objects*, which have a *price* (because they are replaceable by an equivalent), and *persons*, who have *dignity* (intrinsic worth) and are irreplaceable.[1] In Kant's philosophy dignity and autonomy are closely related; indeed, some believe that Kant awards dignity only to human beings who possess the capacity to act autonomously.[2] They therefore believe that non-autonomous persons, such as small children or mentally disturbed persons, do not possess dignity because they are not able to act autonomously. The close tie between autonomy and dignity is also very clearly expressed by the Oxford legal philosopher Joseph Raz, who claims that '[r]especting human dignity entails treating humans as persons capable of planning and plotting their future. Thus respecting people's dignity includes respecting their autonomy, their right to control their future'.[3]

The connection between autonomy and dignity is discussed at length by the US legal philosopher Ronald Dworkin in *Life's Dominion*. He writes that it is in some ways convincing to connect dignity with the capacity for autonomous action. However, Dworkin argues that dignity arises out of the intrinsic worth of human life and thus encompasses all human beings, including those who do not have the capacity for autonomous actions. As he puts it:

> A person's right to be treated with dignity, I now suggests, is the right that others acknowledge his genuine critical interests; that they acknowledge that he is the kind of

1 I. Kant, *Foundations of the Metaphysics of Morals*, London: Hutchinson University Library 1966, pp. 96–97. Quotations are from the English translation, prepared by H.J. Paton and published as *The Moral Law*.

2 S. Andersen, *Kristen etik* [Ethics], in S. Andersen and K.K. Jensen, *Bioetik* [Bioethics], København: Rosinante 1999, pp. 197–306.

3 J. Raz, *The Authority of Law*, Oxford: Clarendon Press 1979, p. 221.

> creature, and has the moral standing, such that it is intrinsically, objectively important how his life goes.[4]

Interestingly, Dworkin also draws on Kant. He refers to Kant's 'categorical imperative', according to which one must always treat oneself and others never merely as a means to an end but also at once as ends in themselves.[5] That two very different conceptions of dignity are based on Kantian thinking demonstrates the uncertainty and vagueness associated with the moral understanding of dignity. Nevertheless, at least two relatively distinct conceptions of human dignity appear at work within moral philosophy: one that relates human dignity to autonomy and the capacity for autonomous action, and another that connects human dignity with the intrinsic worth of human life.

2.2. HUMAN RIGHTS LAW

Human dignity is also important within law. It is not only one of the core human rights concepts but probably *the* most fundamental one. Thus the preamble to the Universal Declaration on Human Rights (UDHR) proclaims that "… recognition of the inherent dignity and of the equal and inalienable rights of all members of the human family is the foundation of freedom, justice and peace in the world". The UDHR continues, in Article 1, by stipulating that '[a]ll human beings are born free and equal in dignity and rights'.[6] Equally, both the UN Covenant on Civil and Political Rights and the Covenant on Economic, Social and Cultural Rights note in their preambles that human rights 'derive from the inherent dignity of the human person'.[7] Thus these instruments explicitly declare human dignity to be one of the foundational ideas in human rights thinking. Interestingly, Article 1 of the UDHR mentions human dignity before rights. This order might indicate that dignity is regarded as more fundamental within human rights thinking than individual rights and freedoms. The Danish bioethicist Anne Mette Maria Lebech says that the drafters of the UDHR recognized that 'left to their own free will, people did not always behave rationally or well'.[8] Clearly the lessons learned from the German atrocities of the 1930s and World War II called for a renewed emphasis on values and principles other than autonomy and liberty.

4 R. Dworkin, *Life's Dominion*, London: Harper/Collins 1993, esp. pp. 236.
5 Kant, *Foundations of the Metaphysics of Morals*, p. 95.
6 UN, UDHR (1948).
7 UN, International Covenant on Civil and Political Rights (1966) and International Covenant on Economic, Social and Cultural Rights (1966).
8 A.M.M. Lebeck, 'Dignity v. Dignity', *Studies in Ethics and Law*, Vol. 7, 1998, pp. 29–38.

Likewise, the UK law professors Deryck Beyleveld and Roger Brownsword argue that human dignity is tied to a cluster of ideas:

> that each and every human being has inherent *dignity*; that it is this *inherent* dignity that grounds (or accounts for) the possession of human rights (it is from such inherent dignity that such rights are *derived*); that these are *inalienable* rights; and that, because all humans have dignity, they hold these rights *equally*.[9]

This line of reasoning closely ties the concept of dignity in the field of human rights to the one in moral philosophy that relates human dignity to the *intrinsic worth of human life*. However, when we look more closely at the various sources of human rights, we can identify at least three separate but interrelated conceptions of dignity: one relating dignity to human freedom and personal autonomy, one relating dignity to the intrinsic worth of each and every human being, and one associating dignity with conditions essential to living a life with dignity.

The case law of the European Court of Human Rights (ECtHR) is of particular interest in this regard. Unlike both the UDHR and the UN human rights conventions, the Council of Europe Convention on Human Rights and Fundamental Freedoms (ECHR) does not explicitly mention 'dignity'.[10] However, the importance attached to human dignity as a foundational idea in European human rights thinking is clearly reflected in the reasoning of the ECtHR. In both *Goodwin v. UK* (para. 65) and *Pretty v. UK* (para. 90) the ECtHR states that 'the very essence of the Convention is respect for human dignity and human freedom'.[11] Here the ECtHR distinguishes between dignity and freedom, thus indicating that its understanding of 'human dignity' separates dignity from human freedom and the capacity for autonomous choice. However, in both of these cases the ECtHR also acknowledges a relationship between dignity and freedom. In the *Goodwin* case, which was concerned with a transsexual person's interest in obtaining legal recognition of her gender change, the ECtHR maintains (para. 90):

> Nonetheless, the very essence of the Convention is respect for human dignity and human freedom. Under Article 8 of the Convention in particular, where the notion of personal autonomy is an important principle underlying the interpretation of its

---

9 D. Beyleveld and R. Brownsword, *Human Dignity in Bioethics and Biolaw*, Oxford: Oxford University Press 2001, p. 13.

10 Council of Europe, Convention on Human Rights and Fundamental Freedoms (1950). Dignity is, however, included in other Council of Europe instruments, e.g. the Convention for the Protection of Human Rights and Dignity of the Human Being with regard to the Application of Biology and Medicine. Convention on Human Rights and Biomedicine (1997).

11 *Pretty v. UK*, Application No. 2346/02 and *Goodwin v. UK* (www.echr.coe.int), Application No. 28957/95 (www.echr.coe.int).

> guarantees, protection is given to the personal sphere of each individual, including the right to establish details of their identity as individual human beings.

Here respect for personal autonomy is treated as a necessary part of acknowledging a person's right to establish his or her identity as an individual human being.[12] This belief is further underlined in paragraph 91, where the ECtHR argues that a 'society may reasonably be expected to tolerate a certain inconvenience to enable individuals to live in dignity and worth in accordance with the sexual identity chosen by them at great personal cost'. Thus the ECtHR observes an intimate link between the right to establish an identity according to one's own preferences and the right to live in dignity.

In the *Pretty* case the ECtHR also affirms the relationship between human freedom and human dignity. The applicant, who was dying of motor neuron disease, argued that her husband's not being permitted to assist her in committing suicide was a violation of her human rights. Her physical condition prevented her from committing suicide without assistance. The court stated (para. 65):

> The very essence of the Convention is respect for human dignity and human freedom. Without in any way negating the principle of sanctity of life protected under the Convention, the Court considers that it is under Article 8 that notions of the quality of life take on significance. In an era of growing medical sophistication combined with longer life expectancies, many people are concerned that they should not be forced to linger on in old age or in states of advanced physical or mental decrepitude which conflict with strongly held ideas of self and personal identity.

Here the ECtHR points to interests that individuals may legitimately have in upholding ideas about self and personal identity in a way that reflects the intimate relation between dignity and the capacity to make autonomous choices in accordance with one's own self-perception.

In both the *Pretty* and *Goodwin* cases the ECtHR establishes a link between dignity and freedom. This link is also evident in *Ribitsch v. Austria*, where the complainant argued that he had been subjected to torture while being arrested by the police.[13] Here the ECtHR stresses (para. 38) that 'any recourse to physical force which has not been made strictly necessary by his own conduct diminishes human dignity and is in principle an infringement of the right set forth in Article

12 See also B.H. Østenstad, 'Grunnverdiar og grunnomgrep i debatten om bruk av tvang mot utviklingshemma og demente' [Legal values and concepts in the debate regarding use of coercion against incapacitated adults], *Nordisk Tidsskrift for Menneskerettigheter* 2006, No. 4, pp. 343–361 (p. 355).

13 *Ribitsch v. Austria*, 4/12, 1995 (www.echr.coe.int).

3'. Thus the ECtHR concludes that the use of coercion in the form of unjustifiable physical force diminishes human dignity.

Elsewhere, however, the reasoning of the ECtHR appears to somewhat disassociate human dignity from the individual's right to exercise autonomy. Thus in *Valasinas v. Lithuania*, which was concerned with the treatment of prisoners – and in particular the practice of performing strip-searches – the ECtHR declared (para. 117):

> ... while strip-searches may be necessary on occasions to ensure prison security or prevent disorder or crime, they must be conducted in an appropriate manner. Obliging the applicant to strip naked in the presence of a woman, and then touching his sexual organs and food with bare hands showed a clear lack of respect for the applicant, and diminished in effect his human dignity. It must have left him with feelings of anguish and inferiority capable of humiliating and debasing him. The Court concludes, therefore, that the search of 7 May 1998 amounted to degrading treatment within the meaning of Article 3 of the Convention.[14]

In this case, there is clearly a restriction of the applicant's personal freedom. But in its reasoning the ECtHR does not refer to the non-voluntary nature of the strip-search. It stresses instead, in more general terms, the relationship between lack of respect for the individual being searched and the debasing treatment involved in the practice of strip-searching.

In *Keenan v. UK* the ECtHR explicitly speaks to the question of violation of dignity in cases in which the victim is unable to make autonomous choices given his or her mental capacity. The mother of a mentally disturbed young man who had committed suicide in prison complained about what she considered the inhuman and degrading treatment of her son by the prison authorities. She also maintained that her son had died from suicide by the prison authorities' failure to protect his life.[15]

The British government argued (para. 87) that such 'protection'– to require that the state protect a person against himself or herself– would be inconsistent with the principles of individual dignity and autonomy underlying the ECHR – thus apparently endorsing the notion that dignity is linked with the expression of personal autonomy. On the one hand, the ECtHR acknowledges (para. 92) that the prison authorities were obligated to perform their duties in a manner compatible with the rights and freedoms of the individual concerned. On the

14 *Valasinas v. Lithuania*, Application No. 44558/98 (www.echr.coe.int).
15 *Keenan v. UK*, Application No. 27229/95 (www.echr.coe.int).

other hand, the ECtHR emphasizes that 'there are general measures and precautions which will be available to diminish the opportunities for self-harm, without infringing on personal autonomy.

The British government also argued (para. 108) that it was not possible to distinguish the suffering resulting from the son's mental illness from any additional injury he might have suffered as a result of the conditions under which he was imprisoned. However, the EctHR concludes (in para. 113):

> While it is true that the severity of suffering, physical or mental, attributable to a particular measure has been a significant consideration in many of the cases decided by the Court under Article 3, there are circumstances where proof of the actual effect on the person may not be a major factor. For example, in respect of a person deprived of his liberty, recourse to physical force which has not been made strictly necessary by his own conduct diminishes human dignity and is in principle an infringement of the right set forth in Article 3 (see *Ribitsch v. Austria*, judgment of 4 December 1995, Series A no. 336, p. 26, §38, and *Tekin*, cited above, pp. 1517–18, §53). Similarly, treatment of a mentally ill person may be incompatible with the standards imposed by Article 3 in the protection of fundamental human dignity, even though that person may not be able, or capable of, pointing to any specific ill-effects.

According to these ECtHR arguments, a violation of a person's right to the protection of his or her human dignity might occur even if that person is not clearly aware of any infringement. Thus in the *Valasinas* and *Keegan* cases the concept of dignity is not exclusively related to personal autonomy or the capacity for autonomous choice. The conception of dignity in these cases appears more closely associated with the notion that *all human beings possess intrinsic worth.*

Finally, we can identify a conception of dignity referring to the *conditions* provided for human beings in special circumstances and consider whether these conditions assure the individual the opportunity to enjoy a sufficiently dignified existence. The ECtHR in several cases stresses that Article 3 of the ECHR imposes a duty on states to ensure that detainees are kept in conditions compatible with respect for human dignity, and that the manner and method of execution of various measures must not subject the detainee to distress or hardship of an intensity exceeding the unavoidable level of suffering inherent in any detention. Furthermore, the court stresses that the detainee's health and well-being must be adequately ensured through such measures as the provision of necessary medical assistance.[16]

Thus the concept of dignity employed in human rights thinking is, in various places, connected with respect for autonomy, respect for the intrinsic worth of all

16 See e.g. para. 94 in *Kudla v. Poland*, Application No. 30210/96 (www.echr.coe.int).

human beings, and the obligation to provide dignified conditions of detention. The rest of this chapter will explore in detail the relationship between these three components of dignity, together with the use of coercion in psychiatric care. However, we first need to take a closer look at coercion.

3. COERCION

Before a new Danish law on coercion in psychiatric care took effect in 2007, coercion in Denmark was defined as 'interventions which the patient opposes'.[17] Before 2007, therefore, legal safeguards against coercion in the course of psychiatric care would have been operative only when a patient actively opposed treatment. By contrast, the new legislation – Act No. 1111 of 1 November 2006, on coercion in psychiatric care – defines coercion as 'interventions for which there is no informed consent'.[18] This new definition widens the scope of coercion: the legal protection from coercion that the act provides is fully operative in situations in which the patient is either unable or unwilling to give informed consent. The different definitions of coercion in these two acts reflect general uncertainty about the meaning of the concept.[19]

However, one can also imagine a range of situations in which a person – without being subjected to force or threats – is persuaded to do something not in keeping with his or her preferences and in which the issue of voluntariness is questionable.[20]

Article 16 of Council of Europe Recommendation Rec. (2004) 10 Concerning the Human Rights and the Dignity of Persons with Mental Disorder defines non-voluntary placement and treatment as measures that a person with the capacity to consent refuses or to which a person who lacks the capacity to consent objects. This definition focuses primarily on the will of the person, not on the use of force or threats. One can, of course, picture an even broader legal understanding of coercion or non-voluntariness – one in which the crucial factor is whether the person in question is able to make a free and informed

17 Sec. 1.2 in Act No. 331 of 24 May 1986, on deprivation of liberty and use of coercion in psychiatric care.

18 Sec. 1.2.

19 References to Danish legislation illustrate the ambiguity regarding a common understanding of coercion. The uncertainty is also reflected in the conception of psychiatric patients expressed in the study by K.I. Iversen, G. Høyer, H. Sexton and O.K. Grønli, 'Perceived coercion among patients admitted to acute wards in Norway', *Nordic Journal of Psychiatri*, 56:6, 2002, pp. 433–439 (force and threats) and in the definition used in the Council of Europe Recommendation Rec.(2004) 19 (overruling will of the person).

20 Studies of perceived coercion of psychiatric patients also point to the use of 'force' and 'threats' as indicators of coercion: see K.I. Iversen et.al., ibid., pp. 433–439.

decision based on his or her authentic preferences. Consequently, in the law there is a vast 'grey area' between measures that are clearly voluntary and measures that are clearly compulsory.[21] Likewise, a gap may exist between the legal understanding of coercion and patient's personal perception of coercion.[22]

Various kind of coercion may be relevant in psychiatric care, including non-voluntary placement in psychiatric facilities, non-voluntary treatment, and the use of seclusion and restraint. These different measures give rise to slightly different considerations with regard to dignity.

4. COERCION AND RESPECT FOR PERSONAL AUTONOMY

Within both moral philosophy and law is a close relationship between dignity and autonomy. Respect for human dignity involves respect for a person's ability to make autonomous choices regarding the future in accordance with his or her own preferences. By this definition, respecting a person's dignity presupposes that the person in question actually possesses the ability to make autonomous choices, i.e. that he or she is mentally competent and can thus be assumed to have legal capacity. But whether psychiatric patients possess legal capacity is not always clear. Some patients suffering from mental disorders are clearly autonomous, whereas others might either temporarily or permanently lack mental competence as a result of the character and severity of their disorder. Consequently, individually assessing each patient's ability to express autonomy is critical. However, within psychiatric care the assessment of mental capability is highly interwoven with the assessment of the character and severity of the disorder. A person's inability to act and reason rationally is one of the symptoms used in diagnosing various mental disorders; once a person is diagnosed with a mental disorder, consideration must be given to the question whether he or she can act autonomously.

The question of whether a person is suffering from a mental disorder must be determined in accordance with internationally accepted medical standards.[23]

---

21 A. Syse, 'Det menneskeretlige vernet mot frihetsberøvelse og tvang i behandlingsøyemed innenfor psykiatrien', *Nordisk Tidsskrift for Menneskerettigheter* [Human rights protection against involuntary detention and coercive treatment in mental health care], 2006, No. 4, pp. 318–342 (323).

22 Iversen, Høyer, Sexton and Grønli, 'Perceived coercion among patients admitted to acute wards in Norway', pp. 433–439.

23 Para. 18–25 in the Explanatory Memorandum to Recommendation Rec. (2004) 10 of the Committee of Minister to member states Concerning the Protection of the Human Rights and

These standards normally develop as a result of both progress in medical research and developments in social attitudes towards mental disorders. As the ECtHR stresses in the *Winterwerp* case (para. 37), Article 5 of the ECHR, which allows for curtailments of the liberty of 'persons of unsound mind', '... obviously cannot be taken as permitting the detention of a person simply because his views or behaviour deviate from the norms prevailing in a particular society.[24] Consequently, the mere fact that a person has views departing from those of the 'average' person will not in itself lead to the conclusion that this person is of unsound mind.

Similarly, that a person is diagnosed with a mental disorder does not in itself imply that he or she is incapable of making autonomous decisions. An assessment of the individual's capacity to make autonomous decisions must be made separately. In Recommendation Rec. (2004) 10, the Council of Europe distinguishes between persons who have the capacity to consent to placement and treatment and persons who do not. Assessment of the patient's capability must thus be based on nationally legislated criteria.[25] Consequently, a mental disorder in itself is not sufficient for establishing that a person does not possess personal autonomy.

The coercion of *autonomous psychiatric patients* will always involve the infringement of human dignity. Here coercion means that the autonomous decision of the patient has not been considered, i.e. that there has been a failure to treat the patient's choice as equal to any other person's. When it comes to the coercion of *non-autonomous psychiatric patients*, violation of the right to dignity – understood in terms of respect for a person's right to make choices for his or her own life – is not necessarily involved: a non-autonomous patient is unable to make autonomous choices, so from this perspective no violation of the patient's dignity can occur. However, as I will soon explain, a violation of the patient's dignity may occur if dignity is understood in terms of respect for the patient's intrinsic worth and right to dignified treatment.

From a *moral* perspective, restricting an autonomous person's right to self-determination is normally justifiable only to protect other personal freedoms and rights.[26] Such restriction may also be justified by paternalistic considerations of the best interests of the restricted individual. Paternalistic interventions may be defensible if a patient is at risk of significant and preventable harm, provided that

---

Dignity of Persons with Mental Disorder. See also Winterverp v. The Netherlands, 24/10 1979, paras. 37–38 (www.echr.coe.int).

24 *Winterverp v. The Netherlands*, 24/10 1979, paras. 37–38 (www.echr.coe.int).

25 Para. 123 in the Explanatory Report to Recommendation, Rec. (2004) 10.

26 T.L. Beauchamp and J.F. Childress, *Principles of Biomedical Ethics*, New York: Oxford University Press 2001, pp. 63–65.

the intervention will probably prevent the harm and that the projected benefits of the action outweigh its cost to the patient. Furthermore, the least autonomy-restrictive alternative for ensuring relevant benefits and reducing the costs must be adopted.[27]

From a *legal* perspective the use of coercion in psychiatric care always needs to be justified – for both autonomous and non-autonomous persons. The human rights legislative framework provides some guidance here. Article 5 of the ECHR states that a person's right to liberty and security of person must be respected. However, deprivation of liberty is justifiable in a number of cases, including the detainment of 'persons of unsound mind'. While the ECHR does not stipulate more detailed criteria for the *legal detainment* of psychiatric patients, the case law of the ECtHR provides some guidance. Most important is the principle of proportionality, which requires that the mental disorder have a character and degree making compulsory confinement absolutely necessary. It also requires that the continuation of compulsion be justified by the persistence of the disorder.[28]

Non-voluntary placement in psychiatric facilities is covered in more detail in Article 17 of Recommendation, Rec. (2004) 10, which states that a person may be subject to non-voluntary placement only if all of the following criteria are met: the person has a mental disorder; the person's condition represents a significant risk of serious harm to his or her health or to other persons; the placement includes a therapeutic purpose; no less restrictive means of providing appropriate care are available; and the opinion of the person concerned has been considered.[29]

As neither coercive treatment, restraint nor seclusion are covered by Article 5, we need to look elsewhere in the ECHR. For *coercive treatment*, both Articles 3 and 8 may be relevant. Article 3 states that no one shall be subjected to torture or to other inhumane and degrading treatment. In the *Herczegfalvy* case the applicant – a prisoner suffering from a mental disorder – claimed that he had been subjected to treatment incompatible with Article 3. He said that he had been forced to

---

27 Ibid., pp. 185–187.

28 The most useful case here is *Winterverp v. The Netherlands*, 24/10 1979, which gave rise to the 'Winterverp criteria' (i.e. except in emergency cases, no one should be deprived of his or her liberty unless the person concerned has been reliably shown to be of 'unsound mind, the mental disorder must be of a kind or degree warranting compulsory confinement, validity of continued confinement depends on the degree and persistence of disorder'. See M. Wachenfeld, 'The Human Rights of the Mentally Ill in Europe: Under the European Convention on Human Rights', *Nordic Journal of International Law,* 1991, pp. 142–145.

29 Furthermore, a person not yet diagnosed with a mental disorder may, under certain conditions, be subjected to involuntary placement for determining whether he or she has a mental disorder that represents a significant risk of serious harm to his or her health or to the health of others: Article 17(2) of Recommendation Rec. (2004) 10.

receive medical treatment and food and had been handcuffed to a security bed for a long period. Although the ECtHR expressed its concern over the length of time he had been restrained, it did not find that the treatment violated his rights under Article 3. Particularly with regard to the use of coercive medical treatment and feeding, the ECtHR argued that the established principles of medicine are decisive, and that 'as a general rule, a measure which is a therapeutic necessity cannot be regarded as inhuman or degrading'.[30]

Counsel for Mr. Herczegfalvy also cited Article 8 to support the complaint about coercion but without success. Here the ECtHR referred to its early reasoning vis-à-vis Article 3. It then emphasized that the information supplied failed to disprove the opinion of the Austrian government that the hospital authorities were entitled to regard the applicant's psychiatric illness as rendering him entirely incapable of taking decisions for himself.[31] The ECtHR thus put the emphasis on the applicant's lack of mental capacity. Had the applicant been mentally competent, a rather different conclusion might have been reached.

Looking at the relevant case law, one might reasonably conclude that the ECtHR relies largely on medical expertise, thus allowing a wide margin of appreciation for assessing the degree of coercion used in psychiatric care.[32, 33]

However, other human rights instruments are more explicit about the justifiability of non-voluntary psychiatric treatment. Article 7 of the Council of Europe Convention on Human Rights and Biomedicine (Biomedicine Convention) states that a person may be subjected to treatment for a mental disorder without consent only if doing so is necessary to prevent serious harm to his or her health. Recommendation Rec. (2004) 10 from the Council of Europe also speaks to the justifiability of coercive medical treatment. It stipulates that such treatment may take place only if there is a significant risk of serious harm to the patient's health or to that of a third party, and if no less intrusive means of providing appropriate

30 *Herczegfalvy v. Austria*, 24/9 1992 (www.echr.coe.int), para. 82.

31 Ibid., para. 86. The ECtHR rejected the notion that coercion used in connection with the applicant's medical treatment amounted to violation of Article 8. However, it conceded that the hospital's practice of sending all the applicant's letters to the curator, who then decided which ones to pass on to the applicant, was a violation of Article 8.

32 The 'margin of appreciation' doctrine has developed in the case law of the European Court of Human Rights. It allows national authorities room to manoeuvre in fulfilling their obligations according to the Convention of Human Rights, esp. in areas where there are cultural and philosophical differences among the signatories.

33 Syse, 'Det menneskeretlige vernet mot frihetsberøvelse og tvang i behandlingsøyemed innenfor psykiatrien [Human Rights protection against deprivation of liberty and use of coercion in treatment of persons with mental disorders], p. 330 and Østenstad, 'Grunnverdiar og grunnomgrep i debatten om bruk av tvang mot utviklingshemma og demente' [Legal values and concepts in the debate regarding use of coercion against incapacitated adults], p. 354.

care is available (Articles 18–19). The opinion of the patient must also be considered, and a number of procedural requirements must apply (Article 20). The difference between these two instruments with respect to risk criteria is striking. The Biomedicine Convention accepts compulsory treatment only where the purpose is to prevent serious harm to the *patient's own health*, whereas the Recommendation allows coercive treatment in cases where there is no risk to the patient's health but a risk to that of *other persons*.

These two instruments apply to both autonomous and non-autonomous patients. Although they allow for paternalistic interventions, they clearly signal that a balance must be struck between the patient's interest in self-determination (autonomous patients) or in participation in decision-making (non-autonomous patients) and the responsibility of society to promote the best interests of the patient. The explanatory report to Recommendation Rec. (2004) 10 contains some thorough and interesting considerations of this delicate balance; it emphasizes that the patient must have an opportunity to choose whether he or she would rather live with some symptoms of the illness than take medication with certain side-effects.[34]

The Biomedicine Convention and Recommendation Rec. (2004) 10 are evidently much more concerned with the protection of the psychiatric patient's dignity than are the ECHR and the ECtHR. It is both a cause of concern and somewhat mystifying that the ECtHR has so far been unwilling to incorporate the principles and criteria set out in these human rights instruments into its own reasoning – especially since the ECtHR itself has highlighted its presumption that human dignity is a foundational principle of human rights.

5. COERCION AND RESPECT FOR THE INTRINSIC WORTH OF ALL HUMAN BEINGS

As the ECtHR emphasized in the *Keenan* case, a person who fails to appreciate or is incapable of detecting an infringement of his or her rights continues to be protected by human rights and thus retains an enforceable claim to respect for personal dignity. Consequently, dignity must be understood more broadly than a matter of merely respecting personal autonomy.

In human rights thinking the right to dignity requires state authorities to regard every human being as having intrinsic worth. Thus the state is also obligated to

34 Explanatory Memorandum to Recommendation Rec. (2004) 10 of the Committee of Minister to member states Concerning the Protection of the Human Rights and Dignity of Persons with Mental Disorders, para. 142.

make special provision for persons who are weak and vulnerable. This aspect of the right to dignity is more complicated than autonomy. Even if one readily agrees that their intrinsic worth requires all human beings to be treated as persons of equal worth, what precisely this understanding implies is far from obvious. For persons suffering from mental disorders, rules and regulations introducing criteria for non-voluntary placement and treatment can be seen as expressions of respect for the dignity of *all* psychiatric patients. However, such regulation does not provide sufficient protection if the rules are administered and implemented in ways that do not equally respect persons with mental disorders.

As an important measure, Articles 17–18 in Recommendation Rec. (2004) 10 requires the opinion of the patient to be considered in all aspects of non-voluntary treatment, irrespective of whether he or she is autonomous. This rule is important, because it obligates hospitals and other authorities to treat non-autonomous patients with the same respect as autonomous patients. However, the treatment of non-autonomous patients as persons of equal worth also creates a duty for ensuring that the patient has the option of living a dignified life. In some situations coercion might be the best way of ensuring that a patient recovers or that his or her condition is improved, and recovery or improvement might be a precondition for respecting the person's right to live a life of dignity. For some psychiatric patients coercive placement and treatment is a necessary part of the journey back to autonomy. Such placement and treatment enables the patient to once again live life according to genuine preferences. For other patients coercion may be perceived as degrading and thus as undermining their perception of a dignified life.

As the Explanatory Report to Recommendation Rec. (2004) 10 emphasizes, a difficult balance must be struck between respecting a person's right to self-determination and the obligation of society to take positive action to protect the rights and health of weak and vulnerable persons[35] However, acknowledging a person's right to express his or her attitude to the anticipated benefits and risks associated with both treatment and non-treatment, and then considering these attitudes, requires respect for the intrinsic worth of that person.

6. COERCION AND DIGNIFIED CONDITIONS

Psychiatric patients deprived of liberty are totally dependent on the conditions provided for them during their detention. These conditions include a variety of elements, such as the physical surroundings (e.g. living space), the opportunity

[35] Ibid., paras. 128–149.

for a certain degree of privacy, the right to keep certain personal belongings, general treatment with regard to food and access to necessary medical care, and the attitude and behaviour of carers and other custodians.[36] If the patient is subjected to compulsory treatment or restraint, the manner and method of execution of these measures should also be compatible with respect for human dignity. The ECHR does not provide strong protection for the psychiatric patient's rights in respect to environment and living conditions.

Some protection, however, may follow from Article 3, which safeguards the patient against inhuman and degrading treatment. This area seems to be one in which there is legal development towards a more protective attitude.[37] In particular, the Council of Europe's Committee for the Prevention of Torture and Inhuman or Degrading Treatment or Punishment has developed standards governing the patient's living conditions and treatment in psychiatric establishments.[38] Equally, Articles 9–10 of Recommendation Rec. (10) 2004 stipulate basic requirements for environment, living conditions, and the provision of health care services for psychiatric patients.

In some situations coercion might be necessary for a person to enjoy sufficiently dignified living conditions. It is not uncommon for persons with severe mental disorders to live miserable lives because they are unable to take care of themselves. For example, such people are frequently unable to manage their housing conditions, food, social contacts, and so on. Although the use of coercion is certainly not the first measure to take here, if other and less intrusive options have proved impractical or ineffective, coercion might be justified in the name of the person's right to a life of dignity. As the Norwegian legal scholar Bjørn Henning Østenstad has emphasized, wholesale rejection of the option of coercion might imply sacrificing the psychiatric patient and his or her fundamental need for care, to support a fundamentalist view of individual autonomy and liberty.[39]

---

36 The Eighth General Report on the Activities of the European Committee for the Prevention of Torture and Inhuman or Degrading Treatment and Punishment (document CPT/Inf. (98) 12) lists a number of factors crucial to the provision of a positive therapeutic environment for involuntary psychiatric patients.

37 P. Lorenzen, L.A. Rehof, T. Trier, N. Holst-Christensen og J. Vedsted-Hansen, *Den Europæiske Menneskerettighedskonvention* [The European Convention on Human Rights], 2nd ed., København: Jurist- og Økonomforbundets Forlag 2003, pp. 120–121.

38 The Eighth General Report on the Activities of the European Committee for the Prevention of Torture and Inhuman or Degrading Treatment and Punishment (document CPT/Inf. (98) 12). In its Sixteenth General Report (document CPT/Inf. (2006) 35) the Committee provides an extensive commentary on the use of restraint in psychiatric establishments.

39 Østenstad, 'Grunnverdiar og grunnomgrep i debatten om bruk av tvang mot utviklingshemma og demente', p. 356.

7. CONCLUSIONS

The relationship between dignity and the use of coercion in psychiatric care is complex. The concept of dignity is multifaceted, and depending on which facet one takes as a point of departure, coercion of persons with mental disorders might either be in conflict with personal dignity or support the right to dignity. Most importantly the legal concept of dignity requires the regarding of all human beings as individuals with intrinsic worth. From this understanding, it is possible to manoeuvre between respecting a person's wishes (autonomous or otherwise) and offering sufficient psychiatric care to vulnerable persons who might otherwise all too easily be treated without dignity.

CHAPTER 7
HUMAN DIGNITY, THE VALUE OF KNOWLEDGE, AND THE LIMITS OF SCIENTIFIC FREEDOM

António Barbosa da Silva

1. INTRODUCTION

This chapter analyzes how the value of 'human dignity' may limit the scope of scientific freedom, especially in medical and health-related research.[1] Whilst 'scientific freedom' is justified by the value attributed to knowledge, scientific freedom can be limited by a number of factors, including the responsibilities of the researcher and the needs of society and humanity. Nevertheless, the intrinsic value attributed to the human being – in the international human rights literature often framed as a concern for the dignity of the human being – ultimately determines the limits of scientific freedom. In other words, human dignity gives the decisive answer as to the limitation or non-limitation of scientific freedom.

This chapter analyzes the relationship between 'human dignity' and 'scientific freedom' from a general standpoint, with the underlying general assumption that issues of freedom are involved in all research. Nonetheless, this chapter argues that the issue of freedom is particularly relevant in medical or health-related research when vulnerable groups are involved as active participants in the research activity. This argument has practical implications: if medical and health-related research is limited by the value of human dignity, what kind of organizations, networks or individuals should be responsible for safeguarding the use of scientific freedom, defending and promoting it, criticizing those who misuse it, and rectifying the results of such misuse?

The next four sections examine the relationship between human dignity and scientific freedom in four ways: by accounting for different justifications of

1 I would like to thank Linda Fisher-Høyrem, Helge Slotten, Bjørn Øyvind Fjeld, and Reidar Salvesen for their useful comments to this chapter.

scientific freedom; by examining differing definitions of human dignity and integrity; by considering the relationship between the value of the human being and scientific freedom; and by discussing alternative approaches not only for monitoring the use and abuse of scientific freedom but also for criticizing and correcting those who misuse, disrespect or violate its limits. The chapter discusses these issues from the perspective of moral philosophy.

2. SCIENTIFIC FREEDOM AND THE VALUE OF KNOWLEDGE

This section clarifies the meaning of the expression 'scientific freedom', and discusses the thesis that the value attributed to knowledge is the foundation of and justification for scientific freedom.

2.1. WHAT IS SCIENTIFIC FREEDOM?

Scientific freedom is the freedom of the scientist, scholar or researcher with regard to his or her inquiry: '[s]cientists should be free to conduct research on any problem or hypothesis. They should be allowed to pursue new ideas and criticize old ones'.[2] According to this concept of scientific freedom, scientists should not be coerced into doing or abstaining from doing scientific research. Freedom in this sense is the same as the absence of coercion. Instead, scientists should be allowed to:

> ... pursue knowledge and research without unreasonable interference or restriction from law, institutional regulations, or public pressure. Its basic elements include the freedom of teachers to inquire into any subject that evokes their intellectual concern; to present their findings to their students, colleagues, and others; to publish their data and conclusions without control or censorship; and to teach in the manner they consider professionally appropriate. For students, the basic elements include the freedom to study subjects that concern them and to form conclusions for themselves and express their opinions.[3]

The Swedish science philosopher Birgitta Forsman maintains that scientific freedom includes the liberty to search for truth for its own sake and to ask any research question, to use any method without asking whether the result is of any

[2] D.B. Resnik, *The Ethics of Science. An Introduction* (Routledge, 1998) p. 59.
[3] *Encyclopaedia Britannica* (CD 2000).

utility for society and humankind.[4, 5] Since the word 'freedom' has different senses or meanings, we need to know the specific meaning here of 'freedom' in the expression 'scientific freedom'. Generally speaking, moral philosophers distinguish between three different meanings of individual freedom: freedom of the will, freedom of choice, and freedom of decision or action.

Freedom or human autonomy in its threefold sense is presupposed in the ethical principles for scientific research.[6] Examples include respect for participants in research projects, including their informed consent, dignity and worth, personal integrity, privacy and identity.

Freedom of decision and action is apparently the issue American ethicist Resnik's statement that '[s]cientists should be free to conduct research on any problem or hypothesis. They should be allowed to pursue new ideas and criticize old ones'.[7] A researcher, by using his or her freedom of will, may think out different hypotheses and methods for solving a given scientific problem. For example, a health care scientist may design his or her research according to the following steps in the research process, each of which requires the use of scientific freedom[8]:

1. *Problem:* Psychiatric patients do not receive adequate treatment in Norway
2. *Hypothesis*: The treatment of mental health problems in Norway is sub-standard compared to that in other comparable countries.
3. *Methods*: Systematic observation, quantitative studies followed by qualitative interviews, comparisons of treatment programs, etc.

The researcher may use his or her freedom of will and choice to choose the method that he or she finds most appropriate for the particular study. The researcher may, for example, choose the method of illegal video- and audiotape recordings of inmates in Norwegian psychiatric institutions to assess whether the patients receive proper treatment. In these and other possible steps of the research process ethical problems or dilemmas may arise. But as long as the researcher has not actually acted on this choice, one cannot attribute to him or her any moral

4 B. Forsman, *Forskningsetik. En introduction* [Research ethics. An introduction] (Studentlitteratur, 1997), p. 105.
5 Resnik, *The Ethics of Science ...*, p. 39.
6 Ibid. and D.D. Runes (ed.), *Dictionary of Philosophy* (Adams and Co. 1974) p. 112.
7 Resnik, *The Ethics of Science ...*, p 39.
8 For a more precise account of and distinction between freedom of decision and freedom of action (liberty), see J. Feinberg, *Harm to Self. The Moral Limit of Criminal Law*, (Oxford University Press, 1986) p. 65. For Feinberg freedom of action includes what he calls '*de facto* liberty', which he identifies with '*de facto* political freedom'.

responsibility or accountability, blame or guilt. At this point, the researcher has only expressed his or her freedom of will and choice.[9]

However, if the researcher uses his or her freedom of decision and action to realize this choice of method, and if no external factor either prevents him or her from acting or forces him or her to act, then the researcher is responsible for his or her actions. If those actions harm the interests of other persons, then the researcher is morally responsible and guilty for his or her action. From a legal point of view, the researcher should be punished if he or she has violated any legal norms. In this particular case, both research ethics and legal norms forbid such investigations, because they violate other people's rights to privacy. Thus, the liberty of the researcher is limited by the protection of the dignity and rights of others.

Other examples of misuse of research freedom occur when an interview is intentionally transformed into the interviewee's confessions of intimate experiences (e.g. child abuse, pornography, a confession of a crime not yet discovered), or when they are forced to do things without their informed consent. Researchers may also deceive participants in an experiment for the purpose of collecting ethically sensitive data.[10]

2.2. THE FOUNDATION OF SCIENTIFIC FREEDOM OF DECISION AND ACTION

This section examines the thesis that the ethical value attributed to knowledge is the foundation and justification of scientific freedom (i.e. the researcher's freedom of action). The section also refines the terms 'intrinsic value', 'instrumental value', 'human dignity', and a person's 'autonomy and integrity'.

2.3. INTRINSIC VERSUS EXTRINSIC VALUES AND THE ISSUE OF ENDS AND MEANS

To indicate the difference between the value of knowledge and that of the human being, as well as their interrelationship, we must first distinguish between two different types of ethical value: intrinsic and extrinsic (or instrumental) values.

---

9 K.E. Tranøy, *Forskning i frihet – men uten ansvar?* [Research in freedom – but without responsibility?] (Centre for technology, innovation and culture, 1989); Knut W. Ruyter, *Forskningsetikk. Beskyttelse av enkeltpersoner og samfunn* [Research ethics. Protection of individuals and society] (Gyldendal Akademisk, 2003) p. 26f.

10 S. Bok, 'Shading the truth in seeking informed consent for research purpose', 5 *Kennedy Institute of Ethics Journal*, 1 (1995), 1–17.

To say that phenomenon X has an *intrinsic value* means that X is an end or goal in itself, which in turn means that X can be searched for, for X's sake alone. In other words, X can be chosen as a goal for human actions. Generally speaking, the following phenomena are regarded as having intrinsic value: human life, human dignity, health, friendship, love, peace, freedom, integrity, truth, non-violence, self-realization, pleasure, well-being, and meaning and quality of life.[11] We desire these phenomena and search for them for their own sake; thus they can be the ends or goals of our actions.

To say that knowledge in general and scientific knowledge in particular has *intrinsic value* means that knowledge should be pursued for its own sake, i.e. as an end in itself. This statement, however, is controversial. Only scholars or scientists who defend basic research at any price regard knowledge as having intrinsic value.

By contrast, scholars who are interested mainly in applied knowledge tend to search for knowledge for its extrinsic or instrumental value.[12] To say that phenomenon Y has an *extrinsic* or instrumental value means that Y can be used as a means of attaining another phenomenon, X, which is regarded as having intrinsic value or which has a greater instrumental value than Y. For example, money, medicine, surgery, or a house is usually regarded as having instrumental value in relation to health, quality of life or life itself.[13] Hence, we use money to buy medicine and we use medicine to attain health. We regard both money and medicine as having only *instrumental value* in relation to health, which is considered as having *intrinsic value*. Everything that has instrumental value can be used as a *means* for attaining an end or goal that is regarded as having either intrinsic value or greater instrumental value than the *means* itself. For example, work may be seen as having lesser extrinsic value than money, and money as having lesser extrinsic value than medicine.

2.4. THE RELATIONSHIP BETWEEN INTRINSIC AND EXTRINSIC VALUE

Both intrinsic and extrinsic values can be ordered hierarchically. Phenomena which have *intrinsic* value may be ordered in relation to one another and constitute a hierarchy of ends and means. The one that has the highest intrinsic value may be regarded as the top of the hierarchy. The other phenomena in the hierarchy

11 R. Holte et al. *Etiska problem* [Ethical problems] (Verbum, Håkan Ohlssons 1977) pp. 48f.

12 Resnik, *The Ethics of Science* ... pp. 39f. As for how to ethically relate things with different values to one another, see J. Jonas, *The Imperative of Responsibility*, Chicago: Chicago University Press, 1984, chap. 3.

13 Holte et al., *Etiska problem* [Ethical problems], pp. 48f.

may function as means to the attainment of the phenomenon that has the highest value. For example, even if freedom, human welfare and quality of life are regarded as having intrinsic value, one may regard freedom as a means in relation to welfare, and welfare can be regarded as a means to a meaningful life, a life with a good quality.

For *extrinsic* values, people usually attribute a greater extrinsic value to medicine, for example, than to money or a car. For example, one may sell one's car to buy medicine if one's health or life depends upon taking that medicine.

As to the difference between intrinsic and extrinsic values, first, no phenomenon with intrinsic value can lose that value, because it is *inherent* to the phenomenon, i.e. it is part of its nature. By contrast, a phenomenon that has only extrinsic (i.e. instrumental) value can lose its value as circumstances change. Human life, health, friendship, freedom, integrity, truth, well-being, and the meaning and quality of life do not lose their value. But things that have only extrinsic value (money, a house) can lose their instrumental value when they do not fulfil the function for which they were designed. For example, medicine loses its extrinsic value when it loses its healing power. Hence extrinsic value is a value 'borrowed' from the end that it is used to attain.

Second, if both human beings and knowledge are regarded as having only extrinsic value, knowledge can still be regarded as a means for the realization of human goals (e.g. happiness), provided that the intrinsic value of human beings is greater than that of knowledge. If knowledge has only extrinsic value, then it can be used as a means to attain some goals, e.g. health and well being, which have either intrinsic value or extrinsic value greater than knowledge, the realization of which can make the world a better place for humans and other living beings. As already indicated, scientists and scholars who restrict themselves to applied research have the tendency to regard knowledge as having only extrinsic, or instrumental, value.[14]

3. HUMAN DIGNITY AND INTEGRITY AS THE ULTIMATE LIMITATIONS ON SCIENTIFIC FREEDOM

The value of the human being and knowledge and their interrelationship have different positions in different perspectives or traditions within moral philosophy.

14 P.P. Kirscehenmann, 'Intrinsically or just instrumentally valuable? On structural types of values of scientific knowledge', 32 *Journal for general philosophy of science*, 2 (2001), 237–256; P. Duncan: (http://plato.stanford.edu/entries/knowledge-value/2007.08.21); W.P. Alston, *Beyond 'Justification'. Dimensions of Epistemic Evaluation*, (Cornell University Press, 2005), p. 31.

In defending the thesis that human dignity is the ultimate limit for academic freedom, I accept Kant's view that everything can have a price except human beings, who have a priceless or infinite value. When Kant talks about the sanctity of human life, he means that the right way to behave towards other human beings is to show them respect or reverence.[15] According to Kant and the later humanists, human dignity is an intrinsic value that is constant, inestimable, unchangeable, inalienable, inviolable, and equal for all human beings. This is the humanistic ethics implicit in contemporary human rights instruments.

Another closely related reason for respecting another person's dignity is implicit in Kant's basic meta-ethical norm, the *categorical imperative*. Kant formulates his categorical imperative in three different but closely related ways. The one most relevant for our purpose here states that one should always treat other persons as ends in themselves, never only as means for achieving one's own interests. Kant is not maintaining that one should never use another person as a means but rather that one should never use another person *only* as a means.[16] That persons are ends in themselves means that they have intrinsic value, i.e. dignity.[17]

The ethical basis of Kant's categorical imperative is his view that human beings are autonomous because they are rational beings and moral agents. For Kant, being autonomous is both a necessary and sufficient condition for the possession of dignity. This view appears implicit in the UN Universal Declaration of Human Rights, Article 1, which is the basis of and justification for the following 29 articles. Article 1 states: 'All human beings are born free and equal in dignity and rights. They are endowed with reason and conscience and should act towards one another in a spirit of brotherhood'.

Another concept closely related to dignity and which is relevant for our purpose here, is 'integrity', which means wholeness, completeness. According to the Danish ethicist Jacob Dahl Rendtorff, '[i]n bioethics and biolaw the idea of integrity [is used] as an untouchable core, the personal sphere, which should not be subject to external intervention.'[18] The person's right not 'to be subject to external intervention' is justified by the person's right to physical integrity (which includes genetic integrity), mental integrity (psychosocial and spiritual integrity,

15 I. Kant, *Groundwork for the metaphysics of morals*, 2nd ed., (Hackett Publishing Company, 1981) p. 41; I. Kant, *Critique of Practical Reason*, (The Bobb-Merrill Company, 1956/1975) p. 95.

16 Kant, *Groundwork for the metaphysics of morals*, p. 41.

17 R. Plant, *Politics, theology, and history*, (Cambridge University Press, 2001).

18 J.D. Rendtorff, 'Basic ethical principles in European bioethics and biolaw: Autonomy, dignity, integrity and vulnerability – Towards a foundation of bioethics and biolaw', *Medicine Health Care and Philosophy* 5 (2002), 28f.

personal domain integrity (comprising privacy and physical and personal integrity of self-determination), and moral integrity (the integrity of character and moral conscience).[19] According to law philosopher J. Feinberg, a 'person of moral integrity is faithful to his [or her] own principles'.[20] Moreover, a person of moral integrity does not use other persons only as a means for the realization of his or her own interests. Therefore, he or she always attempts to do to others what he or she wishes that others would do to him or her.[21]

A person's right to be respected because of his or her integrity is justified by his or her dignity and worth, which gives him or her basic human rights (i.e. the humanistic approach). The Norwegian philosopher Knut Erik Tranøy argues that a person's autonomy, dignity and integrity are so closely interrelated that to disrespect or harm a person with regard to one implies doing the same to the others.[22] In other words, if one does not respect a person's integrity or autonomy, one does not respect the person's dignity. Therefore, from a humanistic viewpoint, respect for integrity, autonomy and dignity sets limits on a researcher's freedom when he or she undertakes research either on human subjects or on anything that may endanger human welfare and life, e.g. atomic research for making weapons.[23] By contrast, a non-humanistic view denies that all humans have equal intrinsic value and evaluates each individual human being according to his or her achievements and contribution to the welfare of the society.

4. THE RELATIONSHIP BETWEEN THE VALUE OF KNOWLEDGE AND THAT OF THE HUMAN BEING

The relationship between the value of knowledge and that of the human being can be described thusly: The value of knowledge is the foundation and justification of scientific freedom, whereas human dignity and worth is the ultimate limit of scientific freedom.

---

19 Ibid.

20 J. Feinberg, *Harm to Self. The Moral Limit of Criminal Law*, (Oxford University Press, 1986) p. 40.

21 A. Barbosa da Silva (ed.), *Etikk og menneskesyn i helsetjeneste og sosialt arbeid* [Ethics and view of the human being in health care and social work], (Gyldendal Akademisk, 2006), p. 67.

22 K.E. Tranøy, *Medisinsk etikk i vår tid* [Medical ethics today] (Sigma Förlag, 1994), pp. 32–48.

23 Einstein and the Pugwash peace treaty of 1957 according to P.L. Cantelon et al. (eds.) *The American atom, a documentary history of nuclear policies from the discovery of fission to the present.* 2nd ed., (University of Pennsylvania Press, 1991); Forsman, *Forskningsetik ... [Research ethics ...]*, pp. 15f.

Whether scientific freedom should be limited depends on the various logical relationships between the foundation of scientific freedom (the value of knowledge) and the grounds for the limitation of scientific freedom (the value of the human being). Arguably the value that one attributes to knowledge and to the human being depends on one's view of knowledge and of the human being. The following analysis proceeds from the assumption that if the human being and knowledge are attributed the same intrinsic value or the same extrinsic value, then they are equally valuable.

We may distinguish between three hypothetical main arguments for the limitation of scientific freedom: According to those who attributed intrinsic or extrinsic value to either knowledge or the human being, or the same type of value to both, scientific freedom should be limited in the case of any of the following possible relationships:

I. If the human being (HB) is attributed intrinsic value, whereas knowledge (K) is attributed *only* extrinsic value,
II. If both K and HB are attributed intrinsic value but the intrinsic value attributed to HB is greater than the intrinsic value attributed to K,
III. If both K and HB are attributed only extrinsic value but the extrinsic value attributed to the HB is greater than that attributed to K.

Furthermore, we find three main arguments against the limitation of scientific freedom. Scientific freedom should not be limited in the case of any of the following possible relationships:

IV. If both K and HB are attributed *only* extrinsic value but the extrinsic value attributed to K is greater than that attributed to HB,
V. If K is attributed intrinsic value but HB is attributed *only* extrinsic value,
VI. If both K and HB are attributed intrinsic value, but the intrinsic value of knowledge is greater than that of the HB.

One last formulation allows an argument in either direction:

VII. If K and the HB are attributed either exactly the same intrinsic or exactly the same extrinsic value.

In this last case, any reasons for giving priority to either of the two will be only pragmatic.

These logically possible relationships between the value of K and the value of HB and their consequences for scientific freedom can be illustrated thusly:

Figure 2

	Intrinsic value	**Extrinsic value**	**View of the human being**
	HB's intrinsic value > K's intrinsic value	K *also* has extrinsic value	*Post-Kantian Humanistic*
	HB has no intrinsic value	HB's value > K's value	*Non-humanistic*
Arguments against limitation of the scientific freedom (cases IV, V and VI)	HB has no intrinsic value	K's extrinsic value > HB's extrinsic value	*Non-humanistic*
	K has intrinsic value	HB has only extrinsic value	*Non-humanistic*
	K's intrinsic value > HB's intrinsic value	HB has also extrinsic value	*Non-humanistic*
No argument in either direction (case VII)	K's value = HB's value	K's value = HB's value	*Non-humanistic*

This figure illustrates various relationships between the value of knowledge (K) and that of the human being (HB). The sign '>' means 'greater than'.

As to the limitation of scientific freedom, first (case I), if the human being is conceived as having intrinsic value and knowledge as having only extrinsic value (Kantian humanism), scientific freedom should be limited. From this viewpoint, the scientist's freedom to search for knowledge – in any form – must be limited or restricted by human dignity. Thus the researcher is free to search for any kind of knowledge to the extent that its value does not conflict with that of the human being and its value is regarded as a means of attaining intrinsic human goals such as health, peace, security or welfare.

Second (case II), if both knowledge and the human being are attributed intrinsic value, but the intrinsic value attributed to the human being is greater than that attributed to knowledge (post-Kantian humanism), then respect for the human value puts limits on scientific freedom.

Third (case III), if both the human being and knowledge are attributed only extrinsic value, but the extrinsic value attributed to the human being is greater than that attributed to knowledge (non-humanism), then the scientist's freedom to search for knowledge must be limited. In this case the scientist is free to search for any kind of knowledge to the extent that its value does not conflict with that of the human being and its value is regarded as a means of attaining human goals. This standpoint implies a non-humanistic view of the human being. This view of the human being does not make a principal distinction between the value of human beings and that of other beings. From this viewpoint the value of certain human individuals might not be greater than the value of knowledge.

Therefore, the researcher should have the freedom to choose his or her research problem and method for when, where and how to publish the results of his or her inquiry. The researcher should also have the freedom of action to make observation, conduct experiments and test his or her hypotheses, according to methodological norms or criteria stipulated by the scientific community and the ethics of scientific research. Thus both the scientist's freedom of choice and his or her freedom of action are restricted by research ethics and methodological principles, e.g. objectivity and truth. Objectivity here is epistemological, not ontological. It implies that the results of scientific research should be assessed according to honesty, carefulness, openness, correctness, impartiality, and inter-subjective testability.[24]

The ethics of scientific research are intended to protect human beings and other living beings through respect for human dignity, integrity, autonomy, and the principles of informed consent, confidentiality, justice, etc. (Helsinki Declaration and Nuremberg codex). All these ethical principles are based on and justified by the Kantian humanistic concept of the human being. Thus an experiment to clone human beings is morally unacceptable and legally forbidden because this kind of research harms human integrity, dignity and worth. The latter values (human dignity and worth) limits scientific freedom of action, thus leading us to the next type of argument.

As to the arguments against the limitation of scientific freedom, first (case IV), if knowledge is conceived as having either intrinsic or extrinsic value that is greater than the value of the human being then the researcher's freedom should *not* be limited or restricted by any consideration used to defend, protect or promote the value of the human individual (non-humanism). Second (case V), scientific freedom should not be limited if knowledge has intrinsic value, whilst the human being has only extrinsic value (non-humanism). In this view, the researcher is not always morally obligated to follow the principles of research ethics, implying that researchers can use human individuals as a means for acquiring knowledge. This is what happened under the Nazi regime in Germany during World War II, when Jews and certain other groups of people were evaluated as having less value than

24 See J. Searle, *The Construction of Social Reality* (Free Press, 1995), pp. 7–10 and 33; I. Hacking, *The Social Construction of What?* (Harvard University Press 1999), p. 105.

scientific knowledge. Therefore, they were not only slaughtered but also used in experiments without any consideration of either their informed consent or their enormous suffering. The Nuremberg doctor's trial established, the Nuremberg code in 1947, and in 1964 the World Medical Association formulated the Helsinki code for research ethics (later amended).

These codes, which cover research on human beings and animals, have their foundation in a Kantian humanistic view of the human being. By contrast, arguments against the limitation of scientific freedom suggest a non-humanistic view of the human being.[25]

Third (case VI), if both knowledge and the human being are attributed intrinsic value, but the intrinsic value of knowledge is greater than that of the human being, there is no principal reason for the limitation of scientific freedom.

Let us now turn to the situation (case VII) in which there are only pragmatic arguments for or against the limitation of scientific freedom. If both knowledge and the human being are attributed exactly the same extrinsic value, or if both are attributed the same intrinsic value, then deciding how to limit the scholar's freedom in his or her search for knowledge is difficult. In such a case, if the researcher's freedom to do research conflicts with the realization of certain prioritized goals, the only way of solving the conflict seems to be the use of *pragmatic* criteria. For example, a government may find limiting scientific freedom necessary for practical reasons, e.g. a state may argue that money spent on research is more useful in health care and education.

The viewpoint that human beings and knowledge have the same extrinsic or intrinsic value implies a non-humanistic view of the human being, as the Kantian and post-Kantian humanists maintain that all human beings have the same dignity and worth, which give them all the same basic human rights: human dignity makes human beings unique in relation to all other beings. A non-humanistic view of the human being denies the uniqueness of the human being.[26] The non-humanistic view denies what both forms of humanism assert, and

25 An extreme non-humanistic view of the human being is defended by philosopher Michael Tooley, who grounds the value of an individual human being in his or her current capacity and ability to exercise his or her autonomy, freedom of will, and freedom of choice and action. Tooley declares: 'I believe that a new-born baby does not possess the concept of a continuing self … [thus] infanticide during a time interval shortly after birth must be morally acceptable' (M. Tooley, 'Abortion and Infanticide', in P. Singer (ed.), *Applied Ethics* (Oxford University Press, 1986) p. 83). Following Tooley means that one can do research on new-born babies without obeying ethical principles or norms.

26 P. Singer, 'All Animals are Equals', in P. Singer (ed.), *Applied Ethics* (Oxford University Press, 1986) 215–228.

emphasizes the difference among human individuals with regard to their acquired extrinsic value.[27] As already indicated, a non-humanistic view of the human being evaluates and may attribute a certain value to each individual according to his or her effort, merit and contribution to society's welfare, all of which presupposes the individual's exercise of his freedom of choice.

5. THE DUTY OF SOCIETY TO PREVENT ABUSE OF SCIENTIFIC FREEDOM

If the arguments for the limitation of scientific freedom are reasonable, then some actors should have the duty and moral obligation to watch over the use of scientific freedom. This section attempts to answer the following question: Who is responsible for watching over the misuse of scientific freedom, limiting it, and criticizing, morally condemning, or taking legal actions against those who disrespect it? In other words, who has the legal duty and moral responsibility to impose limits and accountability on researchers for any disrespect and misuse of scientific freedom? This question is relevant because of the risk that researchers may misuse their freedom in some areas of inquiry, in research dealing with medical, social service or vulnerable groups in the welfare state (e.g., children, persons with disabilities and mental patients). In these cases the state is obligated to ensure the right to informed consent against the possible unjustifiable paternalistic attitude of the researcher.[28] From a humanistic and democratic viewpoint, the following institutions and persons may be responsible for preventing and or punishing the abuse of scientific freedom:

- Institutions responsible for the funding and promotion of scientific research
- The researcher him- or herself (given his or her moral integrity)[29]
- The scientific community (both national and international)
- Committees for research ethics for different fields of scientific inquiry
- Colleagues and peer reviewers (national and international)
- The government, which finances national research projects
- Publishers of the results of scientific research
- Consumers of scientific knowledge

---

27 Ibid.

28 Cf. E. Bogolub and T. Nigel, 'Parental Consent and the Ethics of Research with Foster Children. Beginning a Cross-Cultural Dialogue', 4 *Qualitative Social Work* 3 (2005), 271–292.

29 G. Eriksson, 'Universitet, samhälle och forskaransvar' [University, society and responsibility of researchers], in L. Rydén (ed.), *Etik för forskare. En antologi med utgångspunkt i arbetet med Uppsalakodexen* [Ethics for researchers. An anthology based on the work with Uppsala codex]. Report No. 1 (Swedish National Board of Universities and Colleges, 1990) p. 3f.

Reasons for restricting or limiting the researcher's freedom of action or liberty should be based on the following types of values:

- Human dignity and worth, and fundamental human rights
- The ideals of scientific research, i.e. the search for truth and for publicly verified, valid knowledge
- The integrity and image of the scientific research or enterprise
- The belief that scientific knowledge belongs to humanity as a common good[30]
- The supreme interests of the community, the society, the state and humanity (with regard to security, public health, dignity, integrity, fundamental human rights and individual autonomy, human survival and peace)
- Values implied by laws that forbid certain acts (e.g. 'obscenity, pornography, and libel, also apply to academic discourse and publication')
- Ethical norms that forbid misconduct in scientific research, e.g. plagiarism, fabrication and falsification of data.[31]

Both Kantian and post-Kantian humanism regard human dignity as the foundation and ultimate justification of human rights. The goal of scientific research is to learn the truth about reality and to construct valid knowledge, regardless of how the concepts of truth and valid knowledge are defined.[32] This is an important reason for emphasizing that the misuse of scientific freedom can lead to misconduct, which is ethically unacceptable because it harms science itself and the integrity of research:

> Research misconduct is significant misbehaviour ... that intentionally impedes the progress of research, or that risk corrupting the scientific record or compromising the integrity of scientific practices. Such behaviours are unethical and unacceptable in proposing, conducting, or reporting research, or in reviewing the proposals or research of others.[33]

The belief that scientific knowledge belongs to humanity as a common good and the belief that a common good is one of the supreme interests of the community and humanity are closely related to each other. As the American sociologist Robert Merton argues, scientific knowledge is not the private property of anybody,

---

30 J. Wiesner, 'An interview with J. Wiesner', in L. Rydén (ed.), *Etik för forskare* ... [Ethics for researchers ...], 1990, 91–101.

31 Resnik, *The Ethics of Science* ..., pp. 80f.

32 B. Danermark et al., *Explaining Society. Critical realism in the social sciences* (Routledge, 2002).

33 Integrity and Misconduct in Research: Report of the Commission on Research Integrity (U.S. Department of Health and Human Services, 1995).

but belongs to humanity.[34] Following physicist John S. Bell one may argue that '[m]oral progress is more important than scientific progress', and the researcher should not use his or her freedom, power or privilege to monopolize it.[35] In addition, all the values, explicit or implicit, in point are protected, defended and promoted by the following principles of the ethics of scientific research: respect for human dignity and integrity and participants' identity, autonomy, informed consent, beneficence, non-maleficence, confidentiality and justice.[36]

In sum, given that responsibility implies freedom of action, researchers should use their freedom in such way that they can show respect for the values that apply to them and their research as well as regard for human dignity.

6. CONCLUSIONS

This chapter has defined, presented and discussed scientific freedom and its justification, which include the ethical value attributed to scientific knowledge. It has also pointed out that human dignity and basic human rights limit scientific freedom, especially when the human being is attributed more value than knowledge. The chapter analyzed the relationship between the value of knowledge (as the foundation and justification of scientific freedom) and human dignity (as the limit of scientific freedom) in terms of intrinsic and extrinsic value attributions. The analysis shows a number of logically possible ways in which the values attributed to knowledge and to the human being are related both to each other and to scientific knowledge. These relationships leave us with three main arguments related to the limitation of scientific freedom:

- Scientific freedom should be limited either when the human being is attributed intrinsic value, whilst knowledge is attributed only extrinsic value, or when either the intrinsic or extrinsic value attributed to knowledge is less than that attributed to the human being.
- Scientific freedom should not be limited when knowledge is attributed greater intrinsic or extrinsic value than the human being.

---

34 R. Merton and N.W. Storer (eds.), *The sociology of science: Theoretical and empirical investigations*, (University of Chicago Press, 1973).

35 J.S. Bell, 'An interview with Dr. John S. Bell, November 29, 1983', in L. Rydén, *Etik för forskare ...* [Ethics for researchers ...], 103–105.

36 Cf. Helsinki code, Nuremberg code, Belmont Report 1979 and APA 2002, in K.S. Bordens and B.B. Abbott, *Research design and Methods. A Process Approach* (McGraw-Hill, 2008), 188–215; F. Mishna et al. 'Tapping the Perspectives of Children. Emerging Ethical Issues', 3 *Qualitative Research, Qualitative Social Work* 4 (2004), 449–468.

- No argument exists for or against the limitation of scientific freedom when both knowledge and the human being are attributed either the same intrinsic or the same extrinsic value.

This chapter has also pointed out that individual researchers, the scientific community at large, certain institutions, governments and consumers of scientific knowledge are ethically and legally responsible for limiting scientific freedom on moral grounds. Finally, it has argued that the basic values on which the limitation of scientific freedom should be based and justified are human dignity, individual personal integrity and basic human rights – which in the humanistic view are equal for all human beings.

CHAPTER 8
AUTONOMY AND DIGNITY IN CLINICAL MEDICAL RESEARCH ON ADULTS WITH COGNITIVE IMPAIRMENT

Salla Lötjönen

1. INTRODUCTION

Respect for human dignity and individual autonomy are essential values in medical research.[1, 2] These values have taken many forms in the international regulation of medical research since the middle of the twentieth century. The Finnish Medical Research Act (488/1999) defines 'medical research' as research involving intervention in the integrity of a person for increasing knowledge of the causes, symptoms, diagnosis, treatment and prevention of diseases, or the nature of disease in general.[3] Adding the word 'clinical' narrows the focus as follows: the intervention is now required to involve only the physical integrity of the person, not personal integrity in general (which also encompasses psychological integrity). 'Clinical medical research', however, covers medical research on both the use of pharmaceutical products and other interventions to the physical integrity – such as research into surgical methods.

This chapter analyzes the concepts of dignity and autonomy in the regulation of clinical medical research at the Nordic[4] and European levels. It focuses on medical

1 Legislative changes are through June 1, 2008.

2 The author would like to acknowledge the valuable comments by the editors of this book and by Professor Mette Hartlev (University of Copenhagen), Assistant Professor Beate Hovland (Lovisenberg Diakonale Høgskole), and Professor Elisabeth Rynning (Uppsala University) presented either at the time when the paper was presented in a seminar in Bergen, Norway, in May 2007, or as comments to the manuscript. Any remaining errors, however, remain the responsibility of the author.

3 Medical Research Act (9.4.1999/488), Section 2. In addition to humans, the Act applies to research on human embryos or foetuses, but not on cadavers.

4 Although the Nordic countries comprise Denmark, Finland, Iceland, Norway and Sweden, Iceland has been excluded from this chapter due to the author's linguistic inability to verify the data from original sources.

research on adults with a cognitive impairment, especially those suffering from dementia. Although the diagnosis of illness belonging to the group of symptoms categorized as dementia does not in itself qualify as proof of incapacity for making health-related decisions[5], this chapter starts at the point that the illness has so advanced that the person can no longer make such decisions independently.[6] As medical research with this patient group does not generally require urgent measures, this chapter does not cover the special case of medical research in emergency situations.

2. DIGNITY AND AUTONOMY

There have been many attempts to define 'dignity'.[7] Many have concluded that one single over-reaching definition is difficult to give. International human rights documents also state different, albeit not necessarily conflicting, views on what dignity means. What they all have in common is that they construe 'dignity' as an innate human value, which cannot be given or taken away. This value, which is independent of the will of the person or of any governmental influence, should be inviolable.[8]

Autonomy, likewise, has many definitions.[9] While the most common is that autonomy means 'self-rule' or 'self-determination', views differ on both the source and the content of the right to self-determination. For example, the preparatory documents for the Finnish Constitution state that autonomy derives from the

---

5 A diagnosis of mental illness in itself does not justify restrictions to the exercise of a person's rights. See Principle 3, Council of Europe Recommendation Rec. (1999)4 of the Committee of Ministers to member states on principles concerning the legal protection of incapable adults, and Article 4, Council of Europe Recommendation Rec. (2004)10 of the Committee of Ministers to member states concerning the protection of the human rights and dignity of persons with mental disorder.

6 I have earlier addressed the question of borderline cases in my article S. Lötjönen, *Regulation of Clinical Medical Research on the Decisionally Impaired Adults in Europe*, in *Oikeustiede - Jurisprudentia*, 34, 2003, pp. 355–420.

7 D. Beyleveld and R. Brownsword, *Human Dignity in Bioethics and Biolaw*, Oxford: Oxford University Pres 2001; M. Häyry and T. Takala, *Human dignity, bioethics, and human rights*, in *Developing World Bioethics*, 2005, 5, pp. 225–233, and P. Kemp, *Four Ethical Principles in Biolaw*, in P. Kemp, J.D. Rendtorff and N.M. Johansen (eds.), *Bioethics and Biolaw* (Vol. II - Four Ethical Principles), Copenhagen: Rhodos International Science and Art Publishers and Centre for Ethics and Law 2000, pp. 18–20.

8 The Preamble of the 1948 Universal Declaration of the Human Rights <www.un.org/Overview/rights.html, 27.01.2009, and Note from the Praesidium, Text of the explanations relating to the complete text of the Charter of Fundamental Rights of the European Union, Article 1, www.eucharter.org/home.php?page_id=67, 27.01.2009.

9 T.L. Beauchamp and J.F. Childress, *Principles of Biomedical Ethics* (5th ed.), Oxford: Oxford University Press 2001, p. 57 *et seq.*,Kemp et al. (2000), ibid., pp. 15–18.

concept of freedom.[10] The case law from the European Court of Human Rights (ECtHR) states that self-determination and the protection of physical integrity are an essential part of the right to private life as protected by Article 8 of the European Convention on Human Rights.[11]

This chapter takes the characterization of dignity and autonomy as used by the Council of Europe as its starting point. These same concepts are also used in European Union documents[12] and in medical research, e.g. in Directive 2001/20/EC on the conduct of clinical trials on medicinal products for human use (Clinical Trials Directive).[13] Although the best known and probably the most influential of all Council of Europe conventions, the European Convention on Human Rights (ECHR) does not mention dignity at all, whereas dignity is a central concept in the 1997 Convention on Human Rights and Biomedicine (Biomedicine Convention).[14] Nevertheless, even the Biomedicine Convention does not attempt to define dignity. It merely requires that the parties to it "shall protect the dignity and identity of all human beings and guarantee everyone, without discrimination, respect for their integrity and other rights and fundamental freedoms with regard to the application of biology and medicine" (Article 1). Its Preamble also stresses "the need to respect the human being both as an individual and as a member of the human species". The Explanatory Report to the Biomedicine Convention also affirms that the dignity and identity of a human being have to be respected as soon as life begins.[15] However, it has left the controversial question of when life begins for national signatories to decide. Hence, the scope of respect for human dignity, although considered as "an essential value", grounding most of the values that the Biomedicine Convention emphasizes, is somewhat hazy around its edges.[16] Nevertheless, specific mention of the protection of dignity of human

10 Governmental Bill 309/1993 vp., p. 42.

11 *Pretty* v. *the United Kingdom*, April 29, 2002, ECtHR, No. 2346/02, para. 61, *X. and Y.* v. *the Netherlands*, March 26, 1985, Series A no. 91, para. 22, and *Glass* v. *the United Kingdom*, 9 March 2004, No. 61827/00, para. 70.

12 Charter of Fundamental Rights of the European Union, *Official Journal of the European Union*, 18.12.2000, C 364/1.

13 Directive 2001/20/EC of the European Parliament and of the Council of April 4, 2001, on the approximation of the laws, regulations and administrative provisions of the Member States relating to the implementation of good clinical practice in the conduct of clinical trials on medicinal products for human use, *Official Journal of the European Communities*, 1.5.2001, L 121/34.

14 The term 'dignity' is even included in the long title of the Convention itself – Convention for the Protection of Human Rights and Dignity of the Human Being with regard to the Application of Biology and Medicine: Convention on Human Rights and Biomedicine.

15 Para. 19.

16 The Explanatory Report to the Biomedicine Convention, para.9. See also J. Dute, 'The Leading Principles of the Convention on Human Rights and Biomedicine', in Gevers, Hondius and Hubben (eds.), *Health Law, Human Rights and the Biomedicine Convention*, Leiden: Martinus Nijhoff Publishers 2005, pp. 3–12.

beings occurs with regard to Articles 17 (protection of persons not able to consent to research) and 21 (prohibition of financial gain).

Another central concept in the Biomedicine Convention is that of autonomy. Although the words 'autonomy' or 'self-determination' do not appear in the text at all, one of the most fundamental provisions in the whole Biomedicine Convention is Article 5 (on free and informed consent), which the document refers to throughout. The Explanatory Report states that Article 5 expresses the priority given to the autonomy of the patient over any paternalist approaches that might ignore the wishes of the patient.[17] That report also emphasizes autonomy with regard to Article 6, which discusses the involvement of persons not able to give legally valid consent in decision-making.[18] It therefore appears that the Biomedicine Convention extends the scope of autonomy to also cover persons who are legally considered unable to consent for themselves.[19]

3. DIGNITY AND AUTONOMY IN MEDICAL RESEARCH ON ADULTS WHO LACK DECISION-MAKING CAPABILITY

As previously mentioned, both dignity and autonomy are fundamental to medical research. The Explanatory Report to the Biomedicine Convention particularly links the two concepts to three aspects of medical research: the primacy of the human being, the evaluation of the proportion of risk and burdens against the potential benefits, and respect for the wishes of a person without legal capacity to consent.[20]

3.1. PRIMACY OF THE HUMAN BEING

Article 2 of the Biomedicine Convention states: "The interests and welfare of the human being shall prevail over the sole interest of society or science." The same principle already stems from the 1947 Nuremberg Code and is reiterated in the Helsinki Declaration of the World Medical Association.[21, 22] This rule has many

17 Para. 34.

18 Article 6 of the Biomedicine Convention and paras. 44 and 45 of the Explanatory Report.

19 Para. 106 of the Explanatory Report to the Biomedicine Convention with regard to medical research.

20 Paras. 21, 22, 106 and 111.

21 *Trials of War Criminals before the Nuremberg Military Tribunals under Control Council Law* No. 10, Vol. 2, pp. 181–182. Washington, D.C.: U.S. Government Printing Office, 1949.

22 Principle 5 of the Declaration of Helsinki, Ethical Principles for Medical Research Involving Human Subjects (last amended 2000) www.wma.net/e/policy/b3.htm 27.01.2009.

implications in different contexts. With regard to medical research, for example, it means that research should not be conducted for the sole sake of advancing knowledge but rather for advancing human welfare. It also means that, if the same results could be obtained by other means, research should not be conducted on human beings, let alone on persons who lack the ability to decide for themselves. Examples of non-human research include the use of more laboratory testing, computer modelling, and animal studies.

The principle of the primacy of the human being offers special protection to humans. Closely related to the primacy of the human being is the principle by which medical research must first be conducted on persons who can give informed consent, and that only if these studies cannot provide satisfactory results should persons with cognitive impairment be invited to participate. Hence, persons with cognitive impairment have a special safeguard against abuse.

Both the Biomedicine Convention and the Clinical Trials Directive include restrictions of this kind on conducting medical research on adults who are not able to consent. The Biomedicine Convention states as a precondition in Article 17.1(iii) that medical research cannot be conducted on persons who are not capable of consenting unless "research of comparable effectiveness cannot be carried out on individuals capable of giving consent". The Clinical Trials Directive similarly states in Article 5(e) that medical research on adults not able to give valid consent, who have not given consent before the onset of their incapacity, cannot be conducted unless "such research is essential to validate data obtained in clinical trials on persons able to give informed consent or by other research methods and relates directly to a life-threatening or debilitating clinical condition from which the incapacitated adult concerned suffers".

The rule of conducting medical research preferably on competent persons does not stem directly from the principle of the primacy of the human being but from the interrelationship between dignity and autonomy. When the ability to choose for oneself diminishes, the principle of protection takes over. Hence, if the research entails any additional risk, and it can be conducted with persons who can make an informed decision on accepting the risk, the study should not include persons who have no ability to give informed consent for themselves. Almost by definition, all research includes some additional risk or burden, so the principle of 'absence of alternatives' for research on adults not able to consent has taken form as a rule even without a specific risk assessment.

However, by restricting, as much as possible, the access of adults not able to consent to medical research, are we protecting the person with cognitive impairment, or are we actually excluding them from potential benefits? This question is hard to answer, because the justifications for strict protection are well founded in basic ethical and legal principles of protection of vulnerable individuals. However, the justifications for protection may differ for different kinds of medical research and experimental treatments at different stages of development. In the case of early trials, with very little evidence of efficacy but a lot of uncertainty about potential side-effects, it may clearly be preferable to conduct such studies on persons who can give informed consent to the risks involved. But what about late trials, where the evidence on the efficacy of the treatment brings it close to achieving one or another kind of authoritative approval? In such cases, waiting until the medical statisticians are fully convinced and the product tested on individuals able to consent is not only questionable but morally wrong if the investigators themselves believe that the experimental treatment is beneficial to the targeted patient population. However, the Biomedicine Convention and the Clinical Trials Directive make the inclusion of adults not able to consent even in late trials unacceptable until all studies with competent persons have been finalized.[23]

The question is whether it can ever be morally (if not legally) justifiable to include adults not able to consent in *early* trials? Do scientific questions exist about the treatment of adults *not* able to consent, questions that cannot even begin to be answered by studies on persons *able* to give valid consent? The argument on the differences in adult and child metabolism and physical development, used in the context of defending medical research on children, cannot be used in the context of adults not able to consent, as physical age and related differences with regard to human development itself does not cause the inability to consent, as it does with children.[24] As long as the risks involved are acceptable to healthy adult volunteers, usually recruited into the very early stages of drug development (phase 1 safety studies), there appears no reason to conduct research on adults not able to consent instead. Neither is there sufficient justification for recruiting adults not able to consent into the early efficacy studies in the context of conditions with a slow onset, e.g. most cases of dementia. With dementia patients, persons in the early stages may still be able to make decisions on their own wellbeing or participation in research, although the advanced nature of most forms of dementia will

---

23 However, even experimental treatment may be applied in a *treatment* context outside clinical medical research, if the treating physician is convinced that the treatment is indicated in the best interests of that individual patient and the procedural preconditions set by the national pharmaceutical legislation are applied.

24 See, e.g. *Ethical considerations for clinical trials on medicinal products conducted with the paediatric population, Recommendations of the ad hoc group for the development of implementing guidelines for Directive 2001/20/EC relating to good clinical practice in the conduct of clinical trials on medicinal products for human use,* http://ec.europa.eu/enterprise/pharmaceuticals/eudralex/vol-10/ethical_considerations.pdf, 27.01.2009.

eventually erode that ability.[25] However, do we know enough about the nature of the disease to be certain that potential treatments affect both the early and the late(r) stages of the illness in the same way? If a treatment could potentially at least stop the advancement of the disease, wouldn't those with the more advanced stages have more reason to try any means available to hold on to what is left from their cognitive capacity? These are ethical questions we need to ask when applying the principles of dignity and autonomy to the rule of recruiting adults to medical research only when all other alternatives have been explored.

How have the Nordic countries solved the question of inclusion of adults not able to consent in medical research? First, there is variation in the organization of legal regulations on medical research on humans within the Nordic countries. In Denmark and Finland, one law covers both the clinical trials on medicinal products and other medical research, although both laws partially distinguish between clinical trials with medicinal products and other medical research.[26] In Norway and Sweden, these two groups of medical research are structurally treated differently. In Sweden, clinical medical research is covered by two laws, one dealing with medicinal products and the other with other research on humans.[27] In Norway, until recently, only clinical trials with medicinal products were regulated by law. In May 2008 the Norwegian Parliament adopted the Health Research Act, which is expected to come into force in June 2009.[28] The new Health Research Act will complement the existing provisions on research on medicinal products and medical devices thereby resulting into a similar legislative structure as in Sweden.[29] In addition, the Norwegian National Committee on Medical Research Ethics (NEM) has introduced general guidelines on the inclusion of adults with impaired legal competence in health research already in 2005.[30]

---

25 H. Brodaty, R. Dresser, M. Eisner, I. Erkinjuntti, S. Gauthier, N. Graham, D. Jonker, G. Sachs and P. Whitehouse, *Alzheimer's Disease International and International Working Group for Harmonization of Dementia Drug Guidelines for Research Involving Human Subjects with Dementia*, in *Alzheimer Disease and Related Disorders* 13, No. 2/1999, p. 73.

26 Laki lääketieteellisestä tutkimuksesta (9.4.1999/488) (Medical Research Act), in Finland, and Lov om videnskabsetisk komitésystem og behandling af biomedicinske forskningsprojekter (Nr. 402 af 28/05/2003) (Ethics Committee Act), in Denmark. However, in Finland, the distinction does not concern provisions in medical research on persons not able to consent.

27 Lag on etikprövning av forskning som avser människor (2003:460) (Ethics Review Act) and Läkemedelslag (1992:859) (Medicines Act).

28 Forskrift om klinisk utprøving av legemidler til mennesker (FOR 2003-09-24 nr. 1202) (Regulation on Clinical Trials) and Lov om medisinsk og helsefaglig forskning (Besl. O. nr. 83 (2007-2008), Ot.prp.nr.74 (2006-2007), (Health Research Act).

29 Lov om legemidler m.v. (LOV 1992-12-04 nr 132, Medicines Act), Lov om medisinsk utstyr (LOV 1995-01-12 nr 06, Medical Devices Act).

30 Den nasjonale forskningsetiske komité for medisin (NEM) 2005: Retningslinjer for inklusjon av vokse personer med manglende eller redusert samtykkekompetanse i helsefaglig forskning (hereafter the NEM Guidelines) www.etikkom.no/retningslinjer/samtykke, 27.01.2009.

Despite the differences in legislative solutions, all the Nordic countries have incorporated the rule of absence of alternatives into their regulation on medical research on adults not able to consent, with only slight variation in the wording. The wording used to govern medical research on medicinal products closely follows that in Article 5 of the Clinical Trials Directive, which requires that clinical trials on adults not able to consent must be "essential to validate data obtained in clinical trials on persons able to give informed consent or by other research methods". As prior studies can also be conducted "by other research methods", this suggests that the drafters of the directive did not entirely rule out the possibility that early trials could be conducted on adults not able to consent. Prior studies on persons able to consent is not thus a definite prerequisite but only an option.

However, the Nordic provisions that concern other clinical medical research than that on medicinal products allow only research projects that "cannot with similar benefit be conducted by including legally competent trial subjects of legal capacity" or "projects that can only be carried out by the inclusion of individuals comprised by the age group, illness or condition concerned".[31] Although the formulation of the Clinical Trials Directive appears to give a wider option for early trials with adults unable to give valid consent than the Biomedicine Convention, when one reads them together with other conditions for medical research on incompetent adults under Article 5, both formulations of the principle of human primacy essentially lead to the same result. As all Nordic provisions closely follow either the Clinical Trials Directive or the Biomedicine Convention, no real distinction between the Nordic approaches exists. However, neither is there room in national legislation for the inclusion of adults not able to consent in trials along with competent persons for an unrelated illness (e.g. a dementia patient considered for a cancer trial), even if the preliminary results of that trial would indicate that the treatment is very likely to benefit the participants.

3.2. RISKS VERSUS BENEFITS

Although the requirement of ethics committee approval and the general precondition of an appropriate balance between risks and benefits in clinical medical research protect research participants overall, particular protection has been considered necessary for persons who are not able to give informed consent. According to the Biomedicine Convention, if non-therapeutic research (i.e. where the research has no potential of producing results directly benefiting the health of the person concerned) on persons incapable of giving consent is accepted in

31 See, e.g. Danish Ethics Committee Act, Secs. 13(2) and 13(3).

national jurisdiction, the risk and burden involved can only be minimal.[32] The Explanatory Report to the Biomedicine Convention does not give much guidance, giving a single blood sample as an example of an acceptable risk and burden.[33] The reasoning for the minimal risk requirement is explained to prevent instrumentalization and to protect the dignity of the research participants. In the Clinical Trials Directive, the precondition is even more stringent. According to Article 5(i) of the Directive, a trial with a medicinal product on adults unable to give valid consent must involve grounds for expecting that administering the medicinal product to be tested will produce for the patient a benefit that outweighs the risks or produce no risk at all. Non-therapeutic trials with even a minimal risk appear therefore not allowed by the Clinical Trials Directive, as hardly any medical procedure will satisfy the stringent condition of 'no risk'.

In the Nordic legislation, the approach to the acceptable level of risk again follows the structural decision made as to whether to have separate provisions for clinical medical research on medicinal and non-medicinal treatments.

Finland follows the Biomedicine Convention, allowing even non-therapeutic research, as long as the risk of harming or distressing the subject is 'only very slight'. In addition, unless the research is not likely to directly benefit the research subject's health, it must be likely to be of special benefit to the health of people in the same age group or with the same state of health.[34]

Sweden follows the strict 'no risk' requirement for medicinal products in non-therapeutic trials, allowing them for other research only if its aim is to benefit the subject or somebody else suffering from the same or similar problem and if the research involves only an insignificant risk of harm or inconvenience to the research subject.[35]

The Norwegian Regulation on Clinical Trials does not appear to consider the possibility of non-therapeutic trials: it requires that for the trial to be allowed, there has to be reason for believing that the results will directly benefit the health of the subject *and* that the trial entails only minimal risk or distress for the subject.[36] Both the existing NEM Guidelines and the Health Research Act, however, recognize the possibility of non-therapeutic research on the condition that the risk and burden attached to the procedure is insignificant.[37]

32 Article 17.2(ii).
33 Para. 111.
34 Medical Research Act, Sec. 7.
35 Medicines Act, sec. 13 f(3), Ethics Review Act, Sec. 21.2.
36 Regulation on Clinical Trials, Secs. 4–3(d) and 4–3(f).
37 Health Research Act, Sec. 18.1, and NEM Guidelines, Principle 3.

The Danish Act on ethical review of biomedical research projects is another exception amongst Nordic provisions, because it does not set specific risk levels for research on medicinal products at all; however, non-therapeutic research is allowed (benefit is only required to the *group* of patients instead of each individual patient).[38] In clinical trials with medicinal products, the only provision on risk is the general requirement of a favourable risk assessment by the ethics committee. In that connection, the ethics committee shall carry out the assessment "with due regard to whether the trial subjects are themselves able to give their informed consent" or whether consent from a proxy is necessary.[39] For a research project that does *not* involve medicinal products, non-therapeutic research is allowed on condition that the research project "is expected to be of considerable benefit to the group of patients comprised by the same age group, illness or condition as the trial subject and that the project entails only minimal risk and discomfort for the trial subject".[40] Again, it is somewhat surprising that with regard to research on medicinal products in Denmark, the nature of the research project is much more liberally regulated than for those that does *not* involve medicinal products.

3.3. RESPECTING THE WISHES OF A PERSON NOT ABLE TO GIVE VALID CONSENT

The best illustration of the principle of autonomy in medical research is the requirement of informed consent. The Biomedicine Convention does not give one simple definition of informed consent although Article 5 highlights "appropriate information as to the purpose and nature of the intervention as well as on its consequences and risks". The Clinical Trials Directive defines informed consent as

> a decision, which must be written, dated and signed, to take part in a clinical trial, taken freely after being duly informed of its nature, significance, implications and risks and appropriately documented, by any person capable of giving consent or, where the person is not capable of giving consent, by his or her legal representative; if the person concerned is unable to write, oral consent in the presence of at least one witness may be given in exceptional cases, as provided for in national legislation.[41]

As the definition makes evident, informed consent can be given by the legal representative of the participant, if the participant him- or herself lacks the

---

38 Ethics Committee Act, Sec. 13.1.
39 Ibid., Sec. 12.2.
40 Ibid., Sec. 13.3.
41 Article 2(j) of the Clinical Trials Directive (20/2001/EC).

capacity to give it.[42] Respect for autonomy is often considered to cease with the diminishing cognitive competence to make decisions for oneself. However, both the Additional Protocol concerning Biomedical Research and the Clinical Trials Directive require that the person concerned, even if considered unable to give the legal informed consent, has to be informed according to his or her capacity of the upcoming trial and the risks and benefits involved.[43] Moreover, the authorization from the proxy should consider the person's presumed will and previously expressed wishes or objections.[44]

Indeed, the Clinical Trials Directive even provides an opportunity for the person unable to consent to give a valid informed consent *prior* to the onset of incapacity, an act that would override all additional provisions aimed at protecting the adult not able to consent (including the need for proxy consent).[45] Furthermore, according to the Biomedicine Convention and the Clinical Trials Directive, the objection of an adult unable to consent to participate must be obeyed, although the Directive rather vaguely obligates the investigator to "*consider*" the subject's wish to withdraw or refuse, and connects this obligation to an adult unable to consent but who is still capable of forming an opinion and assessing the information received.[46]

The question is which principles these requirements rely on, if that of respecting the autonomy of a person is already lost by the loss of capacity to consent. The Explanatory Report to the Biomedicine Convention explains that "the rule prohibiting the carrying out of the research against the wish of the subject reflects concern for the autonomy and dignity of the person in all circumstances, even if the person is considered legally incapable of giving consent".[47] Therefore, the Council of Europe's vision of autonomy is *not* restricted only to persons who are legally competent to decide on their own affairs. This vision also appears complemented by the protective view of dignity, which does not require any act of cognitive will from the participant: a sign of distress qualifies as an 'objection' and therefore is sufficient for preventing the continuation of the research procedure.

---

42 In the Nordic countries defining a legal representative, i.e. who can consent on behalf of the incapacitated adult, may also have implications to the emphasis given to the previously made wishes of the subject. This theme is outside the scope of this chapter.

43 Additional Protocol to the Convention on Human Rights and Biomedicine concerning Biomedical Research, Article 15.1(iv), and the Clinical Trials Directive, Article 5(b).

44 Additional Protocol on Biomedical Research, Article 15.1(iv), Clinical Trials Directive 5(a).

45 The introduction to Article 5, which lists the additional conditions for clinical trials on incapacitated adults, states that these conditions only apply to "incapacitated adults who have not given or not refused informed consent before the onset of their incapacity".

46 Biomedicine Convention, Article 17.1(v), Additional Protocol on Biomedical Research, Article 15.1(v), and Clinical Trials Directive Article 5(c).

47 Para. 106.

Again, this sensitive balance of the two principles has been incorporated into law in the Nordic countries with two duties of involving the adult not able to give valid consent in the decision-making: informing the subject and considering the subject's previous wishes and presumed present will, and respecting the subject's objections.

3.3.1. *Informing the subject and considering his or her previous wishes and presumed will*

Each of the existing Nordic laws on medical research includes a provision on giving information to the adult not able to consent, although the subject is considered unable to give independent informed consent.[48] Many of the laws governing this area are so recent that the requirements of the Clinical Trials Directive were already known when the laws were drafted. For acts passed before the Clinical Trials Directive, a later amendment incorporated this provision together with other modifications needed to implement the Clinical Trials Directive into national legislation. However, none of the laws in the Nordic area give independent legal validity to previously expressed wishes (e.g. in the form of an advance directive) for medical research on adults not able to consent (or in connection to medical research in general). The criteria for the specificity of information required from an advance directive to replace informed consent by proxy altogether is indeed difficult if not impossible, to achieve.[49] However, although an advance directive would not qualify as valid informed consent, it could very well function as an aid to the proxy when he or she considers the presumed will of the subject. This will is particularly mentioned as a relevant factor in proxy decision-making in the Finnish, Norwegian and the Swedish provisions on clinical trials on medicinal products.[50]

The Danish formulation requires proxy consent to express 'the interest' of the trial subject, leaving open whether that interest is based on objective or subjective criteria.[51] For the Swedish solution, as with medical research in non-medicinal area, the Ethics Review Act states first that medical research on adults not able to consent is conducted *without* consent (Section 20). Later, however, Section 22

48 Finnish Medical Research Act, Sec. 7.4, Swedish Ethics Review Act, Sec. 22, Swedish Medicines Act, Sec. 13 a(2), Norwegian Regulation on Clinical Trials, Sec. 4-3(c), Norwegian Health Research Act, Sec. 17-6, Danish Ethics Committee Act, Sec. 17.2.

49 S. Lötjönen, *Medical Research on Patients with Dementia – The Role of Advance Directives in European Legal Instruments*, in *European Journal of Health Law*, 13/2006, pp. 235-261.

50 Finnish Medical Research Act, Section 7.3, Norwegian Regulation on Clinical Trials, Section 4-3(b) and the Swedish Medicines Act, Section 13 b(3).

51 Ethics Committee Act, Sec. 17(2), and Ministerial Order No. 806 of July 12, 2004, on Information and Consent at Inclusion of Trial Subjects in Biomedical Research Projects, Sec. 6.2.

states that the subject shall as much as possible be informed personally about the study, and that there has to be *common understanding* with the closest relatives of the subject and the subject's legal representative. As, strictly speaking, no informed consent is required for non-medicinal medical research on adults unable to consent in Sweden (unless "common understanding" is so interpreted), that no legal requirement exists that consent must represent the subject's presumed will is only logical. However, as authorization by a legal representative is a prerequisite in the Biomedicine Convention for medical research on persons not able to consent[52], one must question the compatibility of the Ethics Review Act with the Biomedicine Convention.

3.3.2. Respecting the objection of the research subject

As mentioned previously, the provisions in both the Biomedicine Convention and the Clinical Trials Directive refer to the significance of an objection made by the research participant, despite a difference in its potential effects. Although the Nordic provisions are generally divided between medicinal and non-medicinal research (following the dichotomy of the Clinical Trials Directive and the Biomedicine Convention), this division does not exist for objection by the research subject. All the Nordic countries have adopted the stringent prohibition against continuing research if the subject objects (the criterion of the Biomedicine Convention) in all clinical medical research across the board. Even in Denmark, where Section 7.3 of the Ethics Committee Act states only that "[i]mportance shall be attached to the indications of the trial subject *in so far as these are relevant*", an amending ministerial order clarifies that the study "shall not be initiated or continued on the background of surrogate consent if the trial subject objects to it".[53]

4. CONCLUSIONS

This chapter has analysed the provisions on clinical medical research on adults unable to give valid consent in the Nordic countries and at the European level with regard to dignity and autonomy. Although a systematic review of all provisions relevant to medical research on incapacitated adults has not been possible, the provisions covered here reveal the central dilemma of all regulation

---

52 Article 17.1(iv).

53 Finnish Medical Research Act, Sec. 7.4, Swedish Medicines Act, Sec. 13 c, Swedish Ethics Review Act, Sec. 22, Norwegian Regulation on Clinical Trials, Sec. 4–3(b), Norwegian Health Research Act, Sec. 18–1(b), and Danish Ministerial Order No. 806 of July 12, 2004, on Information and Consent at Inclusion of Trial Subjects in Biomedical Research Projects, Sec. 17.2.

of medical research: whether to emphasize the protective provisions that restrict research or the empowering provisions that give more emphasis on participant self-determination. Both at the Nordic and at the European level the protective emphasis has been chosen with regard to adults who are unable to give valid consent. This choice is understandable, as their ability to decide has been impaired, and the self-determination of the participant has had to give way to the more protective measures. However, seeing that the balance between these two factors is not entirely clear, is essential. The effects of the principle of autonomy do not disappear even if the capacity to give a legally valid informed consent has been taken away. Giving the patient a chance to participate by informing him or her about the project, paying attention to his or her presumed (and previous) wishes, and respecting the signs of objection all exemplify a mixture of both principles – dignity and autonomy.

Overall, given the authority of the Council of Europe and European Union documents, the Nordic regulation on medical research on adults not able to consent seems rather similar. Although no differences between the countries were found under many of the topics investigated, some interesting anomalies appeared. For risk assessment in non-therapeutic clinical medical research, Norway and Denmark are at opposite ends of the spectrum. Whereas Norway does not allow non-therapeutic research with medicinal products on adults not able to consent, Denmark apparently (at least in a literal interpretation of the Ethics Committee Act) allows it without any specific restriction of the risk. Finland uses the minimal risk criterion for non-therapeutic clinical trials on both medicinal products and other treatment methods. Both Finland and Denmark are apparently testing the limits of compatibility with the Clinical Trials Directive, which requires that non-therapeutic clinical trials on medicines should not involve any risk at all.

As for issues involving informed consent and respecting the wishes of the participant, Sweden stands alone by not recognizing informed consent by proxy. However, Denmark has also come up with the 'presumed will' criterion, not merely as a subjective evaluation of the participant's predicted wish, but also allowing a more neutral and objective evaluation of the participant's interest. While one may wonder why Denmark did not formulate the true effect of participant objection at the level of the Ethics Committee Act itself, they did so through a ministerial order. Although the Clinical Trials Directive leaves it to the investigator to consider what effect an objection from a person unable to consent should receive, the Biomedicine Convention requires absolute adherence to objection and immediate termination of the research procedures. As the Biomedicine Convention provisions make no exceptions for clinical trials on medicinal products, it is the Biomedicine Convention provisions that should prevail.

However, despite the letter of the law, only the implementation of the provisions in practice really count when the true value of respecting the dignity and autonomy of a person is tested. No systematic cases of abuse of patients not able to consent in clinical medical research have materialized from the Nordic countries. One hopes to see this pattern continue, as the treatment of adults unable to consent requires more experimentation – and if the public loses its confidence in science and researchers, the likely result is that the conditions for legitimate research will become even stricter.

CHAPTER 9
NORDIC DISABILITY PROTECTION MEETING SUPRANATIONAL EQUAL TREATMENT POLICY – A BOOST FOR THE HUMAN RIGHTS OF PERSONS WITH DISABILITIES?

Rune Halvorsen and Bjørn Hvinden

1. INTRODUCTION

This chapter examines how the evolving supranational equal treatment approach is challenging the profile of Nordic disability policy. We ask whether the adoption of binding disability rights in the Nordic countries will contribute to ensuring the equal treatment, human dignity and autonomy of persons with disabilities. We answer this question in three steps. First, we outline the characteristics of Nordic disability protection and what the Nordic countries have achieved in the social inclusion of persons with disabilities. Second, we examine the empirical support for arguing that the Nordic disability protection model has inherent weaknesses. Third, we consider whether the negotiated compromises of organized interests behind the Nordic welfare model will promote or hinder the successful incorporation of the equal treatment legislation stemming from the initiatives of the United Nations, the Council of Europe and the European Union. The question remains whether the established welfare model could undermine the potential impact of the new legal instruments.

2. NORDIC DISABILITY PROTECTION: A SYSTEM PERSPECTIVE

By disability protection, we refer to the totality of policy measures with intended or unintended consequences for the welfare, living conditions, autonomy, participation and dignity of persons with disabilities in the Nordic countries. In this sense disability protection covers broad areas of policy and sectors of society. Individual countries have not only different welfare policy measures but also differing approaches to disability protection. We argue that comparing the overall systems of disability policy and legislation in the Nordic countries will clarify the strengths and weaknesses of existing approaches and the scope for policy learning and improvements. For this purpose we distinguish between three subsystems of protection that are intended to meet the needs and risks of persons with disabilities:

- The *social benefit subsystem* aims at providing income security for people out of paid work, redistributing monetary resources, and compensating for higher expenses (e.g. diet, transportation).
- The *social services subsystem* aims at both providing benefits in kind to compensate for impairments and offering medical assistance and rehabilitation, education and vocational training, assistive technology, personal assistance, and other services meant to improve the independence and social participation of persons with disabilities.
- The *social regulation subsystem* involves government efforts at influencing the functioning of markets and the behaviour of non-governmental actors through legislation, financial incentives or persuasion, with the aim of promoting social policy objectives.[1]

The social benefit and services subsystems aim at redistributing resources among differing population groups and equalizing life chances. The provisions are intended to give individuals resources that compensate them for disadvantages and that enable them to participate in the labour market and other social sectors. Although the main focus has been on helping individuals to adjust to society and its demands, provisions since the 1980s have emphasized the goal of promoting the autonomy of the person with disabilities. By contrast, social regulation policies aim at remedying market failures.[2] Governments seek to influence the functioning of markets and the behaviour of non-governmental actors, e.g. by setting legal standards for health and security and labour protection or by stimulating the development of industry standards for the accessibility and usability of different products and services. We argue here that the Nordic countries have been characterized by an imbalance among the three subsystems of disability protection.

---

1 M.-L. Bemelmans-Videc, R.C. Rist and E. Vedung (eds.), *Carrots, sticks and sermons* (Transaction Publishers, 1998).

2 G. Majone, 'The European Community between social policy and social regulation', 31 *Journal of Common Market Studies*, 2 (1993), pp. 153–70.

3. THE NORDIC MODEL OF WELFARE AND DISABILITY PROTECTION

In general, the Nordic model of welfare has stood for public responsibility for guaranteeing cash benefits and social services to citizens through publicly funded provisions that cater to all needs and the whole population, financed largely through tax revenues. The Nordic income maintenance systems have been fairly generous, with the official aim of providing benefits enabling people to maintain about the same standard of living during periods of unemployment. To fund these systems, the Nordic countries have promoted as high a labour market participation as possible. Public authorities have taken an active role *vis-à-vis* other main social institutions, especially through regulation of the labour market and intervention in the workings of the economy in general.

The Nordic welfare model has largely made the individual independent of the family, e.g. public authorities have to a larger extent than most other European countries assumed responsibility for providing care services for the sick and elderly and for kindergartens for children.[3] By contrast, policies in other European countries have built on the assumption that the public authorities should generally leave the market to itself and provide cash support or care services only in cases where the family is unable to provide necessary support to their family members.

Not all characteristics of the Nordic model will necessarily be manifest in all areas of welfare policy, e.g. the area of disability protection. Arguably, an 'ideal-type'[4] or model of Nordic disability protection would have the following key elements: first, public authorities would provide universalistic income transfers at a fairly high and predictable level for persons with disabilities who require such transfers. Second, public authorities would strongly emphasize measures for promoting participation in gainful employment for people with disabilities, in terms of both assisting entry for those outside the ordinary labour market and helping those in work to keep their jobs for as long as possible.

Third, public authorities would supply ample social services to enable persons with disabilities to enjoy dignity and autonomy in their daily lives, by not having to rely on family or on charity to meet their care needs. Alternatively, the authorities might grant persons with disabilities cash payments or vouchers,

---

3 G. Esping-Andersen, *Social foundations of postindustrial economies* (Oxford University Press, 1999); A.L. Ellingsæter and A. Leira (eds.) *Politicising parenthood in Scandinavia. Gender relations in welfare states* (Policy Press, 2006).

4 M. Weber, *The Methodology of the Social Sciences* (Free Press, 1949), p. 49.

enabling them to purchase such services themselves. Fourth, public authorities would make systematic efforts to ensure accessibility and usability for all, including persons with disabilities, by regulating the design of the environment and goods and services, e.g. the built environment, transport systems, and information and communications technology. Fifth, the state would seek to coordinate all aspects of disability protection into a mutually supportive and interdependent system.

In practice, Nordic disability protection systems have lived up to these ideal requirements to different degrees. Within some areas, especially *income maintenance*, these requirements appear to have been reasonably achieved. Since the 1980s all the Nordic countries have provided universal and fairly generous cash benefits, granted to a substantial proportion of persons with disabilities. But on closer examination this relative success partly reflects relative failures in other areas, e.g. the promotion of employment participation and removal of barriers for equal treatment and participation. Since the early 1990s the high level of public spending on income maintenance, especially disability pensions, has caused great concern among public authorities in the Nordic countries. A number of reforms have aimed at tightening up the schemes through more restrictive eligibility criteria, a new or reinforced emphasis on the conditionality of benefits, and enhanced efforts at making self-sufficiency through gainful employment a more realistic alternative.[5] Furthermore, a number of reforms have been introduced for improving the Nordic countries' performance in other areas, such as measures for promoting employment participation, accessibility, independent living and service coordination.

It is too early to say whether these initiatives will lead to improved opportunities for participation in society for persons with disabilities. Nevertheless, given that the Nordic countries at least have lived up to some of the 'requirements' of the ideal-type Nordic model of disability protection, we need to ask whether they have done so to the same degree. If there have been large inter-country differences in the degree to which they fulfilled these requirements, we might question the fruitfulness of speaking about a distinct and common Nordic model in this respect.

The next section summarizes the main similarities and differences in achievements of disability protection among the four largest Nordic countries (Denmark,

5 J. Kvist and J. Saari (eds.), *The Europeanisation of social protection* (Policy Press, 2007); B. Hvinden et al., 'Towards activation? The changing relationship between social protection and employment in Western Europe', in M. Kautto et al. (eds.), *Nordic welfare states in the European context* (Routledge, 2001).

Finland, Norway and Sweden) at the start of the 2000s. Unfortunately, this assessment is hampered by the inconsistency in the availability of valid or reliable indicators of success.

3.1. AN ASSESSMENT OF NORDIC DISABILITY PROTECTION IN PRACTICE

3.1.1. Overall policy effort: redistributive provisions

In the early 2000s the Nordic countries did not differ much from other Northern European countries with regard to total expenditures on social protection.[6] However, the Nordic countries gave higher priority to disability issues: at the start of the 2000s they individually spent more on income maintenance and support in cash or in kind for persons with disabilities to engage in social and economic activities than other EU/EEA countries. Whereas the average was 2 per cent of GDP for the EU25, spending on income transfers and other support for persons with disabilities varied within the Nordic group from about 3 per cent of GDP in Finland to about 5 per cent of GDP in Norway. Of the total social expenditures the Nordic countries spent between 13 per cent (Finland) and 19 per cent (Norway) on disability.[7] Given the priority of disability protection in the Nordic countries, all four countries appeared to command the financial resources for providing the best disability protection in the Western world. But did they realize this potential? This section aims to answer this question by discussing how the Nordic countries spent the resources they allocated to disability protection.

3.1.2. The social benefit subsystem: income maintenance

Expenditure: At the start of this millennium the Nordic countries (together with the Netherlands and Poland) spent a larger share of GDP on income maintenance for persons with disabilities than any other European countries.[8] The Nordic countries spent between 3 per cent (Finland) and 4 per cent (Norway) of GDP on disability-related cash benefits.[9] As previously mentioned, governments have introduced several reforms for reducing expenditures and increasing incentives

6 Eurostat, *European social statistics: social protection expenditure and receipts Data 1996–2004* (Office for Official Publications of the European Communities, 2007); *Employment outlook* (OECD, 2007).

7 *European social statistics*, 2007.

8 *Transforming Disability into Ability* (OECD, 2003); S. Grammenos, *Illness, disability and social inclusion* (European Foundation for the Improvement of Living and Working Conditions, 2003).

9 NOSOSCO, *Social Protection in the Nordic Countries 2005* (Nordic Social Statistics Committee, 2007).

for persons with disabilities to seek gainful employment. Eligibility criteria have been made more restrictive and exclusive in terms of the types of diagnoses and conditions accepted. Moreover, income benefits for persons with disabilities are decoupled from old age pension systems and moved into line with short-time benefits, especially unemployment and sickness benefits.

Number of beneficiaries: Although figures for the rates of disability benefit recipiency were incomplete or uncertain, available data suggest that the Nordic countries were among the EU countries with the highest proportion of recipients of income transfers in the working age population (18–64 years) – ranging from 5.4 per cent in Denmark to 10.3 per cent in Sweden.[10] Despite attempts at making the eligibility criteria more restrictive, the share of the working age population receiving disability benefits increased between 1995 and 2005 in all the Nordic countries except Finland, where it decreased.[11]

Overall, redistributive policy in the Nordic countries appears to have contributed to a relatively high degree of equalization of income distribution. The Nordic countries had both the lowest income inequality and the largest effect of social transfers in Europe for reducing the risk of poverty.[12] For the population as a whole, the Nordic countries had a smaller share of poor persons (adults with disposal income below 60 per cent of the median income) after income transference (9–12 per cent) than the average for the EU25 (16 per cent).[13] At the start of this millennium the average disposal income for Nordic persons with disabilities was 80–90 per cent of the average for the working-age population.[14] A recent analysis of data from the European Union Statistics on Income and Living Conditions (EU-SILC) suggests that whereas the proportion of poor people was not significantly higher among Nordic persons with disabilities than in the population as a whole, this proportion was higher among persons with disabilities than in the overall adult population in most other European countries.[15]

---

10 NOSOSCO, *Social Protection in the Nordic Countries (2007)*; *Transforming Disability into Ability* (OECD, 2003).

11 NOSOSCO *Social Protection in the Nordic Countries (2007)*.

12 European Commission, *Joint report on social protection and social inclusion* (Office for Official Publications of the European Communities, 2007); Eurostat, *Europe in figures. Eurostat yearbook* (Office for Official Publications of the European Communities, 2005).

13 'The share of persons with an equivalised disposal income below the risk of poverty threshold, which is set at 60 per cent of the national median equivalised disposal income (after social transfers).' EU-SILC, last update 7 December 2007 (http://epp.eurostat.ec.europa.eu).

14 *Transforming Disability into Ability*, (OECD 2003); J. Ramm, *Inntektsforholdene for grupper med nedsatt funksjonsevne – inntektsregnskap for personer* [Income among groups with disabilities – income statements for persons], Report 18 (Statistics Norway, 2006).

15 T. Ward and S. Grammenos (eds.), *Men and women with disabilities in the EU: Statistical analysis of the LFS ad hoc module and the EU-SILC* (APPLICA and CESEP and ALPHAMETRICS, 2007).

3.1.3. The social benefit subsystem: measures for promoting employment

Expenditures on labour market measures for persons with disabilities: The Nordic countries have generally spent more on active labour market measures (ALMM) than other EU countries (except the Netherlands). ALMM expenditures ranged from 0.6 per cent of GDP in Norway to 1.4 per cent in Denmark, with Finland (0.7 per cent) and Sweden (1 per cent) in the middle, compared to the 0.5 per cent average for the EU25 as a whole.[16] Although the expenditure on ALMM will drain the public purse in the short run, the assumption has been that improved skills and competencies in the labour force will benefit the national economy over time. Public authorities have promoted labour participation through provision of medical rehabilitation, vocational training, and job placement services, and in some cases also publicly subsidized and sheltered jobs.

Available expenditure figures suggest that, among the Nordic countries, Denmark gave the highest and Norway the lowest priority to ALMM overall. However, we get a slightly different picture when we take into account the differing levels of unemployment between the countries and the ways in which the countries spend the resources:

First, there may be good reasons for standardizing ALMM expenditures. Since their unemployment rates varied, the Nordic countries had different 'needs' for spending money on active labour market measures. To compare the overall profile of different countries' expenditures, we can calculate what the expenditure figures would have been if they all had an unemployment rate of 10 per cent. Given that two countries have the same level of spending on active efforts, we can reasonably view the country with the lowest level of unemployment as the more activist of the two, *ceteris paribus*. When we standardize the expenditure figures, we find that Finland (estimated 0.8 per cent) was the least activist and Denmark the most activist (estimated 2.9 per cent), with Norway (1.28) and Sweden (1.3) in the middle.[17] These findings are consistent with those from the late 1990s, when Finland generally spent relatively less on ALMM than the other Nordic countries (after taking into account their unemployment levels).[18]

Second, we also find large differences in how the Nordic countries allocated the resources to ALMM in general. Norway (together with Spain and Ireland) allocated more of their ALMM expenditures to individuals with disabilities than

16 Eurostat, *European social statistics: labour market policy – Expenditure and participants, Data 2004* (Office for Official Publications of the European Communities, 2007).

17 *Employment outlook* (OECD, 2007).

18 B. Hvinden et al. 'Towards activation? The changing relationship between social protection and employment in Western Europe', in *Nordic welfare states in the European context*, (2001).

any other EU country. In comparison, Sweden and Denmark gave higher priority to providing employers with financial incentives (cash benefits and tax reductions) for offering opportunities to jobseekers with disabilities, and were in this respect closer to Continental European countries. Finland was in the middle.[19] Among the Nordic countries Norway and Finland spent more on income maintenance for persons with disabilities while they are participating in qualifying measures, often education.[20] By contrast, Sweden and Denmark emphasized on-the-job experience through support schemes for reasonable accommodation and wage compensation. Although some of these differences undoubtedly are related to differing and inconsistent classifications of expenses across the countries, the broad pattern agrees with past research.[21]

Level of participation in paid work for persons with disabilities: In general, we find a higher total employment rate in the Nordic countries, varying between 69 per cent in Finland and 77 per cent in Denmark, with Sweden at 74 per cent and Norway at 76 per cent, compared to the average 65 per cent in the EU19.[22] Available figures for the employment rates for persons with disabilities are more uncertain and inconsistent, partly because the exact meaning of the questions and categorizations may vary between countries. One set of data suggests that the employment rate for persons with 'severe disabilities' varied considerably among the Nordic countries, with Denmark scoring exceptionally low (28 per cent), Norway performing on average with other European countries (44 per cent), and Finland (56 per cent) and Sweden (58 per cent) achieving better results than most other European countries.[23]

Other data sources on the employment rates for persons with disabilities in general suggest that Sweden had the highest rate (63 per cent) and Norway the lowest (44 per cent).[24] Despite the uncertainties related to the reliability and

---

19 Eurostat, *European social statistics: Labour market policy – Expenditure and participants, Data 2004* (Office for Official Publications of the European Communities, 2007).

20 *Sickness, Disability and Work. Norway, Poland and Switzerland* (OECD, 2006).

21 C. Prinz (ed.), *European disability pension policies: 11 country trends 1970–2002* (Ashgate, 2003); B. Marin et al. (eds.), *Transforming disability welfare policies: towards work and equal opportunities* (Ashgate, 2004).

22 Austria, Belgium, the Czech Republic, Denmark, Finland, France, Germany, Greece, Hungary, Ireland, Italy, Luxembourg, Netherlands, Poland, Portugal, Slovak Republic, Spain, Sweden and United Kingdom, *Employment outlook* (OECD, 2007).

23 M. Blekesaune, *Have some European countries been more successful at employing people with disabilities than others?*, Working Paper 23 (University of Essex, 2007).

24 Statistics Sweden, *Funktionshindrades situation på arbetsmarknaden – 4. kvartalet 2006* [The labour market situation of persons with disabilities – 4th quarter 2006] (the National Labour Market Administration and Statistics Sweden, 2007); B. Olsen and M. Thi Van, *Funksjonshemmede på arbeidsmarkedet. Rapport fra tilleggsundersøkelse til Arbeidskraftundersøkelsen 2.kvartal 2006* [Persons with disabilities in the labour market.

comparability of such figures, there can be no doubt that a large proportion of Nordic citizens with disabilities have been practically excluded from gainful employment. To the extent that they were employed, they more often had marginal positions, e.g. as part-time or temporary workers.

3.1.4. The social services subsystem

Organisation of services for persons with disabilities: Since the 1970s a clear trend has been away from special services such as separate institutions. Public authorities have increasingly incorporated the needs of persons with disabilities into general provisions and services. However, the degree of mainstreaming has varied, depending on the type of impairment. For instance, Norway and Sweden appear to have done more mainstreaming for provisions related to intellectual disability than have Denmark or Finland.[25]

In the Nordic context, Finland has been somewhat of an exception, as Finnish organizations of persons with disabilities (DPOs) have to a greater and longer extent provided services such as medical and vocational rehabilitation, counselling, sheltered work, accommodation, work assessment clinics, and community and social planning. As the economic hardships after World War II delayed the development of the modern Finnish welfare state, DPOs were compelled to develop their own services as substitutes for those missing in the public sector. This situation continues today.

Expenditures on services for persons with disabilities: The Nordic group spent relatively more on services (benefits in kind) than the rest of Europe. The Nordic countries also differed in the balance between public expenditures on cash benefits and services for persons with disabilities. While Norway spent 18 per cent of total disability-related expenditure on services, the corresponding figures for Finland were 26 per cent; Denmark, 31 per cent; and Sweden, 40 per cent.[26] Sweden spent the most on self-directed personal assistance, as Sweden more largely defines such assistance as a legal entitlement, whereas the other Nordic countries tend to consider such assistance a discretionary provision more in line

---

Report from supplementary survey to the Labour Force Survey], *Report 2007/3* (Statistics Norway, 2007); M. M. Miller, J. Høgelund and P. C. Geerdsen, *Handicap og beskæftigelse: Udviklingen mellem 2002 og 2005* [Disability and employment. Developments between 2002 and 2005] (SFI – Danish National Centre for Social Research, 2006).

25 J. Tøssebro, A. Gustavsson and G. Dyrendahl (eds.), *Intellectual Disabilities in the Nordic Welfare States. Policies and Everyday Life* (Norwegian Academic Press, 1996); A. Gustavsson, J. Tøssebro and E. Zakrzewska-Manterys (eds.), *Managing intellectual disability: first person perspectives, policies and services in Sweden, Norway and Poland* (IFiS Publ., 2003).

26 Eurostat, *European social statistics: social protection expenditure and receipts Data 1996–2004* (Office for Official Publications of the European Communities, 2007).

with services that professional helpers define and control.[27] In other words, Sweden more clearly treated persons with disabilities as subjects with legal rights rather than as objects of health and social programmes.[28]

3.1.5. The social regulation subsystem

In the Nordic countries, early regulatory measures included legal provisions giving employers duties in relation to employees with disabilities, such as strengthened job security through the general labour code. While Sweden had one of the strongest frameworks of labour protection legislation, Denmark was among the OECD countries with the weakest job security protection and obligations for employers.[29] Of the Nordic countries, Sweden also appears to have practiced a stricter enforcement of employer obligations for workplace accommodation.[30]

The Nordic welfare model has put stronger emphasis on inclusion through redistributive welfare state provisions rather than through social regulation (e.g. legal duties and financial incentives for employers). However, since the 1990s even the Nordic countries have increasingly been influenced by US-style legal regulation in the disability area, primarily the Americans with Disability Act and the Rehabilitation Act.[31] The US influence has been largely indirect, through policy learning from the British Disability Discrimination Act, and later through the influence of the Article 13 of the Amsterdam treaty and the Employment Framework Directive.[32] Different from the traditional Nordic emphasis on 'mainstreaming', the new social regulation policy has sought to prevent and remedy discrimination on the grounds of disability through separate legal provisions. Rather than compensating for disadvantages, this approach focuses on ensuring equal treatment of all customers and jobseekers in the market.

---

27 O.P. Askheim, 'Personlig assistanse – en nyskapning i den nordisk velferdsstaten' [Personal assistance – an innovation in the Nordic welfare state], 5 *Tidsskrift for velferdsforskning*, 1 (2002), 2–14.

28 Article 19 of the *Convention on the rights of persons with disabilities*, Resolution adopted by the General Assembly, A/RES/61/1 06 (UN, 2007).

29 'Employment protection and labour market performance', *Employment Outlook*, (OECD, 2003), pp. 49–132.

30 A. Inghammar, *Funktionshindrad – med rätt till arbete? En komparativ studie av arbetsrättsliga regleringar kring arbete och funktionshinder* [Disabled – with a right to work? A comparative study of labour law regulations of work and disability in Sweden, England and Germany] (Juristförlaget, 2006); K. Vik, *Employers as a Target Group for Disability Policies: A Comparative Study of the Scandinavian Countries in the 1990s*, MA thesis (Dept. of Sociology and Political Science, NTNU, 1999).

31 P. Blanck et al., *Disability Civil Rights Law and Policy* (Thomson West, 2004).

32 Council Directive 2000/78/EC of 27 November 2000 establishing a general framework for equal treatment in employment and occupation (Official Journal L 303, 02/12/2000, p. 16–22).

Again this policy shift was embraced earlier and more clearly in Sweden than in the other Nordic countries. Sweden has adopted non-discrimination legislation in working life (1999), in higher education (2001), in the trading of goods and services (2003), and in provisions for protecting children and school students (2006). From 2006 the duty of employers to accommodate the workplace also includes new employees. The other Nordic countries have introduced legal provisions against discrimination in employment and occupation: Inspired by Sweden, Norway first adopted legal protection against discrimination in 2001 and later amended the non-discrimination provisions in 2004 to ensure the same level of legal protection as in the EU Employment Framework Directive (2000/78/EC). Finland transposed the employment framework directive in 2004 and Denmark in 2005. While Finland (2000) and Sweden (2002) include in their constitutions a legal provision against discrimination on the grounds of disability, non-discrimination provisions inserted in the penal codes and the constitutions play largely a symbolic role in Europe.[33]

Physical accessibility for persons with mobility impairments: A recent review of policies and regulations requiring accessibility to public transport for persons with disabilities in Norway, Iceland and the EU member states suggests that the Nordic countries are not particularly advanced in this aspect of disability policy, despite their governments' stated commitment to the principle of universal design.[34] Available data suggest that a number of large European cities are more physically accessible than the Nordic capitals for persons with mobility impairments.[35]

As of 2008, the Nordic countries tended to emphasize voluntary commitment, awareness raising and persuasion strategies for promoting universal design and accessibility and usability of goods and services from public and private enterprises and employers. The accessibility requirements in many legal acts are not explicit, leaving one to infer them from the overall purpose of a specific act or through

33 G. Quinn (ed.), *Baseline Study: Disability Discrimination Law in the EU Member States* (European Commission, 2004).

34 A. Tennøy and M.D. Leiren, *Accessible public transport. A view of Europe today - policies, laws and guidelines* (Institute of Transport Economics, 2008); *Regjeringens handlingsplan for økt tilgjengelighet for personer med nedsatt funksjonsevne.* [Norwegian Government Action Plan for Enhanced Accessibility for Persons with Disabilities] (Ministry of the Environment and Ministry of Labour and Social Affairs, 2004); *Uppföljning av den nationella handlingsplanen för handikappolitiken* [Follow-up of the national action plan on disability policy], Report 2005/06:110 (Swedish Government, 2005).

35 *Statusrapport* [Status report] (Norwegian Centre for Documentation on Disability, 2007); *På spåret. Sektorsmyndigheternas arbete mot etappmålen* [On the right track - the work of the sector authorities on the milestone] (Handisam, 2007); A. Tennøy and J.U. Hanssen *Policies, legal frameworks and other means for improving accessibility of public transport systems in the Nordic countries* (Institute of Transport Economics, 2007).

subsequent regulatory guidance or legal proceedings. Alternatively, the actual requirements depend on public employees' use of discretion to decide whether the enterprises comply with the statutory provisions on accessibility.

Given that accessibility for persons with disabilities is considered to have a justifiable economic and social basis, the government may consider accessibility requirements in concessions (e.g. to enterprises in public transport, telecommunication and broadcasting), but this policy opportunity is exercised with caution. Accessibility for persons with disabilities will often come under 'general public interests'. Accessibility may be considered a justifiable interpretation of the general provision, e.g. the interpretation of the general provision in the Norwegian Aviation Act of 1993, which states that 'a concession may be granted only when it is compatible with general public interests' (section 8–2). Under this legal provision, although the Norwegian aviation authorities have the legal competence to include accessibility requirements in the concessions, they exercise it with caution.[36] Opportunities also exist for local authorities to grant exemption from accessibility requirements to buildings and public physical space, e.g. in the Norwegian Planning and Building Act.[37] Therefore, stated norms of accessibility and usability have either been non-binding or not enforced. The Danish government in particular has preferred consultations and voluntary agreements to binding standards.[38]

A major deficit in the Swedish legislation has been the lack of statutory provisions that would define inaccessibility to goods and services as discrimination.[39] Denial of access to a restaurant on the grounds of disability would be discrimination under Swedish law but not lack of accessibility or individual accommodation when the needs arise, such as access to the building, to the restaurant's web page, to menus in Braille, or to the waiter's reading the menu for those with reading difficulties. As of 2008, horizontal non-discrimination legislation for advancing accessibility and preventing inaccessibility for persons with disabilities in all areas of society do not exist in the other Nordic countries. As previously mentioned, the governments rely more on general and less binding provisions in

36 *Likeverd og tilgjengelighet* [Equality and Accessibility Draft statute], Norwegian Official Report, NOU 2005: 8 (Government Administration Services, 2005), p. 57.

37 Ibid. pp. 58–60.

38 Danish IT and Telecom Agency, *Evaluering af handlingsplanen Handicap ingen hindring* [Evaluation of the action plan Disability not a barrier] (Ministry of Science, Technology and Innovation, 2005); Danish government, *Handlingsplan for handicapområdet* [Action plan for the disability domain] (Ministry of Economic and Business Affairs, 2003); C.W. Nielsen, 'Tilgængelighed i nordisk og internationalt perspektiv' [Accessibility in Nordic and International Perspective], 30 *Håndbog for bygningsindustrien, 2003*, 758–764.

39 Inghammar, *Funktionshindrad – med rätt till arbete?* (2006).

the sector legislation, i.e. laws regulating specific areas of society such as aviation or buildings and the built environment.[40]

To date, the accessibility and non-discrimination requirements in public procurement laws are fairly weak in the Nordic countries.[41] However, the 2000s have seen an increasing awareness for how public authorities may use their market power to advance non-discrimination and accessibility: Norway has adopted public procurement regulations – in effect from 2007 – requiring that state, municipal and county authorities, and other bodies under the auspices of a government ministry allow for 'universal design' during the planning of public procurements (corresponding to Directive 2004/18/EC). Whether universal design will be given priority over other needs that the purchaser has to assess is not clear.

In 2006 the Swedish government issued an executive order concerning the use of anti-discrimination clauses in public contracts. The order recognizes that EU public procurement directives, and thus Swedish public procurement law, allow government agencies to include contract terms that relate to social and environmental issues. The order specifies that the 30 largest government agencies must include anti-discrimination clauses in their public contracts for services or building contracts if the contract is for eight months or more and has a value of at least 750,000 Swedish Crowns (about 80,000 euro). The new Swedish Public Procurement Acts that went into effect on 1 January 2008 'recommend' that government authorities include demands related to accessibility in their contracts.[42] Denmark and Finland were less advanced in their public procurement policies, relying more on local initiatives to apply the opportunities in the EU public procurement directives.

Thus far none of the Nordic countries has required public employers to anticipate the needs of employees with disabilities to ensure workplace accessibility. Neither has any required that a party contracting with a public authority for the procurement of goods or services take affirmative action to employ and promote qualified individuals with disabilities.[43] In comparison, the US has adopted both

---

40 Sector legislation refers to statutory provisions that regulate a specific sector or area of society, e.g. broadcasting or telecommunications. By contrast, horizontal non-discrimination legislation is by definition cross-sectional, i.e. the laws provide general rules of non-discrimination across a number of policy areas.

41 C. McCrudden, *Buying Social Justice. Equality, Government Procurement, and Legal Change* (Oxford University Press, 2007).

42 *Lag om offentlig upphandling* (2007:1091) [Act on Public Procurement] and *Lag om upphandling innom områdane vatten, energi, transport och posttjänster* (2007: 1092) [Act on procurement within the domain of water, energy, transport and postal services] (Notisum, 2008).

43 However, the Norwegian government has proposed that public employers, private employers who regularly have more than 50 employees, and the social partners should have a legal duty to work 'actively', in a 'goal-oriented' way, and 'systematically' to promote equal opportunities and

policy instruments in federal legislation that regulates the behaviour of public authorities (sections 503 and 508 of the US Rehabilitation Act).

The new statutory non-discrimination provisions of 1999–2007 have thus far led to few court cases in the Nordic countries. Sweden was the first to adopt non-discrimination provisions (1999) and an ombudsman's office (1994). Most complaints from persons with disabilities concerned alleged discrimination in employment and access to employment services, insurance, restaurants and housing. In most cases the Swedish Disability Ombudsman concluded that there was no sufficient basis for summoning the parties to voluntary negotiations or to court; often the evidence was considered insufficient, or whether the case fell within the scope of the law was unclear. Consequently only a handful of cases on the grounds of disability discrimination have been tried in the Swedish Labour Court.[44]

Even fewer cases have arisen in the other Nordic countries. Norway established a general equality and anti-discrimination ombudsman in 2006. However, Denmark and Finland have hesitated to introduce a separate appeal system outside the administrative appeals system (which is operated in agreement with the social partners and the ordinary courts of justice), even though such a system has already been established for enforcing legislation against discrimination on grounds of ethnicity in both countries. At the time of writing (December 2008) all Nordic countries have considered introducing new and more extensive non-discrimination and accessibility legislation.[45]

4. THE INHERENT WEAKNESSES OF NORDIC DISABILITY PROTECTION

Our assessment of the similarities and differences in disability protection among the Nordic countries has shown persistent differences in *de facto* priorities among the Nordic countries. Sweden has adopted the broadest repertoire of policy measures within all three disability protection subsystems (dealing with social benefits, social services and social regulation). While Norway spends relatively

prevent discrimination against persons with disabilities, *Om lov om forbud mot diskriminering på grunn av nedsatt funksjonsevne* [Norwegian law bill on prohibition of discrimination on grounds of disability], Ot.prp. 44 2007–2008 (Ministry of Children and Equality, 2008).

44 *Årsredovisning* [Annual report] (Swedish Disability Ombud, 2006).

45 Norwegian law bill *Om lov om forbud mot diskriminering ...* [On Prohibition of Discrimination] (2008); Swedish Law Bill *Ett starkare skydd mot diskriminering* [Stronger protection against discrimination], prop. 2007/08:95 (Ministry of Integration and Gender Equality, 2007).

more resources on cash benefits, other Nordic countries spend more on services. Of the resources allocated to ALMM Finland and Norway in particular spend an unusual high share on income maintenance for persons on vocational training, and relatively less on financial support to employers and suppliers of ALMM services. Whereas Nordic policy-makers assumed and expected a mutually supportive and interdependent relationship between the three subsystems, we have found several indications that redistributive and compensatory measures are more strongly developed than social regulation measures for influencing the preferences and behaviour of the market actors.

Does the underdeveloped social regulation policy reflect an inherent weakness in Nordic disability policy? We answer this question in two steps. First, we discuss whether the emphasis on voluntary commitment from market actors to the inclusion of persons with disabilities has been sufficient to achieve an accessible, inclusive market. For this purpose we use as an example policies that promote labour market participation by persons with disabilities. Second, we account for how the emphasis on voluntary commitment from business and industry is related to Nordic industrial relations.

4.1. SOCIAL REGULATION AS A NEGLECTED ASPECT OF NORDIC DISABILITY PROTECTION: POLICIES TO PROMOTE LABOUR MARKET PARTICIPATION

We have seen that substantial sections of the working age population with disabilities are excluded from the ordinary labour market. In some cases vocational training schemes may have been more important for renewing participation rights to income benefits than for increasing the job-relevant qualifications of the participant. Participation in vocational training and education may have become compensation for absence of labour market participation rather than effective assistance for finding a job. The bias towards redistribution in Nordic disability protection may be criticized from two perspectives: a costs perspective and a rights perspective.

From a costs perspective many today argue that Nordic disability protection is too expensive and creates disincentives for persons with disabilities to find paid work.[46] In a similar vein, a Norwegian study suggests that social security benefits may be a disincentive for students with disabilities when seeking summer jobs.[47]

46 *Transforming Disability into Ability* (OECD, 2003); *Sickness, Disability and Work. Norway, Poland and Switzerland* (OECD, 2006).

47 Ø. Lorentsen and A. R. Berge, *Hørselshemmede i arbeid* [Persons with hearing disabilities in work]. Rehab-Nor (Directorate of Health and Social Affairs, 2006).

Unlike the situation for other students, having a summer job will not make a difference in the economic situation of students receiving disability-related benefits. In such cases, young people with disabilities may not be stimulated to achieve the labour market experience that other young people normally receive.

Another Norwegian study assesses the economic gain from work for social benefit recipients.[48] Estimates of the salary a person on social security may earn by working full- or part-time demonstrate that about one in four have relatively little to gain from working. The large majority, however, will improve their economic situation if they find employment. In many cases the balance will depend on the extra costs associated with employment, such as travel expenditures and kindergarten fees. Norwegian economist Elisabeth Fevang and team argue that the economic gain from work can be improved by increasing the basic tax-free allowance on income but not on the social security benefits.[49] Improving the economic incentives for persons with disabilities will, however, have little effect if there are no job opportunities corresponding to the competence and capacity of the jobseeker, if persons with disabilities are excluded from working-life, or if the workplace is not accessible.

From a rights perspective one may argue that a relatively well-functioning cash benefit system has become an excuse for different governments and shifting majorities in the Parliament – and an opportunity for employers – to evade responsibility for inclusion of persons with disabilities and to recruit and keep the employees they prefer. A survey among Norwegian companies with more than ten employees demonstrates that few employers are likely to call jobseekers who are blind (10 per cent of the employers) or who use a wheelchair (37 per cent of the employers) for a job interview even if they are highly qualified for the job. Employers who already have employees with disabilities appear more likely to call jobseekers with disabilities for an interview.[50] The reluctance among employers is likely to be the result of stereotypes about the working capacity of persons with disabilities, reinforced by general risk aversion.

Moreover, available macro-data about the employment situation of persons with disabilities show no clear trend towards increased employment rates since the 2001 signing of the tripartite Agreement on an Inclusionary Working Life between

---

48 E. Fevang et. al., *Formelle og totale skattesatser på inntekt for personer med svak tilknytning til arbeidsmarkedet* [Formal and total tax rates for persons with a weak connection to the labour market], Report 3 (Frischsenteret, 2005).

49 Ibid.

50 *Telefonundersøkelse om betydningen av nedsatt funksjonsevne ved ansettelser i arbeidslivet* [Telephone survey on the significance of reduced functionality for appointments in the labour market] (Synovate for the Norwegian Centre for Documentation on Disability, 2006), N=600.

the social partners and the government, despite substantial provision of new financial support from public authorities and strong backing from the main employers' federations and trade unions in Norway.[51] Few Norwegian enterprises appear to have written plans for recruitment, human resource management or corporate social responsibility where the inclusion, accommodation and career development of persons with disabilities are explicitly mentioned.[52] In Norway, if any of the qualified jobseekers state that they are disabled, employers in the public sector have an obligation to call at least one of them for an interview.[53] Although the employer may choose to hire a qualified jobseeker with a disability rather than a more qualified person without a disability, this option is rarely chosen.[54]

There are also signs of insufficient policy coordination in the Nordic countries. For instance, for several decades Norway has had a national insurance scheme for financing or reimbursing costs involved in on-the-job accommodation for employees with impairments. Under given circumstances the full costs can be reimbursed. But a closer examination reveals a striking under-use of the scheme, partly from an overzealous effort among the staff in the local offices of the Norwegian Labour and Welfare Organization (NLWO) to prevent abuse of public funds. Local staff in the Labour Inspectorate appear to lack basic knowledge about this possibility and the Labour Inspectorate is barely coordinated with the NLWO.[55] Finally, as the employers have no strong legal duty to accommodate persons with disabilities, they have few incentives to seek financial support for this purpose.

Consequently, a disproportionately large part of Norwegian public expenditures is used on improving individual vocational qualifications or compensating for the individual's lack of labour market income. As employers are usually not required to make the workplace accessible before the need arises, the danger exists that they may use limited access or usability in the existing premises or environments as a pretext for not recruiting any job applicants with impairments. Thus, the

51 C.H. Anvik et al., *Kunnskapsstatus for IA-avtalens delmål 2: Rekruttere og beholde personer med reduserte funksjonsevne* [Knowledge status for the IA-agreement subgoal 2: Recruit and keep persons with disabilities] (Nordlandsforskning, 2007).

52 S. Brandi et al., *Inkluderingsledelse: utnyttelse av mangfold i arbeidslivet* [Incluive Management: taking advantage of human diversity in working life], (Scandinavian University Press, 2004); *Telefonundersøkelse om betydningen av nedsatt funksjonsevne.* (2006).

53 Civil Servants Act, administrative regulation, sec. 9, in *Statens Personalhåndbok* (Norwegian Ministry of Government Administration and Reform, 2008), Chap. 2.3.2.5.

54 H. Bull and T. Alm Andreassen, *Oppfølgingsundersøkelse om ansettelse av funksjonshemmede i staten* [Following-up survey on the employment of persons with disabilities in the government], Report 7 (Work Research Institute, 2007).

55 B. Hvinden 'How to get employers to take on greater responsibility for the inclusion of disabled people in working life?' in B. Marin, C. Prinz, C. and M. Quiesser (eds.), *Transforming disability welfare policies: Towards work and equal opportunities* (Ashgate, 2004).

need for adjustments in the workplace may never arise unless job applicants with disabilities manage to use the anti-discrimination regulations to force the employer to undertake these alterations. Similar experiences have been reported in Denmark.[56]

Unfortunately, few comparative studies exist of the difference that the social regulation system can make to the social inclusion of persons with disabilities. One exception is a cross-national study (Denmark, Germany, Israel, the Netherlands, Sweden and the US) by the Dutch social scientists Bukje Cuelenaere and Rienk Prins from the 1990s.[57] The results are of particular interest here since it involved the two Nordic countries with the weakest and strongest systems of protection against dismissal. The researchers collected longitudinal data about the extent of work resumption among people with back problems and factors and interventions that had affected their return to work over two years. The findings showed striking differences among the six countries, in both the extent of work resumption in general and the extent to which there was return to a job with the same employer.

In Denmark and Germany about 40 per cent returned to work within the two-year period, while the rate for Israel, Sweden and the US was about 60 per cent and for the Netherlands over 70 per cent. In Denmark and Israel somewhat less than half of the work 'resumers' had returned to their former employer, whereas in the US the proportion was about 60 per cent, and in Sweden, the Netherlands and Germany more than 80 per cent. Many of the work 'resumers' in Denmark and Israel ended up in jobs of lower quality. In Denmark more than 60 per cent were dismissed by their original employer during the two years; in Israel, about 30 per cent, and in the other countries less than 20 per cent. According to the researchers, 'the rates of work resumption, both at the older employer and at a new employer, seemed to be conditioned by the job protection rules in effect in the respective countries'.[58]

Several observations are relevant here. First, the overall results were not particularly impressive in the two Nordic countries (Denmark and Sweden), especially compared to the Netherlands. Second, the findings from these two countries were strikingly dissimilar. No uniform 'Nordic-ness' appears. Third, one claim often advanced about job protection is that strict job protection rules are to one's advantage if one already has a job but they exclude one if one is

56 T. Clausen et al., *Handicap og beskæftigelse – et forhindringsløb* [Disability and employment – a series of barriers], *Report No. 3* (SFI – Danish National Centre for Social Research, 2004).

57 B. Cuelenaere and R. Prins, 'Factors Influencing Work Resumption', in F.S. Bloch and R. Prins (eds.) *Who returns to work and why? A six-country study on work incapacity and reintegration* (Transaction Publishers, 2001).

58 Ibid.

applying for a job – especially if one has a health problem or an impairment. Employers are expected to be reluctant about engaging a job applicant with an assumed high risk of sickness absence or prolonged incapacity, especially if they have limited possibilities for dispensing with this person. The findings indicate that the likelihood of finding a job with another employer was not particularly promising in Denmark, one of the three countries with relatively weak job protection legislation and thus the prime Nordic example of 'flexicurity' policies, i.e. a combination of easy hiring and firing (flexibility for employers) and generous benefits for the unemployed (security for employees).

More generally this study indicates the need for more attention to go to regulatory measures within the overall system of disability protection in the Nordic countries. A movement in this direction will probably be stimulated by the evolving international equal treatment policy regime. Interestingly, we see an evolving regime of binding statutory regulations, not only recommendations.

After the statutory approach to equal treatment of persons with disabilities first emerged in the US, we now see a global trend in this direction:

- Since the mid-1990s the European Union (EU) has developed a social regulation policy for ensuring equal treatment for all, independent of disability or impairment, very much inspired by the US.[59] The social regulation policy – pursued through a broad set of legislation, financial incentives and persuasion strategies – is concerned with removing the physical, organizational and attitudinal barriers that limit or preclude participation or hinder an assessment based on an individual's qualifications or achievements. The employment framework directive is the main advance in the EU thus far on the rights of persons with disabilities.[60] Additionally, separate disability-related provisions have been included in an increasing number of general directives and regulations for safeguarding and advancing accessibility to goods and services for persons with disabilities.[61]
- In 2006 the United Nations adopted the Convention on the Rights of Persons with Disabilities, which covers both proscriptions against unfair treatment and substantive rights. The convention contains both classical liberal rights,

59 R. Whittle and R. Halvorsen, 'From disabling barriers to participation: the opportunities created by the EU equality strategy', in B. Hvinden and H. Johansson (eds.), *Citizenship in Nordic Welfare States* (Routledge, 2007).

60 Council Directive 2000/78/EC establishing a general framework for equal treatment in employment and occupation.

61 L. Waddington, *A New Era in Human Rights Protection in the European Community: The Implications [of] the United Nations' Convention on the Rights of Persons with Disabilities for the European Community*, Maastricht Faculty of Law Working Paper No. 4 (Maastricht University, 2007).

such as access to justice, and material rights such as the right to work and education. It is a legally binding instrument that will require both immediate reforms and progressive achievement of results. The objective is not to create new human rights but to ensure that all existing rights are made equally effective for persons with disabilities.[62]

- Additionally the Council of Europe (CoE) has adopted an 'Action Plan to promote the rights and full participation of people with disabilities in society'.[63] The recommendations will be followed up through exchange of information, experience and best practice among the Member States, and review of progress made in the implementation of the action plan.

The evolving human rights approach to disability implies that the supranational organizations and the adhering state parties recognize that persons with disabilities have the same human worth, dignity and integrity as other people – including the freedom to make their own decisions.[64] It is animated by the view that persons with disabilities should be recognized and treated as subjects who hold rights, not as objects of welfare or medical care. Persons with disabilities should enjoy the same participation opportunities as other people.[65] In some cases the supranational instruments not only require that the states remove the formal barriers to participation for persons with disabilities but also establish the necessity for creating real opportunities for using those rights. The underlying norm is not to turn a blind eye on disability but to recognize that people are different and therefore have different abilities and needs.

As Irish law professor Gerard Quinn has noted, the evolving supranational equal treatment policy resembles the Aristotelian conceptualization of equality: to fully recognize the difference of disability will sometimes entail positively accommodating that difference.[66] Although the principle of non-discrimination is essential in the understanding of what should count as equal treatment under the UN disability convention, it does not preclude specific measures that are considered necessary for accelerating or achieve *de facto* equality for persons with

---

62 *Convention on the rights of persons with disabilities*, Resolution adopted by the General Assembly, A/RES/61/1 06 (United Nations, 2007); G. Quinn, *The UN Convention on the Human Rights of Persons with Disabilities*, conference paper (Berlin, 2007).

63 Recommendation Rec (2006)5 of the Committee of the Ministers to member states on the Council of Europe Action Plan to promote the rights and full participation of people with disabilities in society: improving the quality of life of people with disabilities in Europe 2006–2015 (CoE, 2006).

64 Council of Europe Action Plan, 2006, Art. 2.7; *UN Convention on the rights of persons with disabilities*, Art. 3; *Charter of Fundamental Rights in the European Union*, C 364/1 (Official Journal of the European Communities, 2000), Art. 21 and 26.

65 *UN Convention on the rights of persons with disabilities* (2006).

66 G. Quinn, *Achieving eAccessibility: The Role of Equality Legislation and other Measures*, Paper to European Workshop (Brussels, 2006).

disabilities.[67] The principle of accessibility (universal design and reasonable accommodation) is paramount in the disability policy of all three institutions: the UN, the CoE and the EU. The UN disability convention marks the first time that accessibility is mentioned and comprehensively defined in an international human rights instrument. Article 4.1.b of the UN convention states that the states parties shall take all appropriate measures (including legislation) to tackle discrimination with respect to the various rights contained in the disability convention. Thus Article 9 on accessibility must be read in the light of 'reasonable accommodation'. What this effectively means is that where universal design is not (yet) available, alternative means must be provided. If not, then reasons exist for arguing that Nordic legislation is under-inclusive and thus failing to pass muster under the Convention.

The three institutions – the EU, the CoE and the UN – have different rationales and mandates, as reflected in how they justify and frame their disability policy. The EU is the most integrated: membership is more binding, and more power is deferred to the supranational decision-making level. The EU has a double rationale for its disability policy – not only the human rights perspective but also the commitment to enhance the economic competitiveness of the European communities. Thus the economic rationality for the disability policy reforms is more explicit in the EU compared to the UN and the CoE, as the EU has adopted statutory market regulations both to prevent discrimination and to advance the employment, self-sufficiency and enjoyment of market opportunities of persons with disabilities. In the EU, according to Quinn, the human rights provenance of the EU employment framework directive should have priority if there is a conflict with the market rationality of the directive.[68]

The UN disability convention is the first human rights convention which the European Community has signed, intends to ratify, and will be bound by.[69] Discussions are also ongoing as to how the Disability Action Program of the CoE may support the implementation of the UN disability convention. Despite their past and present differences, the three institutions are moving in the same direction, thereby also stimulating the Nordic countries to give more attention to the regulatory measures within their disability policies.[70]

---

67 *UN Convention on the rights of persons with disabilities*, Art. 5.4.

68 G. Quinn, 'Disability discrimination law in the European Union', in H. Meenan (ed.), *Equality Law for an Enlarged Europe: Towards a Greater Understanding of the Article 13 Directives* (Cambridge University Press, 2007).

69 Waddington, *A New Era in Human Rights Protection in the European Community* (2007).

70 G. de Burca, 'Beyond the charter: how enlargement has enlarged the human rights policy of the EU', in O. de Schutter and S. Deakin (eds.), *Social Rights and Market Forces* (Bruylant, 2005); G. Quinn, 'The European Union and the Council of Europe on the Issue of Human Rights: Twins Separated at Birth?', 46 *McGill Law Journal* 2001, 849–873; G. Quinn, 'The European Social Charter and EU Anti-Discrimination Law in the Field of Disability: Two Gravitation

5. THE INSTITUTIONAL CONTEXT OF NORDIC DISABILITY PROTECTION

We now need to ask whether the weaknesses of Nordic disability protection have at least partly been generated by some limitations in the Nordic welfare model as constructed after World War II. At that time, the expansion of the Nordic welfare states demanded strong and continued economic growth, with steps to improve productivity and profitability negotiated primarily between employers and trade unions at both central and local levels.[71] Similarly, real increases in wages were largely achieved on the basis of organizational strength and skilful collective bargaining, rarely on that of conflicts and strikes. Collective wage bargaining was substantially central and coordinated. In this negotiated order, the employees and their organizations enjoyed the certainty that they would get a proportion of the productivity gains and some degree of co-determination, e.g. in relation to plans for reorganization of production. In return, organized labour did not contest 'employers' prerogatives' as these were interpreted or constructed.

More generally the Nordic system of cooperative industrial relations made social democratic parties, with their close relations to the trade unions, reluctant to challenge or confront employers and business interests too strongly. Again, in practice, the emphasis was on voluntary commitments and negotiated solutions, even if the parties officially adopted a tougher, more confrontational rhetoric. Thus policy-makers have repeatedly suggested that legal regulation would be an infringement of market freedom and the prerogatives of producers, despite emerging findings to the contrary from studies in the US and elsewhere.[72] Ironically, the reluctance to enforce obligations has also applied to the state itself in its role as a major employer and entrepreneur.

As a result, social democratic governments, in their assumed role as the driving force behind welfare state expansion, have been more effective in developing public income maintenance systems and vocational rehabilitation services than in obligating employers and business interests to be responsible for providing work and accessible and usable standards for persons with disabilities. Nordic governments have encouraged voluntary commitment to 'corporate social responsibility' from business and industry in their capacities as employers and

Fields with One Common Purpose', in G. de Búrca and B. de Witte (eds), *Social Rights in Europe* (Oxford University Press, 2005).

71 M. Wallerstein et al., 'Unions, employers' associations and wage setting institutions in Northern and Central Europe, 1950–1992', 50 *Industrial and Labour Relations Review*, 3 (1997), 379–401; J.E. Dølvik, *The Nordic regimes of labour market governance: From crisis to success-story?*, Report No. 7 (FAFO Institute for Labour and Social Research, 2007).

72 Blanck et al., *Disability Civil Rights Law and Policy* (2004).

suppliers of goods and services. Nordic governments in varying degrees have offered financial support as an incentive for employers, along with information and persuasion rather than legal means, combined with restrictive sanctions such as fines.[73]

The first priority of the Nordic labour movements has, of course, been to protect the interests of the wage earners or those already in employment as an undifferentiated collective. Trade unions have paid attention to the requirements and needs of persons with disabilities mainly in so far as they were 'insiders' – that is, already employed but in danger of losing their job as a result of reduced capacity to work. In relation to 'outsiders', the organizational capacity has been more limited, e.g. in terms of mobilizing support or putting pressure on employers to employ persons with disabilities without paid work and without previous labour market experience.

Some important differences also exist within the traditions of industrial relations. We have noted a stronger political will to impose social responsibilities on employers and a more confrontational style in Sweden than in the other Nordic countries. Both the organizing of political interests and differences in political culture may account for this divide, as Sweden has had the strongest trade union movement in the Nordic countries, with heavy and large-scale industry more developed. Swedish unions have been sector-based, not divided in different occupations and sectors as in Denmarkor divided in political fractions as in Finland.

The industrial relations have also structured the space for agency among DPOs and the realistic opportunities for DPOs to influence the disability protection system. As pressure groups the DPOs have developed competence for extending the social service and cash benefit subsystems of the welfare state. Encompassing and generous social services and benefits guaranteed by the state have stimulated a benign view of the state among the DPOs. In particular, organizations of people with well-defined diagnoses have enjoyed high legitimacy in the political sphere. These organizations have had faith in the political system and in their own ability to influence it. The larger organizations have achieved close, informal and cooperative relations to the civil service; individuals move between positions in the organizations and the civil service, and their representatives share many values, judgments and opinions. Close ties to public authorities have compensated for relatively meagre collaboration with the social partners.

73 Anvik et al., *Kunnskapsstatus for IA-avtalens ...* [Knowledge status for the IA-agreement ...] (2007).

For the DPOs, the safest option has been to continue pursuing the strategies they had successfully applied previously. Earlier events and experiences have induced further steps in the same direction. The organizational leaderships have developed particular loyalties and vested interests, along with perceptions of social problems coloured by their experiences with welfare state institutions.[74] Hence the characteristics of the established disability protection system are reflected in 'path dependent' behaviour on the part of the Nordic DPOs.[75] The feeling of being centrally positioned in the Nordic political-administrative systems has encouraged the larger DPOs representatives to take a 'gradualist' approach to social policy reforms; they emphasize step-wise reforms and formulate themselves in a language considered neutral, detached, balanced and factual, so as to be perceived as non-controversial, 'serious' and 'responsible', rather than 'too demanding' or unreasonable.[76]

In this collaborative system, litigation has been viewed as unnecessary, confrontational and 'noisy', drawing attention and resources away from collaborative relations with the authorities and potentially leading to increased social distance between DPOs and the public authorities. DPO leaders would have to confront a large number of market actors directly, engage with the court system, and lean less on the authority of the government as a predictable counterpart. Nordic DPOs have had variable experiences, interests, skills and competencies in handling legal rights on behalf of their constituencies, and thus also different degrees of self-confidence and belief in the fruitfulness of pursuing a legal non-discrimination strategy.

This diagnosis, if correct, has implications for comparisons with non-Nordic countries. Scholars in comparative welfare state research tend to see the strength of the labour movement, either on its own or through alliances with others such as agrarian interests, as essential for the establishment, scope and impact of the Nordic welfare model. Other political parties, especially Conservative and Christian-Democratic parties, have usually had strong close links with the organized interests of employers and business. From a Nordic perspective it is a paradox that a number of European countries in which Conservative and Christian-Democratic parties dominated after World War II, and in which the

74 B. Rothstein and S. Steinmo, 'Restructuring Politics: Institutional Analysis and the Challenges of Modern Welfare States', in B. Rothstein and S. Steinmo (eds.), *Restructuring the Welfare State* (Palgrave, 2002).

75 M. Levi, 'A model, a method and a map: rational choice in comparative and historical analysis', in M.I. Lichbach and A.S. Zuckerman (eds.), *Comparative Politics* (Cambridge University Press, 1997).

76 J. Galtung, 'Foreign Policy Opinion as a Function of Social Position', 1 *Journal of Peace Research* 1964: 206–231.

trade unions have had fewer members than in the Nordic countries, have adopted stronger obligations for employers to provide work for persons with disabilities (e.g. through quota schemes for employees with disabilities). Moreover, it was under a Conservative government in the mid-1990s that the UK became the first European country to introduce legislation against discrimination on the grounds of disability in employment. Likewise, it was a Republican president who signed the Americans with Disability Act of 1990.[77]

6. CONCLUSIONS

This chapter has examined the overall Nordic disability protection system, distinguishing among three subsystems; social benefits, social services and social protection. We have demonstrated that while Nordic governments have made great efforts to develop and modernize the social benefit and social services subsystems, they have been more reluctant to expand that of social regulation. Governments on both the left and the right have greeted proposals for more forceful social – and especially legal – regulation of this area with uncertainty. The business community in particular has expressed strong reservations against stronger legal duties for employers, while the trade union movement has given this issue low priority. We have argued that this bias is at least partly due to the nature of industrial relations in the Nordic countries: the institutionalized profile of Nordic disability protection has been associated with path dependencies reflected in the preferences and priorities of the Nordic governments and the DPOs.

We have also seen that existing statutory social regulations have tended to be neglected or watered down by frequent exemptions. Arguably there is a risk that such enforcement deficits will be repeated in any new statutory social regulations.

To what extent do the Nordic countries comply with the overall objectives of the evolving rights approach in supranational disability policy? The Nordic countries have different policy traditions and regulatory approaches. In certain respects Sweden has been more advanced in protecting individual autonomy and giving persons with disabilities a legal standing to challenge the way in which they are being accommodated (e.g. in relation to individual choice of personal assistance, rights to education, employment protection rights, and reasonable accommodation in the workplace). Our reading of available data is that Swedes

77 T.F. Burke, *Lawyers, Lawsuits and Legal Rights. The Battle over Litigation in American Society* (University of California Press, 2002).

with disabilities have been attributed a stronger legal standing to negotiate the content and form of the delivery of their entitlements. In general Sweden has been the leader in developing statutory non-discrimination provisions for persons with disabilities, whilst the other Nordic countries have set a higher premium on the exercise of discretion by the public administration in the allocation of resources. Thus Swedish disability law and policy could be seen as more in accordance with the human rights perspective as expressed in the Convention on the Rights of Persons with Disabilities.

In our view the evolving supranational equal treatment policy challenges the underlying assumptions of the Nordic system of disability protection. When the Nordic welfare states have adopted new statutory social regulations since the 1990s, they have largely responded to the evolving supranational social regulations for ensuring equal treatment for all, including persons with disabilities. However, although the Nordic tradition of industrial relations was built on assumptions of voluntary agreements and collaborative relations between the social partners, along with a benign view of the state, the regulatory traditions of other countries have been driven by legal adversarialism.[78]

According to American political scientist Thomas Burke, adversarial legalism involves 'formal adversarial procedures, punitive sanctions, costly forms of legal contestation, and complex legal rules that are subject to frequent controversy and change'.[79] Full and effective use of statutory social regulations requires the development of new competencies and working methods. In this context, Nordic DPOs and individuals with disabilities cannot appeal to or lean on public services to take care of their needs or protect their interests. Non-discrimination laws specify complaint and adjudication procedures and some form of sanction mechanisms, often fines or financial compensation. The person or group claiming to have been discriminated against has to take legal action against the alleged violator of his or her rights. In this sense, non-discrimination regulations are likely to create a more adversarial climate of disability policy, involving a confrontational style of dispute resolution unfamiliar to the Nordic traditions of tripartite and collaborative industrial relations.

Yet this argument should not be overstated, as the Nordic countries (especially Sweden) already have fairly extensive general statutory job protection. The important task is to examine the practical implications of the underlying

78 Ibid.; R.A. Kagan, *Adversarial Legalism* (Harvard University Press, 2001).

79 T.F. Burke, 'On the Rights Track: The Americans with Disabilities Act', in P.S. Nivola (ed.), *Comparative Disadvantages? Social regulations and the Global Economy* (Brookings Institution Press, 1997), p. 244.

assumptions in Nordic industrial relations. For the new social regulation policy measures to be effective, the Nordic countries need to find new solutions to the recurring fear that the costs associated with making workplaces fully accessible and accommodating them to the requirement of workers with disabilities will represent a disproportional burden for business and individual employers. We need more systematic studies of what costs such accessibility and accommodation actually involve. With their strong tradition of public responsibility for compensating the personal disadvantages associated with having a disability, the Nordic countries ought to have a good point of departure for finding ways of socializing or sharing all costs related to ensuring accessibility and accommodation.

Comparative research suggests that other affluent countries have different ways of mixing redistribution and regulation than the Nordic ones. Some scholars have indicated that social regulation dominate too much in some countries like the US, at the expense of public redistributive measures (e.g. in the form of subsidies for mandated accommodation).[80] An advanced social regulation system may ensure accessibility and prevent attitudinal, physical and social barriers to participation for persons with disabilities without eliminating the need for social benefits and services.[81]

A substantial challenge for the Nordic welfare states is to find fruitful ways of combining the new forms of social regulation policy with the most viable parts of their established redistributive policy in the disability area. The main achievements of Nordic disability protection are fairly equal standards of living and low poverty risk for persons with disabilities. Yet the potential remains for policy learning on the part of the Nordic countries, as they have different profiles and priorities in their social protection systems. Denmark and Sweden allocate more resources to subsidies for employers and service providers than Finland and Norway. Sweden has been more advanced in providing legal protection against employment discrimination and inaccessibility. Finally, the Nordic countries have much to learn from other Western countries with regard to improving regulatory measures for promoting equal treatment, dignity and autonomy for persons with disabilities.

---

80 Ibid.

81 Blanck et al., *Disability Civil Rights Law and Policy* (2004); *The Impact of the Americans with Disabilities Act: Assessing the Progress Toward Achieving the Goals of the ADA* (National Council on Disability, 2007).

PART III
CONCLUSIONS AND CHALLENGES

Henriette Sinding Aasen, Rune Halvorsen
and António Barbosa da Silva

The ethical and legal dilemmas discussed throughout this volume are closely interrelated at their core. They all point to a fundamental question: what is human dignity, and how should it be protected in situations where different human rights, values and interests are at stake?

Modern health care ethics and law is founded on the Kantian notion of human dignity, in which the human being is considered as an end in himself or herself and therefore has a right to be treated with basic respect in all situations.[1] This principle is of utmost importance in health care and social services, where people are often vulnerable to humiliation and loss of control over their personal lives, even in the absence of coercive measures. Medical treatment, care and social assistance or protection are not only acts of beneficence but also interventions into the personal sphere of human beings whose individual rights to private life, self-determination and liberty are in danger. This dilemma is typical in a modern welfare state characterized by public policies directed towards improvements of health and living conditions for its citizens. Even though these policies are positive for the possible enhancement of public health and social welfare, they may be experienced as, and even result in, unjustified interventions at the personal level.

History has proved that neither good intentions nor professional or scientific qualifications can guarantee that medical personnel or other professionals treat other human beings with respect and dignity. Therefore, the main rule and normative strategy for the protection of human dignity in modern health care and social law is the protection of individual autonomy, expressed in the requirement of informed consent to health care and other interventions in the physical or personal sphere of the individual. The requirement of having informed consent and individual participation as far as possible in decision-making processes is a basic pillar of modern health care ethics and law, as well as in social welfare law.[2]

However, several of the chapters have shown the normative strategy of informed consent and participation is not sufficient in all situations, especially when the person concerned – due to age, serious mental illness, or cognitive impairment – is not able to give valid consent to proposed treatment or care. In these situations, protection of only individual autonomy and privacy is likely to result in serious threats to life and health. When the principle of autonomy or self-determination cannot be fully applied or applied at all, human dignity must be protected by other means. Our overall argument and conclusion is that human dignity in these situations must be upheld and protected through a balancing of human rights.

1 See chapter 1 (Barbosa da Silva).
2 See chapter 2 (Aasen).

The balance must favour the rights most likely to uphold and protect human dignity for the person concerned. More concretely, when the right to autonomy and informed consent cannot protect the dignity of the person, other human rights become more relevant and important, such as those to life and health. As these rights can still protect the dignity of the person, they therefore must be given due weight. The 'best interest' principle in the Convention on the Rights of the Child is an example of balancing rights and interests for making decisions that protect the overall interests of children[3], who are usually dependent upon decisions made by others, for example parents or child protection authorities.

Modern health care is based on developments in modern medicine. Scientific freedom is a fundamental principle in all societies where knowledge is promoted as a basic value, and research is an essential tool for ensuring continued progress in treatment opportunities.[4] The requirement of valid informed consent is a basic requirement for ensuring the necessary protection of research subjects. However, if some exceptions are not allowed, this requirement would imply that individuals who cannot give valid consent themselves are excluded from benefits that other groups enjoy, such as the possibility of improved treatment and care. The long-term consequence could be that health care services are not fully adapted to the needs of particular groups.[5] This possibility illustrates how the unconditional requirement of informed consent could have negative effects on other rights, such as that to adequate health care. Therefore, we need to think twice before we make protective regulations that completely exclude certain groups from participation in medical or other kinds of research.

Classical civil rights such as autonomy and privacy are born from an individualistic view of human beings, picturing the autonomous person as an independent agent with full responsibility for his or her own life. The idea of the autonomous person is typical in Western societies as a normative ideal for human beings. However, the individualistic view of the human being does not fit situations in which the individual is in a state of dependency, vulnerable to the power of others, typically doctors, nurses and social workers. Such situations occur when the person concerned, for example someone with a serious mental disorder such as dementia, lacks the capacity to take proper care of his or her own interests or make adequate decisions under specific circumstances.[6] Persons who have their mental capacity fully intact but who, due to physical disabilities, need more personal assistance

3 See chapters 3 (Sandberg) and 4 (Skivenes).
4 See chapter 7 (Barbosa da Silva).
5 See chapter 8 (Lötjönen).
6 See chapters 5 (Aasen) and 6 (Hartlev).

than others for functioning in daily life, will also experience situations of dependency and vulnerability, although of another kind.[7]

All human beings are, have been or are likely to be in a situation of dependency at some point in their lives, either as children, when sick, if disabled or when old. Thus, the situation and experience of dependency and vulnerability is not exceptional but rather an ordinary part of being human. But society has yet to acknowledge and recognize the full implications of human dependency and vulnerability. Not only sick, disabled or unskilled individuals are dependent upon others but also the most competent and strong-minded amongst us: we all need electricians, farmers et al. for our personal and economic survival. Even the strongest and most capable person will experience times of dependency and vulnerability, for example in childbirth, childhood, severe illness, or disability.

In the context of health care and social services, the individuals concerned are more or less dependent and vulnerable. Even the competent patient whose capacity to consent to proposed treatment is fully intact depends upon receiving proper information and adequate treatment and care from health professionals. Thus, the right to autonomy must always be supplemented by other rights protecting the dignity of human beings. If a person cannot give valid consent to treatment, the right to autonomy must be balanced towards other rights, such as the right to life, health and dignified life conditions.

Social welfare rights – to health, social security and an adequate standard of living – are essential human rights for protecting human dignity.[8] These rights also strengthen the realization of civil and political rights. The recognition of social human rights is especially important for vulnerable individuals who depend upon public services for being able to live with basic human dignity. The mere lack of state interference in private life ('negative' rights) cannot fully support the protection of human dignity with regard to individuals who are in constant need of services and assistance to maintain an acceptable level of life quality. For example, persons with physical disabilities will be able to enjoy more autonomy and social participation if adequate personal assistance or social support for extra expenses related to the impairment is available, and if the appropriate social infrastructure, places, goods and services are accessible and usable. Extended social and personal support for individuals with cognitive impairment may also enhance their potential for autonomy and social participation. However, the importance of social rights as 'real' human rights, with the same normative status

---

7 See chapter 9 (Halvorsen and Hvinden).

8 Articles 12, 9 and 11 of the International Covenant on Economic, Social and Cultural Rights. See also the European Social Charter (Council of Europe, revised charter of 3. May 1996).

as classical civil and political rights (or 'first-generation' human rights) is yet to be acknowledged worldwide. As the Vienna Declaration and Programme of Action states, '[a]ll human rights are universal, indivisible and interdependent and interrelated'.[9]

The modern challenge of welfare states is to protect human dignity in all spheres of life and for everyone without discrimination. As all human rights are equally important, they must be given due weight and balanced against each other according to the particular situation and circumstances. As their purpose is to protect the dignity of human beings, they must always be applied with that dignity in mind.

9 United Nations: 12. July 1993. Para. 5.

INDEX

C

E

F

G

H

I

J

K

L

M

N

O

P

www.ingramcontent.com/pod-product-compliance
Ingram Content Group UK Ltd.
Pitfield, Milton Keynes, MK11 3LW, UK
UKHW051927100926
8556IPUK00022B/1410

9 789050 958776